▶▶▶ Rave Reviews for *The Golden Highway* ◀◀◀

"...accurate information, well illustrated and also fun and entertaining to read . . . "The Golden Highway, Volume I," . . .

. . . To report accurately, one must . . . go directly to the . . . actual words of those who were there and experienced what happened. That is what Jody and Ric Hornor have done in "The Golden Highway Volume I" . . .

. . . you will become involved and actually feel the joy, anguish and determination of the brave people who settled this land. . ."

Mountain Democrat, Placerville

"This is **a collection of incredible stories** found in actual historic documents and journals as well as **hundreds of restored photographs** taken by some of the first photographers to document the settling of California. Indexed, with a photo on every page, **a must have** for the local history buff."

The Union, Nevada County

. . . the Hornors have done a wonderful job of putting this book together."

Mountain Democrat

A 2007 Bronze Medal winner from the
Independent Publishers Association

▶▶▶ Reviews for *The Golden Highway, Vol. II* ◀◀◀

►►► Rave Reviews for the Golden Corridor ◄◄◄

"...lots of authentic, historical pictures. ...a wonderful job of putting this book together.

...you will actually feel the joy, anguish and determination of the brave people who settled this land...

"*The Golden Corridor*" is beautifully organized...

...**this is the one book you need to have.** You will spend hours reading the writings of those who were here and delight in the restored pictures of that era."

Mountain Democrat, Placerville

"Fans of old photographs...will love "The Golden Corridor." The book is filled with amazing black and white photos that bring early Northern California to life.

Sidebars on each page give fascinating quotes from diaries, journals and newspapers, as well as anecdotes.

I am a lifelong resident of Northern California and I learned from this book... "The Golden Corridor" is well worth checking out."

The Union, Nevada County

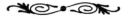

...a captivating study of 19th century people who helped shape the times.

Sacramento Bee

"... this amazing collection of firsthand testimony... Sidebars offer amusing quick vignettes from the era! **Enthusiastically recommended reading...**

Midwest Book Reviews

"...**educational and entertaining.** Profusely illustrated..."

Auburn Journal

[The Golden Corridor]...
...is the one book you need to have. You will spend hours reading the writings of those who were here and delight in the restored pictures of that era."

Mountain Democrat

▶▶▶ Rave Reviews for the Golden Quest ◀◀◀

This book is exciting . . . What makes these books wonderful is not only the words, but the abundance of authentic, historical pictures. These are not the grainy scratched photos . . .These have been carefully restored to look new.

The Golden Quest is beautifully organized, starting with a look at El Dorado County – Lake Tahoe and the High Sierra. Then, into Nevada . . .there is a discussion of events not often covered, the Indians and their wars in Nevada.

The Golden Quest not only describes what went on, but makes you a part of it . . . you will spend many enjoyable hours reading the writings of those who were there and delight in the restored pictures of that era.

Mountain Democrat

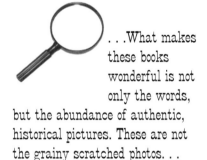

. . .What makes these books wonderful is not only the words, but the abundance of authentic, historical pictures. These are not the grainy scratched photos. . .

Mountain Democrat

The Golden Quest and Nevada's Silver Heritage . . . The text comes from history books of the 1880s and from letters, journals, diaries and newspaper stories of the era.

They liked the writing style in the historical books . . . as a way to deliver the "flavor" of the times, as well as the information. . . . The goal was . . . To bring together things that are not currently available unless someone wants to spend hours sitting in a library . . .

Reno Gazette-Journal

GOLDEN HIGHWAY
Highway 49, Volume I, North

Written by:
California pioneers and 19th Century historians.

Researched, compiled by Jody & Ric Hornor
Photo restoration by Ric Hornor & Steve Crandell

Published by:

Century Books

An Imprint of Electric Canvas™
1001 Art Road
Pilot Hill, CA 95664
916.933.4490

www.19thCentury.us

GOLDEN HIGHWAY
Highway 49, Volume I, North

19th Century Northern California including El Dorado, Placer, Nevada, and Sierra Counties

Including Coloma, Placerille, Auburn, Grass Valley, Nevada City, Downieville and smaller communities in between.

Written and photographed by the people who lived and made Northern California's history.

Acknowledgements

This book is dedicated to the thousands of pioneers who wrote California's history, the early photographers who captured the scenes and the hundreds of historians who have preserved it over the years.

This work would not have been possible without the help of dozens of libraries, librarians and archivists including:

Bancroft Library

Downieville Historical Society

El Dorado County Historical Museum

Folsom Historical Society

Kentucky Mine Museum

Library of Congress

Placer County Museums

Searls Library

Steve Crandell

Yale University Library

As we searched the vast libraries for the appropriate photographs, we found many of the same photos in different archives. The attributions are based on the archive from which we actually obtained the image. Any corrections or suggestions are welcome. Our apologies for any real or perceived errors.

We'd also like to thank our fact checkers and experts who helped assure the accuracy of this publication.

Lee Adams, Downieville Historical Society

Carmel Barry-Schweyer, Placer County Museums

Daniel M. Sebby, Command Sergeant Major, California Center for Military History, California State Military Department

Foreward

I love history! And, I really love the the early history of the Mother Lode of California – the communities that generally lie along the appropriately named Highway 49. Best of all, a book that is based on accurate information, is well illustrated as well as fun and entertaining to read, is a real plus. *The Golden Highway, Volume I*, is one of these books.

Like many others, I write history, which is what historians do. I have been doing it for a dozen years or more for the *Mountain Democrat*, which is in Placerville and now the oldest continuously published newspaper in California.

I point out that historians write history, and rarely report it, because most do not search out the original or earliest documents relating to the event or events about which they are writing. What happened then, and still happens, is that several people wrote about an event and many decades later someone writing a new story or book about the subject finds just one of these accounts and stops searching. Thus, it becomes the "truth." Years later historians pick up this information and it continues to be the "truth," whether it is or not. Unfortunately, most all other versions of the story are forgotten or simply ignored if discovered. To report accurately, one must bypass these later writings and go directly to the basic information or, better yet, the actual words of those who were there and experienced what happened. That is what Jody and Ric Hornor have done in their previous books and in this their latest exciting book, *The Golden Highway, Volume I*.

As a part of the writing I do for the *Mountain Democrat* I have been privileged to have had the opportunity to review a number of books on the subject of early California and the West, including both of the two previous books by the Hornors, *The Golden Corridor* and *The Golden Quest and Nevada's Silver Heritage*. What impressed me then with both of these books, and now with this third book, is the length to which the Hornors have gone to find and relate to the reader as accurate information as possible.

As with their previous books, the Hornors have done a wonderful job of putting a book together. They don't claim to be the authors; they modestly point out that they are but the researchers, compilers and editors. The real authors they tell

". . .the Hornors have done a wonderful job of putting a book together. They don't claim to be the authors; they modestly point out that they are but the researchers, compilers and editors. The real authors they tell us, are the people who wrote the letters, journals and books that they use as the text and often quote directly."

us, are the people who wrote the letters, journals and books that they use as the text and often quote directly. Similarly, they credit the very early photographers who took the hundreds of vintage photographs. These they have either themselves or with the assistance of Steve Crandell, a talented restorer of photographs in Placerville, CA, painstakingly brought back to life from their scratched, faded and grainy condition and included to illustrate their books. In other words, this is 19th century history written and photographed by those who made and lived it. As a result, when reading it you will become involved and actually feel the joy, anguish and determination of the brave people who settled this land and created the State of California.

The Golden Highway, Volume I, covers the northern part of the Mother Lode along Highway 49. For ease of reading each county is given a separate chapter, starting with El Dorado and working northward to Sierra County. The history of each of these counties and the cities and towns within them generally served by Highway 49 is provided to the reader in the Hornor's unique way – in a fun and interesting manner.

To assist with the reading experience, the Hornors have included visual clues for additional information. A picture of a quill pen identifies text from personal letters; stories about crime are identified by a hangman's noose; quotes from diaries and journals have a picture of President Taft's personal journal beside them and call outs, text that is highlighted for emphasis, appears with a magnifying glass.

The Golden Highway tells the history of a region in an interesting and exciting way that involves the reader completely as if they were there. Carefully selected photographs from the era complete the experience.

Like their books before, *The Golden Highway* tells the history of a region in an interesting and exciting way that involves the reader completely as if they were there, along with carefully selected photographs from the era to complete the experience. The Hornors started out to do this with the first of their planned six books and by this, their third, they are succeeding beyond their expectations.

If you are interested in the history of California and its growth from simple beginnings into the great state it is now; if you are interested in the adventure and intrigue of the early days of California; or if you just enjoy reading well written and well thought out, interesting history books, you too will love this book.

Doug Noble, Placerville, California, 2006

Table of Contents

Although some hunting and fishing might have been part of this outing based on the equipment in the camp, photography was clearly one of the major goals of the expedition. There are three stereo cameras visible. This photo was shot by a fourth camera that was not stereo, as we can tell by its horizontal format. Even with the major difficulties of lugging lots of equipment, photographers of the 19th century captured thousands of scenes that allow us all to envision what life was really like in the 1800s. This scene, probably in the 1880s, was shot at a logging camp on Slab Creek near Georgetown in what is now El Dorado National Forest.

Introduction

Trappers, adventurers, pathfinders, emigrants . . . even before the Gold Rush began there was a trickle of the truly hearty, wildly adventurous and amazingly tenacious people who began to settle California.

The discovery of gold in 1848 ignited hopes and dreams of thousands of people from the "States" and around the world. For a handful, those hopes and dreams came true. Most, however, battled bitter elements, a lawless society, disease and famine. Thousands suffered immeasurable hardships. Hundreds died. And a few -- a lucky few, made their "pile."

It is on the backs of their labors, the graves of their dead, and the dreams of their dreamers that these early pioneers turned California into one of the most desired places to live and work in our country.

Feel the joy, anguish and determination of the brave people who settled this land. Enjoy their humor, admire their flair.

As you read about their adventures, in their own words, you'll be amazed by their ingenuity, resiliency, and stamina. You'll feel their heartbreak and pain. You'll laugh at their antics. And you'll wonder if you could have conquered the challenges these hardy pioneers faces every day.

This is their story, in their words with their photographs.

Culled from roughly 5,000 pages of primary source documents, in *The Golden Highway*, you witness the many monumental accomplishments, brave souls, and exciting times that made Northern California what it is today.

With the exceptions of the photo captions, forward and introduction, this book was written in the 19th century style. Key points of history are delivered in the colorful language of the time.

Also, as you read the core text in the chapter, the diary entries, letters and newspaper articles, you'll may find many different formats and writing styles. That's because the main body of text in each chapter comes from one source unique to that chapter and the side bar materials come from many different writers. Words were often spelled differently in those days. Punctuation and sentence structure were also different. Because of the many contributors and their individual writing styles, you'll find some that are challenging to read. But, they're well worth your effort. Our goal is to preserve these styles for you to enjoy, so we have intentionally done nothing that will make the chapters consistent in their presentation, punctuation, spelling or format as it would eliminate each contributor's personal style and flavor in doing so.

There were huge cultural biases that are reflected in the text. As ingenious as these brave pioneers were, they had yet to invent "political correctness." As degrading and disheartening as some of the terms and stories are, they do reflect history.

Keep in mind that history, as it was recorded in the 19th century, was often done so subjectively. Many of the county history books (from which most of the core text is taken) were underwritten with the support of the people whose lives were chronicled within them. Thus the poor or not so vain may have been omitted unless they were truly newsworthy.

Our goal is to preserve these styles for you to enjoy, so we have intentionally done nothing that will make the chapters consistent in their presentation, punctuation, spelling or format as it would eliminate each contributor's personal style and flavor in doing so.

See page 211   See page 123

Photo restoration examples. These are the originals.
See the noted pages for the restored versions.

We're fortunate that there were a number of photographers, especially after 1860, who traveled extensively through the area and took hundreds, if not thousands, of photographs. Even so, finding the one image that exactly illustrates a point in the text is often impossible. We must sometimes go out of the specific geography or era to give you the best illustrations of the places and events being discussed.

Many of the original photographs are so damaged that it's nearly impossible to see the detail in them. They are carefully restored to uncover details that have faded over the years. Sometimes we make amazing discoveries in the restoration process. Other times there's a tinge of disappointment that we can't fix the many years of degradation. Even so, some of those images are included because they illustrate important points of our history.

Hundreds of hours of restoration have gone into the photographs used in *The Golden Highway*. Many of the original photos are in the public domain and available through the organizations noted with each image. Some are from private collections. In all cases, the restoration work is copyrighted. If you'd like copies of these images for your own use, you must contact the libraries or archives noted and obtain them directly from the respective institution.

So have fun wandering *The Golden Highway* in the 19th century. Get a taste of the rich history. And, if this book has whet your appetite for more, pick up a copy of *The Golden Corridor,* which covers the area from San Francisco to Lake Tahoe, or *The Golden Quest* that covers Lake Tahoe and Northern Nevada. Or use the bibliography as a guide and find yourself a library with a good California reference section. Have fun with your studies!

Side Bar Legend

Most of the side bars provide new information that is not contained in the main body of text. The nature of the information is denoted by the following icons:

Text from personal letters will appear in this script font with the quill pen.

Stories about crime will appear with the hangman's noose.

Quotes from diaries or journals will appear with this image of President Taft's personal journal.

Call outs, text that appears in the main body of content, highlighted for emphasis, appears with this magnifying glass.

You'll also occasionally find direct quotes from old newspaper articles which are in this font and quoted and sourced.

Miners moved frequently, sometimes every few days. Moving this tent was pretty easy, but even when frame construction became popular, it wasn't uncommon to either pick up the frame shack or disassemble it by sections to move on to the next mining camp.

Chapter 1: El Dorado County — Coloma, Placerville, Georgetown, Cool, Fair Play & vicinity

El Dorado county was one of the most prosperous of the mining counties. It is estimated that the vast product of the gold-fields of California at least $100,000,000 was taken out here. Scattered all over the Union are hundreds of men, now rolling in wealth, who made their "stake" in the placers of El Dorado county. The industrious thousands who once swarmed in these canyons, digging for the precious metal, have vanished, leaving ravished stream-beds and abandoned camps, as the only monuments of their presence.

There were no distinctions in society; dress did not indicate wealth or poverty. The most filthy and ragged looking ''ombre'' might have the biggest pile.

Luther Melanchthon Schaeffer, 1851

Steve Crandell Collection

Coloma was a bustling town when this photograph was taken in 1857. Even though many miners were located outside the actual town, it was still a hub of commerce for the thousands of miners in surrounding areas. Note the covered bridge in the background. It was one of several in the area.

The roads were so wretched that supplies could be got to the mines only by pack-animals. A dollar per pound was the customary rate to Coloma and to Hangtown, which were about the same distance from Sacramento.

Gold dust was the universal currency, and the "blower" and the scales were a fixture in every place of business. The weights were often home-made, and of very dubious specific gravity.

David Leeper, 1849

OLD COLOMA! The town with some history--no, the starting point of a history of El Dorado county, and of the total revolution in the history of the whole State, throwing her out of the lethargy and quietness of hundreds of years in a feverish excitement that kept her enchained for about twenty-five years. The discovery of gold in the race of the Coloma mill, however, did not stop with the revolutionizing of California; no, it became epidemic and infected the whole civilized world. The alarm was given out, and Coloma became the motto of the day, Coloma the longing of millions, and Coloma the endpoint of the travel of thousands, whose starting points had been most every where on this globe. And right here it may be allowed to put the question: Has California been benefited with the discovery of gold at Coloma, and all the circumstances that followed? The discovery of gold was inavoidable, it would have been made sooner or later. But there can be no doubt that California would be better off nowadays, if the discovery had not been made before the State became more settled and thicker populated, or if the discovery would have been kept a secret as Capt. Sutter had proposed it. A slow development would have avoided the outgrowing of all those monopolies under which the State is suffering now. What did those miners of early days care for the welfare of this country? More than nine out of each ten came here to make their pile and march home with it.

Coloma is located on the South Fork of the American river, in an altitude of 900 feet above the level of the sea, on the upper end of the Coloma basin, which is surrounded by hills from 800 to 1,000 feet higher up.

For the first few years after the discovery of gold all the new arrivals were bound for Coloma, and though the mines in the vicinity were rich and plenty of them, the population was growing so fast that soon many had to be turned away to look out for other diggings. But a large business was done here in support of a population that numbered into the thousands. The first business places in town were Capt. Shannon & Cady's, the New York Store, S. S. Brook's store, and John Little's emporium on the North side of the river. Warner, Sherman & Bestor, of the United States army, kept a store here during the winter of 1848-'49. The first hotel was the Winters Hotel, Messrs. Winters & Cromwell, proprietors; A. J. Bayley, now of Pilot Hill, attended bar there. Sutter's saw-mill had been finished and was put to work by Messrs. Winters, Marshall & Bayley, doing a fine business. A large two-story building had been erected for a theater in 1852. Capt. Shannon was Alcalde of the township, and John T. Little first Postmaster, a Post office having been established already in 1849. This then was the principal Post office in California.

Mr. Sinclair, who had two hundred acres of fine ripe wheat, left it and took the Indians who were to have harvested it to the mines; the gold he found could be measured by the bushel, I was told.

Heinrich Lienhard, 1849

Placer mining near Coloma. Note the various styles of hats. Clearly there are two Chinese in this group, but the styles of other hats indicates this was truly a multinational group working together on this claim in 1851.

El Dorado County Historical Society

El Dorado County Historical Society

Bendfeldt Mine in Smith Flat

The following is the estimated amount of gold as taken from some of the bars on the Middle Fork of the American River:

Valcano Bar	$1,500,000
Greenhorn Slide	1,000,000
Yankee Slide	1,000,000
Sandy Bar	500,000
Menken Cut Bar	200,000
Mud Canyon	3,000,000
Nigger's Bluff	500,000
Gray Eagle Bar	800,000
Eureka	100,000
Horse Shoe Bend	2,500,000
Boston	100,000
American Bar	3,000,000
Willow Bar	600,000
Junction Bar	150,000
Missouri Canyon	800,000
Grizzly Canyon	300,000
Otter Creek	400,000
From all the hills	300,000
Total	$16,750,000

Six pony expresses were running between Coloma and the mines all around, to deliver the half-monthly arriving mail, charging one dollar a letter for the delivery. [One rather interesting letter follows.]

Coloma, 1st July, 1850

Dear Lawrence,

Again I write you from this ... town. As far as I am able to judge from observation and "talks" with operating practical miners here, I am of the opinion that this portion of the South Fork of the American river will give more than its average of gold this season; miners at work on the banks of this stream average an ounce a day within three miles of Coloma. West from here, claims yield to the man from one to three ounces a day; more may be expected as the river is yet high. Mr. Little's enterprise of cutting a canal and turning the river, is progressing rapidly; he has fifty workmen employed; on his own shoulders he has taken the responsibility, and I trust the experiments will meet with success. Coloma has much to thank this same Mr. Little for; he built her bridge, encouraged "capitally" her mill, aided materially in giving her a good road to Georgetown, supplies her with a full assortment of desirable merchandise, feeds the hungry in his hotel, and has been foremost in aiding all improvements for her welfare. The road to Georgetown is in good order though much traveled; a stage coach runs daily from Coloma there.

Mr. Brown, partner of Heufmeir & Co., (proprietor's of the Digger's Hotel) took out in three days last week, $1100 in gold *dust from this fork from where I am now writing. A body was found in the river some two miles west from here, but it was so mutilated as not to be recognized. Muller is getting up to a new restaurant in keeping with our fast improvements. Great preparations are being made to keep alive in the spirit of the Fourth, an oration is to be delivered, a dinner and ball come off at Winters, a military turn out is to happen and sundry other movements are to take place to perpetuate the memory of men whose deeds won our nation's freedom.*

'In a promenade this morning, I was struck with the number of ladies I encountered; and I can with truth speak in praise of the beauty of the fair of Coloma. I think seriously of calling this town my home for a month or two; no girls, prepare yourselves for my polite attentions. I will find leisure to write again soon, and tell you how "the Fourth" slid off with us.

Yours truly, Nedwin of Nedwin

One of Sutter's iron howitzers is still decorating the front of Meyers' Hotel. It was here that the first plan for obtaining water by artificial means was derived, and the first ditch in El Dorado county and California was built. Sutter's old saw mill was working at full speed from 1849 to 1852 or '53, thereaf-

After quitting work for the evening and having supper, the time would be passed round our campfires in singing and telling yarns till it was time to go to bed. Everyone seemed happy and full of hopes. No quarreling or fighting took place.

John Swan, 1848

Hydrauliic Mining in El Dorado County, 1850s.

El Dorado County Historical Society

The Palace Hotel in Greenwood.

The hostlers and station-keepers treated the really powerful conductor of the coach merely with the best of what was their idea of civility, but the driver was the only being they bowed down to and worshipped. How admiringly they would gaze up at him in his high seat as he gloved himself with lingering deliberation, while some happy hostler held the bunch of reins aloft, and waited patiently for him to take it! And how they would bombard him with glorifying ejaculations as he cracked his long whip and went careering away.

Mark Twain, 1872

ter it was not used any more and commenced to go to pieces. Pieces of the old mill were used to transfer them into presents for memory and relics, which will be highly valued by the coming generations.

Notwithstanding the great accumulation of all classes of people from all different nations, Coloma was a very quiet and peaceful mining camp; but very few incidents of violence are known to have taken place here.

Coloma has not only a place in history, but also in the hearts of all romantic visitors. There is no hamlet in the Sierras more serene and poetic; the air is perfectly ethereal, during the day mellow and golden, during the night silver and purple. Then the moon rises over the hills, arraying orchards and piney summits and quiet cottages with veils of silken radiance. Vineyards and orchards line the hillsides as high up as water for irrigation can reach, and the sunny grape draws its sparkling juice from among soil sprinkled with virgin gold. And, though, the Coloma basin has lost a great richness in the shape of gold, it has copiously made up in permanent improvements. The fruit grown in this vicinity and on this soil is unsurpassable in juice and flavor.

GREENWOOD was originally called "Long Valley," and a trading post opened there sometime either in 1848 or the Spring of 1849, by John Greenwood; the first general store there was opened by Lewis B. Myers, Nathan Fairbanks and Louis Line.

El Dorado County Historical Society

On the 25th of March, 1850, a son was born to Lewis B. Myers and the town was called Lewisville after the first-born child in the township. The name, however, was changed when a Post office was established, on account of there being another Louisville in the county, and Greenwood Valley substituted therefore.

It is located in one of the loveliest little valleys of the foot-hills of the Sierra Nevada; about five miles south of George-town, on the highway from Cave Valley to Georgetown. Here in early days a nice and lively village developed in a considerable short time.

There existed quite a number of large mercantile houses. Bloom & Partner kept the Illinois Exchange, afterwards the Nation. Mr. Bloom was the first Post Master, and being himself quite illiterate, he used to look at one or a couple of letters and after that would ask the caller to look for himself; this, however, was no hindrance to his endeavor for a seat in the State Legislature which he was running for.

The Penobscott House, one of the oldest public houses and stopping places in the township, owned by L Myers, from 1851 to 1854, sold to Page & Lovejoy, who also bought Doctor Thomas' line of stages from Georgetown to Sacramento by way of Pilot Hill and Salmon Falls. Mr. Page's aspirations were running faster than the stage trot and higher than the highest stage seat, and did not let him rest until he succeeded with a seat in the Hall of legislature.

Miners along the American River, 1852.

Steve Crandell Collection

I drove to Mormon Island. I had passed about five white miners washing gold in their camps, and one of them, noticing the watermelons in our wagon, came over and helped himself. I told him to put it back; and his comrades, too, advised him to return it; but he merely sneered at us. The miner who stole the melon was a stalwart, disreputable, one-eyed man whose attitude showed me he was a law-breaker. As long as he knew he would not be caught or punished, he intended to take advantage of us. I knew that if I got into a fight with the man I could not rely on more than half of my Indians, and that the four stalwart friends of the melon thief would undoubtedly come to his assistance. So I drove on, after remarking that I was willing to give melons away, but taking them was nothing more than thievery.

Heinrich Lienhard, 1849

Main Street in Greenwood was bustling with activity when this photo was taken in 1880.

 I got to a stopping place six miles from Coloma. There I met a man with a long beard, slouched hat, and sash around his body, a flannel shirt, evidently a miner. I had a long talk with him. He posted me about the gold diggings and I him about the news from the States. As we were about to part, he asked me to take a drink. He inquired of the proprietor if he had champagne? He said, yes, at $10 a bottle. The man said, pass us down a bottle, which we drank together. He, evidently, had struck good diggings. We parted, as I was anxious to get to Coloma before dark, which I did, just as the sun was setting, having made twenty-five miles in one day on foot. I found a regular tavern here, kept by a man from Mississippi, with his family. I sat down to a regular table for my supper, which seemed quite a treat. He informed me that he had no bed-room for me; that I could sleep on the dining-room floor, or in his barn. He had just had some new hay put in. I chose the latter. It was a kind of a shanty building, but the soft bed of new hay was a luxury after my twenty-five miles walk.

Daniel Knower, 1849

Greenwood Valley was by far more fortunate than its sister mining town, as far as the destruction by fire is concerned; the first fire of any magnitude originated in Charles Nagler's house, where it was caused by an ash barrel standing at the corner of the house, and bid the entire business part of the town in ashes, in 1858. On February 3d, 1876, at an early hour, a box filled with combustibles etc., was discovered on fire placed to the front of Felice Ricci's store, and had it not been for Chas. Nagler's watchdog, whose restless noise alarmed the clerk sleeping in the store, there would have been a big blaze, but under the circumstances it only could be called a close call, as the flames were subdued in time with the assistance of some neighbors. Nothing could be found out about the originator, and whether it was done with the intent to burn the town and get a chance for robbing or to gratify a personal grudge against Ricci. There speaks a great probability for the latter argument, however, if we consider the circumstances under which the premises of Messrs. Nagler and Ricci were set on fire June 3d, 1878; about two years afterwards, and residences, stores etc., with all contents were totally destroyed.

The principal support consists in mining, and there are the richest mining claims close onto town. The Nagler or French claim, first a seam mine, worked after the hydraulic process. North of the French claim there is the Bower mine, run by eastern capital and pushed with great vigor. A Chinese agent some years ago came up here from San Francisco, offering the sum of $100,000, for this property as it stood at the time, while about a year before that, it could have been bought for perhaps $15 or $20. The Argonaut mine, upon which as long as 1852 prospecting was done to a limited extent in search of the quartz ledges.

UNIONTOWN first called "Marshall," as Coloma was called Sutter's mill, below Coloma, once a mining community of some note. There were not less than one thousand men engaged here in mining, partially on the South Fork of the American river, partially on the neighboring Granite and Shingle creeks, supporting ten or twelve large boarding houses, and a number of stores. The first store was opened by Inglesby & Merrill. Benjamin Smith also kept a store. Another store was kept by Franklin Prague, who also built the first Uniontown bridge. A saw mill, the second one in El Dorado county was erected on what was then known as saw-mill slough. Dr. Doolin kept a drug store besides his practice as a physician. Law and Stevens kept the first bakery, and furnished the very smallest loaves of bread in the winter of 1850, when flour was worth $50 per 100 lbs., and a pound freight was charged 16 cents from Mormon Island to Coloma. Herrick Jacobs was probably the first blacksmith in town. In 1853, Mr. A. Lohry opened a general store here and a few years after erected the brick store still occupied as such.

Mormon Island with tents in the mid-1850s This was one of more than 30 gold mining camps that were in the area that is now covered by Folsom Lake. Mormon Island had a population of more than 2,500 by 1855. After the Gold Rush the community focused on ranching and agriculture until the mid-1950s when Folsom Dam was constructed and the lake was filled.

Steve Crandell Collection

Fragments of a human skeleton were found, including quite a number under a tree near the flume; here and there also particles of clothing attached to or near some of the bones were found, and at a point, where it appeared very likely the body had originally lain, by digging away the dead leaves and rubbish, a pocket-book and a few half and quarter dollars, amounting in all to $2.25, were discovered. The pocket knife and some strips of a woolen shirt were identified as having belonged to Jesse Hendricks, the ditch tender, whose mysterious disappearance in June, 1870, cause quite some little excitement. No doubt he had been murdered; by whom, however, never has come to light up to this day.

The Indians of the vicinity of American and Columbia Flats had a "big eating" on Irish creek, on Wednesday, July 27, 1870. White Rock Jack could not withstand the temptation of being present. He left his mountain hiding place and repaired to the place of feasting. The Indians, had procured liquor, and Jack's appetite again getting the better of him, he got beastly drunk. Two Indians then came to the storekeeper of Columbia Flat informing him that Jack was near by and in what condition. They help[ed] to bind him; whereupon he was brought to Placerville, and delivered into jail. Thus this savage desperado, for whose capture the Supervisors of El Dorado county had offered a reward of $500. His trial came up in the District Court on March 3, 1871, he pleaded guilty of murder in the second degree, and was sentenced by Judge Adams to hard labor in the State Prison for the term of his natural life. Jack received his sentence with the characteristic Indian stolidity, but, it is said, when reaching his cell, he wept at the cheerless and hopeless future of a lifelong incarceration within the walls of San Quentin. Jack was then 23 years of age and a superior specimen of the Digger Indian.

El Dorado County Historical Society

This ditch tender, Ed Stanton, and his donkey were in the Georgetown area. In most areas ditch tenders were usually spread out at 4-5 mile intervals. Their job was to remove debris, repair flumes and keep water flowing to the mines at all cost or the mine would have to shut down.

A Post office was established here January 6th, 1881, with the store keeper, as Post Master, the Post office is called "Lotus" on suggestion of Mr. Lohry.

GEORGETOWN in early days was the prettiest town in the mountains. Georgetown is and always will be a mining town in the full sense of the word, the high elevation as well as the character of the country don't recommend it for an agricultural centre. The first mining work on this divide was done by a party of Oregonians under the leadership of Hudson; they were mining in what has since been known as "Oregon canyon" and "Hudson's gulch" in July 1849, but, though they took out a large amount of gold at both these places they did not stay. They were followed by a party of sailors, among whom was one George Phipps, who first pitched his tent near the head of what since has been called "Empire canyon," and from him derived the original name of George's town, just as John's town lower down in the same canyon, at its junction with Manhattan creek, was named after another man of the same party. The afterwards famous "Sailor Claim" in Oregon canyon, however, did not obtain its name from the Phipps party.

The first log house in the young George's town was erected about September 20th, 1849 and the first store opened therein; other buildings followed, and by January 1st, 1850, their number had increased to a dozen, occupied chiefly as stores, among whom were Graham and Hull; John T. Little's branch of the Coloma store; old Tom Clegg; Gushing and Grammer. Mr. Grammer also started the first letter express, and during the summer of 1850, Mr. Graham had a stage line running between Georgetown and Coloma; this however, finally emerged into a through line of stages to Sacramento City. The "Georgetown Cut-off" road opened in 1850, furnished a great opportunity to a portion of the overland emigration to reach the valley below by passing this way, and the location of the place proved to be a very favorable one, if not a necessity, as the highway junction for all those rich river bars on the Middle Fork of the American river; as Ford's, Volcano, Big, Sandy, Junction, Gray Eagle and other bars, and the distributing point for supplies, etc., to those who were working on those bars and all those flats and other mining camps beyond Coloma.

Meantime the town, imbeded in the native wilds of surrounding material wealth, made up of log cabins, shake houses and canvas tents, was growing until a traveling photographer, in his attempt to take a photograph of a deceased miner, by accident set the frail building or tent on fire, July 14th, 1852. The fire originated in the "Round Tent," a gambling saloon kept by Pete Valery, where N. Lothian, formerly leader of the famous Lothian Band, of New York, furnished the music. The flames spread with such rapidity that it was only under difficul-

Ford Copper Mine near Georgetown

Steve Crandell Collection

Here we are, at length, in the gold diggings. Seated around us are a group of wild Indians, from the tribe called "Diggers," so named from their living chiefly upon roots. These Indians are of medium size, seldom more than five feet and eight or ten inches high; are very coarse and indolent in appearance, of a dark complexion, with long black hair which comes down over the face; are uncivilized, and possess few of the arts of life. They weave a basket of willow so closely as to hold water, in which they boil their mush, made of acorns dried and pounded to a powder, or their flour, purchased at some trading tent.

They have brought us in some salmon, one of which weighs twenty-nine pounds. These they spear with great dexterity, and exchange for provisions, or clothing, and ornaments of bright colors.

We were induced to come to this place by the accounts we received of the success of two brothers who, in a few weeks, made $3000 here, and are now on their way home.

Daniel B. Woods, Salmon Falls, South Fork of the American River, July 4th, 1849

El Dorado County Historical Society

Georgetown Cash Store owned by Warren C. Green. Note the signs for the Bell "Telephone Pay Station" and "Star Tabacco." Photo 1889.

We had no vegetables. One day we heard that they had dried apple sauce at the hotel at Coloma for dinner. The next day, Sunday, three of us walked eight miles to get there to dinner to get a taste of it. We paid $2 apiece for our dinner, and they had the sauce; it tasted so good that we did not begrudge the price of the dinner and the walk back again.

Daniel Knower, 1849

ties, that the corpse could be saved from cremation, and in one half hour the business portion of the town was almost entirely laid in ashes.

The pioneer miners from the surrounding camps generously volunteering time and labor, came with axes and other implements, and under their heavy blows the pines fell with thundering crash and the thick under brush was cleared away.

The town then was in the most flourishing condition, with rich placer mines surrounding it in every direction; the crude surroundings of its birth place were fast thrown off and a better condition of society established.

A second big fire visited Georgetown on July 7th, 1856, the day after Placerville had been destroyed by a big blaze. It originated in the rear of what was known as Pat. Lynch's saloon, midway on Main street. The flames spread with such rapidity that scarcely anything could be saved. Stores, hotels and dwelling houses on Main street, melted away like snow before the sun, and only by almost superhuman efforts was it possible to save the rear portion of the western part of town. But again the indomitable spirit of the people arose in triumph over their misfortune, and, phoenix-like, from its ashes a new town sprang up. Again on the 16th of August, 1858, the principal business portion of the town was destroyed by fire; the greatest damage was done on the east side of Main street, which was only partially rebuilt. The last time Georgetown has been visited by the fire fiend was on May 28th, 1869; the fire was discovered in the old

Miners' Hotel, on Main street, shortly after midnight, and the flames spread with such rapidity that the proprietor of the hotel, Mr. Stahlman, barely escaped out over the roofs with his eldest child; but his wife, three children and Miss Stanton perished in the flames.

The west side of Main street was partially destroyed, also the Catholic church and the Town Hall. Stahlman, suspected of arson . . . the jury deliberated and gave a verdict of not guilty.

Mining in this district was first confined to the canyons and gulches, and to the bars on the Middle Fork of the American river. Then came the "Hill diggings," worked by drifting. The first strike was made at "Bottle Hill," which was opened up in 1851, Mameluke Hill followed in 1852, and even richer deposits were discovered in 1853 and '54 at Cement and Jones' Hill. At each of these mining camps thriving towns were built up, and regular stage and telegraphic communications with Georgetown established. But the days of wild excitement have passed by.

Next came what has been termed "seams diggings," a peculiarity of the vicinity of Georgetown, worked principally by the hydraulic process; with great promise in the constancy of

Tahoe Saloon in Georgetown, owned by Frank Scherrer. Signs in the background advertise "Wm. Penn Havana Cigars," "Jesse Moore AA Wiskey" and "Star Tobacco." Coffee mugs in the background appear to have individual patron's faces painted on them, probably for their exclusive use. Photo 1897.

El Dorado County Historical Society

Dear Lawrence,

Tis said that a Benedict citizen of this town returned a night or two since from a business tour to Sacramento City, with open arms ran to his wife's boudoir, herald of his own return, when in his horror he saw a pair of boots going out at the window. 'Tis said, also, that said boots contained an "hombre." "Beauty and the beast" are names by which the newly married couple of this town are known. I have seen the pair and can vouch for the personal attractions of the lady, the partner of her bosom out-uglys our brother Pete. The owner of a more awful mug can rake my pile.

Yours truly,
Nedwin of Nedwin
Coloma, 1st July, 1850

In the latter part of August, 1852, I went to Placerville for supplies. After I had completed my purchases I discovered two desperate characters on horseback parading the streets. Both were, or pretended to be, intoxicated, and flourishing large revolvers, they rode furiously while shouting to people on the streets, "Hunt your holes! Hunt your holes!"

Hoping to avoid an encounter with them, I remained some time in the store; but at last ventured out. I left the store when here they came flourishing their pistols and howling at the top of their voices.

A large, well-proportioned man walked a short distance in advance of me. His claystained clothing indicated that he was a miner; attached to his belt a large revolver hung at his back; and on the seat of his pantaloons was a large patch, evidently a piece from a flour sack, as it bore the mark EXTRA FINE. He would first meet the reckless rider, and I hesitated to see what would be the result.

Nearer came the man on horseback. A shot from the horseman's pistol glanced along the side walk. The miner's hand had been laid upon his pistol; now it was instantly drawn and fired.

The rider threw up his arms; then he made an effort to grasp the saddle, but fell heavily to the sidewalk; the horse shied into the middle of the street and the rider on the opposite side went quietly down to the South Fork, a noted gambling headquarters. The fate of his comrade seemed to have tamed or sobered him.

Rev. John Steele, 1850

The Pilot Hill Post office building was originally the McLaglen Store and then the Nance Store and Bar in the late 1800s. Numerous advertisements are visible. Hires Root Beer (began in 1876), Cambell's Soup (began in 1897), and Copenhagen Tobacco (began in 1822) are some of the more well known names advertised. But, it's the Zerolene Gas & Oil sign that best dates this photo as sometime after 1907.

their character. The "Beatty Seams Claim," at Georgia Slide, for instance, was opened in 1854. Nearly all the small divides between the canyons and gulches contain deposits of this description. The Woodside mine was worked to the depth of 225 feet, and the amount taken out of the mine was over $50,000. The Eureka had a shaft sunk to the depth of 230 feet. The Taylor mine was a good paying property some years ago. The location of Georgetown is on the regular divide, being the water shed of the two rivers.

The water of the Georgetown divide is controlled for the most part by the "California Water Company," their main supply is a system of lakes situated at a high altitude in the eastern portion of the county, having an aggregate of 300 miles of ditches, flumes and iron pipes.

Incidents of an exciting character have been quite rare at Georgetown, though the town has been notorious for stage robberies and burglaries—on account of which Wells Fargo & Co., discontinued their office in town—at an immense cost to the county in not convicting.

Judge lynch held a carnival here two or three times, only once with fatal precision.

CENTERVILLE. The old town of Pilot Hill was located further north and nearer the base of Pilot Hill. Originally called Centerville, but now known as Pilot Hill, it has retained more of the character of a mining camp of old, than most places in the country. The town is located at the north-eastern base of Pilot Hill, from which it derives its name. The first mining was done in 1849, and the first little store was opened here the same year in a common log building. Rich placers had been discovered, but as there was no water on hand, the mining work had to be delayed until the winter of 1850, when miners flocked in here from the river bars and a lively business began.

Talcott & Rose started the first regular store in this mining camp, making this their head quarters for the winter, while they tended to their other places of business on the river during the summer season. Among the first ones, that came here to try their fortune at Centerville, was John Woods, of New York, he came up here from Salmon Falls in the fall of 1849, at which time there were plenty of grizzlies around here. The first house in town was built by Samuel Stevens in the earliest part of 1850. John Brown and Wilson kept one of the first boarding houses here, and did a splendid business. Another store was kept by Henry Stevens and Conrad Thompson, the latter known as "Topside," as he was an old sailor. Another boarding house was opened by Charles Tudsberry. Of other old residents

This is the Cool and Placerville Stage in 1915. Cool was called Cave Valley until 1885. It was renamed after Aaron Cool, who traveled the Gold Country as a circuit preacher administering the gospel to miners and their families.

Our habitation was simply some posts placed upright in the ground, supporting a roof of boughs. It made a good shade and as there was no rain in summer we enjoyed the outdoor air. A tent was pitched beside our booth, but was seldom used.

We were greatly annoyed by fleas; they seemed to be everywhere, but more especially where we fixed our bunks and tried to sleep. We were advised to place our cots on a pile of the branches of a kind of black alder, which fleas avoid, and in doing so we were much relieved.

Rev. John Steele, 1850

Library of Congress

The Bayley House in 1890. In 1861, A.J. Bayley erected the roomy three story brick mansion that was touted as "the most exquisite building in the county," believing that the railroad would go through the area and the "mansion" would do a booming hotel business. But the railroad did not pass through and the mansion speculation soon became known as "Bayley's Follies." This famous Pilot Hill home is still standing... barely. It's awaiting funding for a $3 million restoration.

Peter borrowed my saddle to go to Sutter's Fort to see an old acquaintance of his. There was no Sacramento City then. He had a horse of his own, or borrowed one. He went to the fort, got on the spree, and then went down to San Francisco and kept on the whiskey line so long that he had the delirium tremens and jumped into the bay in one of his fits and was drowned.

John Swan, 1848

at Pilot Hill out of the year of 1850, we have to mention A.J. Bayley and F.B. Peacock.

The first school in Pilot Hill School District was a private school supported by Bayley and others, and was located near Bayley's residence.

John Bowman was the first blacksmith in this community, since the Spring of 1852. He moved around considerably and finally settled on Bayley's ranch.

The present hotel, a two and a-half story frame structure was built in 1854, and occupied for some years by Mr. Creque. Mrs. Jane McLagan is the present proprietor.

There are still three stores kept here, two in town and Mr. Bayley's on Bayley's ranch about a quarter mile northeast of town, where Mr. Bayley, in 1860, erected the present magnificent and roomy three story brick mansion of the Bayley family, without any doubt, the most exquisite building in the county.

The Pilot Hill mining district, once as noted as the far seen Beacon Hill, from which it takes its name, situated between the North and South forks of the American river, seems to be one of those lost mining camps; and why so, we are unable to give an answer. The alluvial deposits in its ravines, flats and gulches have been immensely rich and plentifully diversified with large nuggets and rich specimens of golden quartz. Near the top of the hill--from which in clear weather a magnificent view is presented of Sacramento with the Capitol and the whole Sacramento valley, with the river like a silver ribbon running through, the Marysville Buttes and the Coast range in the back ground, forming a beautiful panorama-- is situated the Pilot Hill mine. A number of auriferous quartz seams run through the location, and several shafts have been sunk, which brought the owners several thousand dollars in return for their work.

NEGRO HILL. The first mining work done in the vicinity of Negro Hill was on the east side, adjoining the river, by a company of Mormons, in the year 1848. Little Negro Hill paid from two to three ounces per day to the hand, the dirt being carted to the river and washed through a long tom. About this time (fall of 1849) three men, Messrs. Vosey, Long and French started a store and boarding house, the house being known as the Civil Usage House, and a good business was done here. Soon after Mr. Fish built another store in the vicinity and did good business up to 1852.

In the spring of 1852, Conrad Benniger, Harvey Smith and Darius Clark sunk holes on the second bench back from

The Fair Play Hotel and McKees Saloon, 1879

Steve Crandell Collection

One dark night and no moon, after talking till it was time to go to sleep and some of the miners had spread out their blankets and some laid down for the night--most of the conversation had been about bears and other animals--something was heard coming down through the bushes towards the water and afterwards towards the log cabin. And as most people's thoughts were on bears and it was too dark to see, of course everybody thought it was a bear; and what few arms there was being unloaded, there was a scattering. Some got up trees; some stowed behind them and bushes; and some got over the walls of the log cabin into it; and I, being small, got through the window. But while some nearly got jammed trying to get through and others getting over it, up came the animal, and it proved to be Haggerty's big black mule. And if ever a mule got a cursing it did that night, and then there was a general laugh at their own fears.

John Swan, 1848

About five o'clock, we stopped at what was termed the "Mormon Camp" for supper, and while discussing the goodly fare of the dames who prepared it, my horse, who was famous for such exploits, wandered off and could nowhere be found. One of my medicine chests was loosely suspended at the saddle-bow. In this, for safety, as the medicine gave out, the bottles were replenished with "dust," and now contained the all in gold of two or three individuals, whom it had cost no little time and labor to accumulate. Search was made in every direction for the missing horse, with no little dread of the result, but in vain, and night came on before he was found, quietly enjoying a little herbage which his sagacity had discovered nearly three miles off, unconscious of the severe pangs his absence had inflicted on one at least of the party, who vowed "he should be his banker no longer."

James L. Tyson, 1849

Gold panning, 1889

the river, and found good dirt, it being a large flat. In one week after, there was every foot claimed and staked off for mining, and two Negroes from Massachusetts started a store and boarding house, around which quite a Negro village sprung up, and was called Big Negro Hill. On another portion of the flat the white men built quite a town, representing the present Negro Hill. Here Thos. Jenkins and Richard Rickard built a store, and Thomas Bennett and Wm. Trengove built a boarding house, being each the first one in town.

In the year 1853, Leander Jennings and Alexander Fraser built a ditch from Salmon Falls to Negro Hills, a distance of eight miles, which carried about 300 inches of water, sold at $1.00 per inch, by which nearly the whole of the top of the hill has been sluiced off, and paid well. In 1855, Messrs. Clark, Boyd, Richards and Eastman built another ditch from near Salmon Falls, running it to Negro Hill, Growlers Flat, Jenny Lind Flat, Massachusetts Flat, Chile Hill, Condemned Bar and Long Bar, all of which are in a circuit of three miles; so as a matter of course all the miners came to Negro Hill to buy their goods, and the result was, that business men did well for five or six years. After that the mines fell gradually in the hands of the Chinese and business rapidly declined. All the white men who remained in the district, with the exception of two or three, are now engaged in farming.

MURDERER'S BAR. The derivation of this name as told by Mr. D. Fairchild, an old pioneer of 1849, is showing a true picture of early mining events: "Among the pioneers of 1848, was Thomas M. Buckner, now a resident of Spanish Dry Diggings, El Dorado county, who emigrated to Oregon from Kentucky, in 1845. When the news of the discovery of gold in California reached Oregon, several parties were immediately fitted out with the purpose to start for the gold-fields. Buckner was a member of one of these companies. Having obtained unmistakable directions as to the route and distance, they left the fort about the 10th, of August.

"Knowing nothing about dry or ravine diggings, and believing the tales of trappers and others, that it would be impossible to winter at the mines along the rivers, Buckner went to San Francisco and thence to the redwoods, known as San Antonio, in the hills back of the present site of Oakland, where Redwood-peak is, here he found employment making shakes, pickets, whip-saw lumber etc.

"Among these homogeneous spirits who were temporarily inhabiting the redwoods was Capt. Ezekiel Merritt, ... during the winter an intimate friendship sprang up between Buckner and Merritt, and they determined to blend their fortunes into a venture to the mines.

My duty was now to carry stones and dirt in a bag, on my shoulder to the rockers, about twenty yards distant, and the first step I took, I slipped, and my foot pressed clear through my shoe. On I kept, and when I was about to tumble the load down, I hardly remember which fell first, the bag or myself, and a more mud-bespattered individual is rarely to be seen. Of course, my fall and appearance caused the crowd to shout with laughter.

Luther Melanchthon Schaeffer, 1851

Miners panning gold at Coloma, 1850s.

Steve Crandell Collection

One day in December, '49, a crowd came trooping down the street to Captain Shannon's mansion, having in custody a vagabond sailor, charged with having stolen from a miner $600 in dust contained in a purse, demanding the exercise of the judicial authority of the Captain as Alcalde. The latter without ceremony opened his court, selected a jury of six reputable men, appointed prosecution attorney, etc.; the prisoner was given a full opportunity to establish his innocence. The case, after the charge of the Alcalde, was given to the jury. After due deliberation, through their foreman, the jury rendered a verdict as follows:

1. We find the prisoner guilty of the charge.
2. In consideration of the poverty of the complainant, if the prisoner will make restitution of the property and depart the "diggings," he may be discharged.
3. If he does not accept the offer, then and there he shall receive 25 lashes, well laid on, be imprisoned with ball and chain for a space of 10 days, and then, if he restores the money and departs, be discharged.
4. At the expiration of the imprisonment he shall receive 25 lashes and leave the diggings.

"The prisoner declined to return the money and suffered the full penalty; after which he vamosed to parts unknown.

Motherlode miners in 1852

"Meritt and Buckneer, packed up their animals, and advancing in a northerly direction, crossed the South Fork of the American, and descended into the canyon of the Middle Fork.

"There were no evidences of any work having been done by white men, but while traveling, the little party had observed signs of Indians, and, deeming any they would there meet would be hostile, on account of their small number a sharp lookout was kept. They had proceeded but a short distance, when they reached the head of a large bar, situated upon the South side of the river, there upon the pebbly bar above high water mark, among evidences of a plundered camp, was the white man's hair, strewn around with that of the Indian, silent evidence that the life of the superior race had not gone out to the great unknown unavenged and without a struggle. No bodies were found, but an ash heap close by, in which were calcined bones, told the story of the white and red man together.

"Upon this discovery, the point of rocks ahead became a barrier post, beyond which the white men dared not go for fear of an ambuscade, but no Indians in sight. Thereupon all three, with arms in readiness in case of necessity, sallied forth for further explorations down the river. Scarcely had they passed the point, before some sixty or seventy Indians appeared upon the bench or higher bar, above them, yelling and gesticulating in a frightful manner, but as they were only armed with bows and arrows, dared not attack. Now that the enemy were in sight all fear of ambush passed away, and with "Rachel," as Merritt called his old-fashioned rifle, poised for business, the white men watched the yelping savages until the latter apparently became convinced that they could do no harm to the former, and in the course of a few hours, retreated upon the mountain and disappeared from view.

"He accordingly took his pocket knife and cut upon the smooth and easily slipped bark of an alder tree, "MURDERER'S BAR " by which the spot has ever since been known. But Merritt and Buckner did not deem it prudent to remain there. They preferred to camp in some more open spot less liable to be approached by the Indians under cover, and crossing the river in a dug-out canoe, they established themselves with animals and paraphernalia upon the Placer county side of the Middle Fork at Buckner's Bar, with the river between themselves and their dangerous foe. Who the men killed were, has never been satisfactorily determined. They probably met their fate late in the fall of 1848."

There were some companies of miners working on this bar in the summer of 1849, but most of them left on account of the commencing raining season. Five men built cabins on the bank, as they thought sufficiently high up to be out of the reach of the high water; but were surprised by the rising of the water on January 9th, 1850, which drove them as fast as they were able higher up on the hill, without giving them time to save anything out of the cabins, the waters of the river, rising sixty feet in one day, took away all their property.

Lumber wagon at Smith Flat, 1879

Steve Crandell Collection

The hanging of Devine [in Georgetown]. In the fall of 1850, for shooting and killing his wife while in a drunken frenzy. Devine was an Englishman, a deserter from the English army; he came to California in 1849, and used to live on Oregon canyon in 1850, at that time belonging more to the town. Mrs. Devine was a woman of fine presence, dignified and somewhat reserved, kind and thoughtful to those around her, in marked contrast with the course and, as the sequel proved, brutal disposition of her husband. There were only two women in town at that time. He had threatened her before already, and when he reached for his gun, she attempted to escape and was shot when passing out of the door in the rear of the building. One Joe Brown, a noted character, and a few other persons determined that Devine was guilty of murder, and that justice would only be satisfied by life for life; consequently he was hung by this mob from the limb of an oak tree on the hill, south side of the head-waters of Empire canyon, opposite the old town. The tree still stands there, a monument to the, so-called justice.

Hearing the sounds of the violin from the old man's cabin, which was near our tent, we went to the door and looked in. This was an enclosure of upright logs, or slabs about ten feet by fifteen, and roofed by the same. In one corner of the ground floor, seated on a saddle, was John Greenwood, fiddling away in first rate style, for two or three of his friends; opposite stood a rude cot, which they had made for the old man, while the other corners contained the ever-present rifle, and two or three rough shelves, filled with bottles of liquor and sundry drinking cups of every shape and variety, for Old Greenwood did not often indulge in Adam's ale.

Soon after the whole party rode in, young Greenwood as he passed our tent unloosing from his saddle bow an Indian scalp, the long, black, bristly hair clotted with blood, and tied with a leather string, by which he flung it to us. Disgusted with the spectacle we quickly threw it in the race, and turning to inquire as to the result of the expedition, ascertained that they had killed four, made several prisoners, burnt the rancheria, and carried off some gold dust.

Theodore Taylor Johnson, 1849

Rattlesnake Bar Bridge, 1866. This bridge crossed the North Fork of the American River between the Pilot Hill area to what is now Auburn-Folsom Road. Perhaps the most famous person from the area was Richard H. Barter, who worked as an honest miner at Rattlesnake Bar "until he was led astray." He transformed into the famous bandit known as Rattlesnake Dick.

In 1850, the miners of Murderer's Bar, for the purpose of working on a large fluming process, consolidated with the miners of New York Bar, Vermont, Buckner's Bar and Sailors Claim, to join flumes and work all together on shares: Stephen Tyler and Lefingwell, of Murderer's Bar, took the contract to build the flume of twelve feet wide by three feet high, and over a mile in length, and a very busy time began in the canyon of the Middle Fork of the American river. There were not less than six hundred men engaged in different kinds of work on those five river bars, including of the construction, etc., of the big flume, and about one half of them accounted for Murderer's Bar.

The population of Murderer's Bar was growing constantly; in 1855 the town had over five hundred inhabitants, and always represented one of the liveliest mining camps up to the year of 1860. Lee and Marshall's National circus made an excursion down into the canyon once, and gave exhibitions here and at Rattlesnake Bar. The gold found at this and the neighboring bars was all fine scale gold of very rich quality; never was any large pieces found.

SPANISH DRY DIGGINGS is situated in the northern part of El Dorado county, on the summit of the hill above the Middle Fork of the American river.

In 1848, Dan Andreas Pico, brother of ex-Governor Pio Pico, organized a company of Mexican miners, chiefly Sonorians, for the purpose of a prospecting tour through the Sierras, to test the extent of Marshall's discovery of gold. The company thus organized under the leadership of Don Andreas, proceeded north to the Yuba river, and from thence south to the Stanislaus, traversing and superficially prospecting all the since celebrated mineral belt known to the world as California's richest placer diggings.

In the course of his trip Don Andreas passed through what is known as Spanish Dry Diggings. Resting a short time here, the most experienced of his men were at work in the ravines, obtained rich prospects in course gold of a quartz nature.

Aside from these seam diggings there is the celebrated Sliger quartz claim, a true and well-defined quartz lode, a claim, undoubtedly among the best in the county if not in the State. The owners are content to themselves, quietly working their claim without the aid of outside capital.

Between Anderson's store, Columbia Flat, and Johntown, two small boys, sons of Mr. Davey, in 1878 took out more than a hundred dollars worth of gold; they having there mine in full arrangements, with sluice boxes, and everything in a diminishing shape; The oldest of these promising young miners, at that time was not more than ten years old.

Icicles crown the Ohio House at Main and Sacramento Streets in Placerville in 1889.

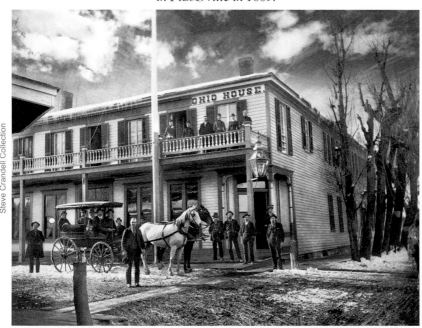

Steve Crandell Collection

Making ice blocks for the Placerville Soda Works, 1889.

Robert E. Draper was the pioneer mail carrier for the village, he was the best walker in the State. Sometimes he would leave Pilot Hill at 6 A.M., carrying the mail to Sacramento, got his mail and returned with it to Pilot Hill at 7:30 P.M., a distance of near 40 miles. He carried letters for one dollar each, and papers for 50 cents each.

MICHIGAN FLAT. On the North side of the South Fork below Coloma there were the following mining camps: Red Hill, Coyote Diggings, Rich Gulch, all together called Michigan Flat since 1854. Charles Smith kept here the first store, on the South Fork at the mouth of Greenwood creek, in a canvass tent, in 1849, and a butchershop, together with a hotel and boarding house, etc., was kept by one Tutsbury, a drink here was 50 cents in 1849. On the flat Charles Dusenberg was the first merchant, his store in 1850, was built of canvass. It was here where the Stanford brothers laid the foundation of their wealth. Thomas W. Stanford attended to a store here, a round topped live-oak tree marks the spot near which the store stood, while Leland Stanford was looking after the interest of another store, which the brothers kept in partnership together. Another store was kept by John Haas, there were also two or three boarding houses and a bakery.

KELSEY. The old town of Kelsey is located about seven miles in a northwesterly direction from Placerville, occupying an elevated plateau on the higher side of the South Fork of the American river. In the flush times of placer mining it was the business center for an extensive and a wonderfully rich mining district, embracing a large number of creeks, ravines, gulches, flats, etc. In those days the old town supported twelve stores, perhaps twice that number of saloons and gambling houses, half a dozen hotels and hay-yards, and other places of business in proportion. The placer mines of this district were wonderfully rich; and in a large proportion had small fragments of quartz attached to the particles of gold, indicating to thoughtful observers, that the places where it was found, were not far remote from its original place of repose in a quartz ledge. But in large proportion the old brood of placer miners were not the men to follow up such indications. With them it had become a habit, which gradually assumed that the character of second nature, that they could not wait longer than a week to "clean up" and realize the result of their labor.

SPANISH FLAT has always been the most important; and while most all those above named are entirely gone or shrunk into one single settlement, Spanish Flat has preserved quite some townlike appearance. The town is located on the stage road from Placerville to Georgetown, about six miles south of the latter place. The richest diggings here were near the site of the village, first worked by the Spaniards, from whom the name was derived. This same claim was known afterwards as the "Frazier Claim" or "Deep Hole," over $100,000 have been taken out of this claim.

No murder or lynching occurred here; the resolute miners kept the Spaniards down, and other rogues away.

COLD SPRINGS. The first diggings at this place were discovered sometime in 1849, and soon a road was laid down to connect the camp both ways with Placerville and Coloma, which became the main traveled road between both these places;

Spanish Flat, 1880

I next turned my steps to the Mormon Island diggings, emerging altogether from the hills into a handsome rolling country, beautifully wooded, and decked with several lovely flowering shrubs, and manzanita rushes, with their handsome bunches of crimson berries, under which the quail were as thick as chickens in a poultry-yard, not caring to take wing as you came upon them, but running in amidst the thicket. I now came upon a well-beaten road, leading from the mill to Sacramento city, which presented a great growing thoroughfare of miners and waggons, carrying goods from one town to the other. There was no lack of houses of call either on the way, for every hollow tree was the nucleus of a grog-shop, while in the neighbourhood of every spring, or stream, a sort of tavern sprung up as from the soil, "like a rose-tree in full bearing."

William Redmond Kelly, 1849

Steve Crandell Collection

This blacksmith shop operated in El Dorado County in the 1800s. Blacksmiths went well beyond just making horseshoes. Virtually every metal tool, including wagon wheels, ax and pick heads, and farm equipment were made and repaired by blacksmiths well into the 20th century.

Here, within 100 yards of the old millrace, we built a wingdam in the river for the purpose of turning its waters, hoping to strike it rich in the natural channel. The fact that only a small volume of water was flowing at that season made the operation easy. Our anticipations were not realized, however, only a small amount of gold being obtained. We continued prospecting down the stream until "Mormon island" and "Nigger hill" were reached, near where the town of Folsom now is.

David Agustus Shaw, 1850

Cold Springs was the half-way station on this road. The condition of life and existence, the natural spring water, had caused the start of several other camps in the direct neighborhood, which became named after their springs; just the same with Cold Springs, which derived its name from a spring of cold and good water, located near the edge of Cold Spring creek, in the upper end of the town. This camp soon became a great attraction, and in the Summer of 1850, was settled with from 600 to 700 miners who camped in tents or slept under the trees, and only those who intended to stay for the winter season made arrangements to build cabins. They all were working in the bed of the creek, where a mining claim then was called 15 feet square. So soon as it had been ascertained that the gravel of the creek bed was rich in gold and there would be great probability for a permanent mining camp, some enterprising men started in business.

This was a very quiet and peaceful camp, more inclined to society life than to make up excitements. Cold Springs had a singing school connected with a singing society; the school district was established in 1851, and school regularly taught since; church services were held in the school house.

George Mull, a representative of the sunny South, who came here with his negro slaves intending to introduce into

California the institutions of the slavery States, had camped while his negroes had to work for him in the creek bed, without discovering the rich placer mines on which his camps stood. A German by the name of Stakemeyer, who was killed afterward near Grizzly Flat, was working a claim out of which he produced quite an amount of loose quartz mixed in between the gravel, which he threw out of his long tom having no better use for. Judge Kenfield, passing by, inspected this quartz pile found it full of gold and took up a quartz claim. A company was formed to work it, shafts were sunk and a mill was erected, but it never paid for the amount invested in the construction of mill, etc.

Few excitements happened and they were of minor character. A gambler generally known by the name of Crowbar, in 1852, had swindled a number of miners out of considerable money, and quite a little excitement arose the next day, when he tried to get out of town with his booty; the difficulty, however, was quietly settled under assistance of some brethren of the gambling fraternity, from Hangtown; a few of the miners got their loss restituted.

Cold Springs in early times of the golden era, was one of the liveliest mining camps of the country, which had a population of about two thousand souls, with a direct stage connection

Some difficulties about a mining claim between one Beck and one Walker, in 1850, led to an earnest hostility and ended in the murder of Beck, who was shot by Walker with a shotgun across the river, Walker was on the El Dorado county side, while Beck stood on the Placer county side.

Miners working near Placerville in probably the late 1800s. There were people from virtually every part of the world seeking their fortune in California gold.

El Dorado County Historical Society

Grizzly Flat, c. 1850

Dysentery made its appearance in its most malignant form, soon prostrating the majority of the miners, carrying off many, and reducing all who were attacked to the lowest possible state of bodily feebleness.

William Redmond Kelly, 1849

to Sacramento, running a four horse coach daily, besides stage connections to Coloma and Placerville.

GRIZZLY FLAT. Sometime in the summer or fall of 1850 Lyc. L. Ramsey, better known as "Buck Ramsey," with a company of prospectors was searching for gold on the mountains between the North and Middle Forks of the Cosumnes river. The party were enjoying their evening meal near one of those noble springs, that abound in the vicinity, relishing after a hard days toil the usual miner's feast of those times—bread, bacon and coffee. The repast was not ended before an unexpected visitor, parting the brush and cracking the dried limbs and leaves under his tread presented himself. He was a magnificent specimen of Sierra's nobelest beast—a grizzly bear. His intrusion lasted but a moment. Rapidly, but perfectly self possessed, "Buck" grasped his rifle, and with a ringing shot sent his majesty tearing through the underbrush, over the flat and down a steep declivity where he was subsequently found, a trophy of the skill and coolness of the lamented pioneer. This incident furnished the appropriate name which the village bears. The flat proved to be rich in gold. Ramsey and his party did not, however, remain, but others soon followed and in the Spring of 1851 placer diggings, rich and extensive, were found for miles around, and though distant and somewhat difficult of access, the camp grew in number.

Grizzly Flat is situated about 23 miles a little south of east of Placerville, between the two Middle Forks of Cosumnes river. The North Fork of the Cosumnes, heading well in the Sierra Nevada, lies three miles north-west of the village; Steely's Fork of the same river, but one half mile distant to the southeast. "String Canyon" was one of the richest that has been in the district heads directly in town and flows 3 miles westerly to join the Cosumnes. In 1852, the ridge leading down from Leak Springs and between the Forks of the Cosumnes was adopted as one of the principal roads by the emigrants of that year; nothing but a dim trace of this old thoroughfare can be discovered, and its solitude is broken only by the annual pilgrimage of the dairymen or sheepherders. The usual red soil predominates, yielding liberally, as often proved, to miner and farmer both. Grand forests of spruce and sugar pine extend up to the summit.

It was soon found that our golden treasures were not confined to the beds of our rivers and canyons. Our quartz veins traverse the earth throughout the whole region, and many of the most extensive and costly enterprises have been in this branch of mining.

Among the earliest and most extensive operators in quartz was Victor J. W. Steely. In March, 1852, he discovered and located one of the many ledges in the district, and in the prog-

Grizzly Flat with mining equipment.

On Christmas day, 1850, a young man from Pilot Hill, by the name of Avery, took his rifle and went out to kill a deer; but about a quarter of a mile from Bayley's he was murdered by Indians for his gun, which they carried off. The camp became alarmed at his not returning and some went out to look after him, but not finding any trace of the missing man, returned and gave the report that in their belief Avery had been killed by Indians. A meeting was held in the evening and A. L. Parker, once a Texas ranger, was appointed captain of a company, which at daylight sallied forth for the Indian camp, surrounded it and captured the chief and five others; but no threatening whatever could move them to confess what they had done with Avery, notwithstanding his rifle was found in searching the camp. The prisoners, one of them being a boy 12 years old and the son of the chief, were taken to Pilot Hill. One of the party took the boy aside and he took them to the spot where Avery's body had been secreted under a pile of leaves and sticks. He had been shot three times and his brains were beaten out; most all his clothing were taken away also. The Indians [were] put on trial. J.D. Galbraith was elected Judge. Five Indians started for court; one of them broke and ran, but at his third jump he fell down dead, five balls had pierced his heart. After a speedy trial the jury found a verdict of murder against the remaining four, and the Judge sentenced them to an immediate execution. They were placed on a wagon and by this means carried under a tree and by removing the wagon, Pico, chief of Piutes, and three of his braves, were launched into eternity.

Steve Crandell Collection

Fair Play, 1881

''Here, here, doctor, doctor, come quick; the bank has caved in, burying poor Sherwood--run!'' We all started off and found, just as I had predicted, the bank caved in, poor Sherwood covered up entirely, and Dr. P_____, of New York buried to the waist. We pulled the doctor out, who, although much bruised, was not seriously hurt, and we then rapidly and cautiously sought for Sherwood. The crowd assembled around were painfully excited; not a word was spoken. We all feared the worst, but still hoped. At last I espied the hat of the unfortunate man; and I saw the brains scattered around, and discovered that the very stone he was warned to look out for, had killed him!

Luther Melanchthon Schaeffer,
1849

ress of his work erected two mills at different points upon that branch of the Cosumnes that bears his name; from these he built a wooden railroad nearly a mile in length to his mines which lies about three-fourths of a mile south-west of the village. In these improvements he spent large sums of money; he was a man of great energy of character, persevering, and full of hope. All of his own capital, and the means of many of his friends and of the employees were cheerfully and confidently loaned to help the enterprise. But years of trial and industry, which in those days meant experiment, finally ended in failure, and the ruin of the old mills on Steely's Fork.

From that day to this quartz mining, with varied results, has been one of the principal industries of the district. The Eagle Quartz Mine, located the same year as the Steely, was famous in its day for the wealth it poured into the hands of its lucky owners.

From 1853 to '57 the fever of quartz mining prevailed, but not to the exclusion of placer or river mining, which held their own in the contest for supremacy. Among other notable mines was the Roberts' lead, struck in 1855 by that man, which proved rich for a season. Also the Valle del Oro, operated in 1867 by Captain Gedge, now of the steamer *New World*. This is a southern neighbor of the Mount Pleasant, and had a forty stamp mill, hoisting works, etc., erected on the ledge, when work ceased, the mill and other property sold, carried off and rebuilt twenty miles below, upon a worse mine.

Early in 1853 while working the rich surface of Spring Flat, half a mile north of Grizzly, the rivers of the adjacent hills were touched, which paying well led to explorations in the hills themselves.

In 1866 the village met with its first calamity, being nearly destroyed by fire, but few houses remained. In 1869 the village was again destroyed by fire. This fire originated in an outbuilding where a drunken Indian was sleeping, and it is supposed his attempts to light some matches during the night and carelessness in extinguishing them, was the immediate cause; his body badly burnt and life extinct, was discovered next morning.

In 1856 Kine's and Hereford's saw-mills were in full blast. They made but little sunshine, however, in the surrounding dense and magnificent forest. The first water ditch brought into the camp was dug by the Eagle Mining Company in 1852; Bartlett & Co.'s ditch one year later. The zenith of prosperity was reached in 1856. At the election in the fall of that year over six hundred votes were polled, and the population probably exceeded twelve hundred.

From 1855 to 1857 two semi-weekly stage lines were maintained.

Grizzly Flat, like other mining towns, has had its share of vicissitudes. It has always been a pleasant place to live in, and its citizens possess the usual characteristics of Californians— hospitable, generous and obliging. For a border town, but little outlawry and but few reckless and desperate characters have flourished at any time in its history. But one murder was ever

The payment of rent has always annoyed me, and I had often wished that I could turn into a snail and carry my house on my back. In California, my wish came true; for everyone arrives with his blankets slung over his shoulder and immediately sets up his hotel wherever he pleases.

Herman Scharmann, 1849

Grover's Saw Mill on Bear Creek

El Dorado County Historical Society

El Dorado Station

I rode on through the valley, now and then taking shelter under the huge oaks, and arrived at Mormon Island early in the evening, before the miners knocked-off working, as they term it. They take their name from being first discovered and worked by a body of Mormons, who got out great quantities before the public came to find it out. There was not room, I may say, for another man there at the time of my visit, its convenient position and easiness of approach leading all new comers to it.

William Redmond Kelly, 1849

committed in the place: Hiram Palmer, while drunk, killed an Indian in 1873.

The patriotism of the young men of Grizzly Flat became electrified before those of any other place, when, in the fall of 1857, the Mormons became troublesome. They organized a volunteer company to operate against them, on January 11th, 1858, and elected E. C. Springer captain. A resolution was also adopted at the meeting, requiring the captain to report the company ready for service and for marching to Utah at the shortest notice. The members of this company were called the "Grizzlies."

INDIAN DIGGINGS was first discovered by a company of white men from Fiddletown (Oneida), who were on a prospecting trip, in the fall of 1850. They found several Indians there at work panning out gold in the bed of the creek, which was suggestive of the name adopted. A town soon sprang up, rich gravel deposits having been discovered in the hills north of where the town is now situated. Indian Diggings creek, upon whose banks the town was built, was among the richest surface or creek diggings in this part of the State, and have paid well by tunneling and by hydraulicking also. At one time (in 1855) the town there were nine stores, five hotels, the usual number of saloons, etc., with a population of fifteen hundred persons.

On the evening of August 27th, 1857, the town was totally destroyed by fire, including every store and hotel of the place. Another big fire, that laid in ashes a large portion of the town, occurred in 1860. The history of the town is not entirely without those incidents that were the greatest necessity to make up a first-class California town.

In the summer of 1855, a ditch superintendent left town, taking with him the funds of the company and another man's wife. He was overtaken at Nevada City and gave up the coin but stuck to the woman.

In the fall of 1855, a man was shot at a circus by a man who had taken the wife of the injured party to the performance. The audience was considerably alarmed. After firing several shots, the party fled, and, by the aid of friends, escaped. The wounded man finally recovered, though crippled for life.

A duel was fought to settle a dispute about a game of ten pins. Pistols were used without effect, when one party went back to his cabin for his rifle, with which he would "fetch him." The difference was settled by friends.

In the flushest mining time the town had quite a communication with other parts and the outer world. In 1855 there were three stages running between the town and Sacramento, two of them daily, one tri-weekly--all doing a good business.

An excitement turned up when a man who had been a mason of the higher grades, disappeared in a house of ill-fame, and some spots of blood suspiciously were connected with his disappearance. By thoroughly investing the case, however, nothing could be found and the bloodstains were said to have been poured out from a neighboring butcher shop.

Steve Crandell Collection

*Hydraulic mining
at Indian Diggings
in 1870.*

Watkins wagon at the Diamond Springs station.

An accident happened to the senior partner of the firm Sudson & Goodenough, early in 1852, that came near enough to result fatal. Returning from Sacramento with a big load of goods drawn by a four horse team, Mr. Sudson wished to be home before night, and when coming up to Weber Creek, in the dusk, he found it running with a big flood. Trusting his strong team and the heavy load he was driving, and underestimating the flood, he thought he would be able to cross the creek. He had hardly reached the middle of the roaring stream when his wagon was upset and carried down by the flood; his horses were drowned and though he held on to the wagon, on account of being unable to swim, the force of the water made him give up his hold and he was swept down with the swift current until he got a hold on some willows, from where he was rescued by a party that had been alarmed.

DIAMOND SPRINGS took its name from a group of springs with beautiful clear water, which were located on that now mined out ground on the north side of Main street, in the center of town, opposite the livery stable. The emigrants passing over this (Carson) road from the earliest times made this a favorite stopping or camping place. No attempt, however, had been made towards permanent settlement on this point. The latter part of the summer of 1850, when a party of emigrants from the State of Missouri, numbering about two hundred, came down this way and took a fancy to stop here for a few days; but being satisfied with the location, as they found beautiful and plenty of water and pasture, and after they had learned to mine, discovered that the mining here was paying well, they concluded to make this a permanent camp and went on to build clap board houses.

It commenced growing as a worthy rival of the neighboring "Hangtown," concerning numerical strength, business and society life. In 1854, when the star of Coloma began to go downward, Diamond Springs was the rising star. The proprietor of the Miner's Advocate sold out at Coloma only to publish his paper at Diamond Springs; and of the size of the trade the town commanded, the many stores and other business places, that were doing a flush business, gave sufficient proof.

On August 5, 1856, about 9 o'clock A. M. flames were discovered to issue out of the Howard House, a large building in the heart of the town of Diamond Springs, built of the most combustible material, a strong breeze helped the flames to spread with fearful rapidity, sweeping everything before them. Scott's brick house, and the office of Wells, Fargo & Co., on Main street, escaped uninjured.

Another destructive fire visited Diamond Springs on the 23d of September, 1859.

MOSQUITO VALLEY. A flourishing settlement, exists in Mosquito Valley, about six miles southeast from Garden Valley, or nine miles east from Placerville, having nearly the altitude of Georgetown. The visitor is astonished to find in this hidden place so many enterprising and well-to-do farmers, as may be seen without inquiry, observing the fine dwellings, large barns and thrifty fields of grain and clover; the numerous cattle, sheep and hogs, and fine looking orchards. As early as 1849, mines were discovered in Mosquito canyon and the placers worked; the population of early days settled in two different places or villages; one called Nelsonville, and the other known as the Big House or Lower town, the latter was built and inhabited by Spaniards principally. At Nelsonville two or three stores had a good trade. The mining paid well here in early days, and especially Little Mosquito was noted for chunks of gold found there from 2 oz. up to 100 dollars weight. At the present day [1883] quartz mining is going on to some extent. To provide the canyon with a stream of water a ditch had been built in 1853 or '54, at an expense of above $20,000 owned by the Mosquito Ditch Co. A saw-mill was built here in One Eye canyon,-- named after the first man engaged there being one-eyed,--in 1851 or '52.

Bowman and Crocker House near Placerville, 1865.

Steve Crandell Collection

In a little oak grove about three miles from Sutter's Mill, [we] killed a deer, ate a hearty supper, spread our blankets on the ground, and slept quietly and peacefully beneath a star-studded and cloudless heaven. Next morining we went into Culoma, the Indian name for the territory around Sutter's Mill, and here we were to purchase our provisions previous to going to the river. Three stores only, at that time, disputed the trade as what is now the great centre of the northern mining region; and where now are busy streets, and long rows of tents and houses, was a beautiful hollow, which, in our romantic version, we named as we were entering it, "The Devil's Punch-Bowl." Surrounded on all sides by lofty mountains, its ingress and egress guarded by an ascent or decent through narrow passes. Here it was that gold was first discovered in California; this was the locality where was commenced a new era, and where a new page was opened in the history of mankind; and it is proper that I should turn out my mules to browse on the sunny hill-side shrubbery, while I stop to tell how, from this remote corner of the globe, a secret was revealed to the eyes of a wondering world.

Edward Gould Buffum, 1849

In 1851 or '52 some crooked industry was commenced, one Moffatt, an early store keeper, went in with Darling, an old steamship engineer, to fabricate gold dust out of lead, coating it with gold by the way of galvanizing. The scheme worked remarkably well, Moffatt bought goods at Sacramento for which he paid with the dust, and smaller quantities were disposed of at the home trade; but finally it was discovered by running the dust into bars, or by coining money out of it, either. The result was the Moffatt lost everything he had, his partner Darling, the instigator, skipped the country in time to escape punishment.

Culbertson's Store in Placerville opposite the Bell Tower

LATROBE is located in the lower part, far southwest, of the county, where the character of the country in its transformation comes nearer to that of the plains of Sacramento valley. It is the youngest town acquisition of El Dorado county, and owes its origin to the Placerville and Sacramento Valley Railroad, which established a station for the benefit of the neighboring Amdor county here on the crossing of the roads. The town started on completion of the railroad in 1864, and was surveyed and platted by Chief Engineer F. A. Bishop, who also suggested the name of the town, after Latrobe, the civil engineer in the construction of the first railroad in the United States.

The population in a short time accumulated to 700 or 800, supporting three blacksmith shops, one wagon and carriage factory, there were three doctors in town. For quite a while the town controlled the whole trade of Amador county, and eight daily stages in connection with the railroad run, for the accommodation of the traveling people.

PLACERVILLE. Hangtown under which it was going for several years, known by all miners of California up to this day, and not seldom used even now after about thirty years. We have got different statements of the affair that caused the above name… [we] make space here for [one of three] of them.

"[This] version [of how it received its name] had its origin in the hanging by a mob, in 1849, of two Frenchmen and a

Spaniard, to an oak tree at the northwest corner of Main and Coloma streets. The victims had been arrested for highway robbery on the Georgetown road. While being tried by a jury of citizens for this offense, and while it was doubtful what penalty would be inflicted on them, an officer from one of the lower counties arrived, in search of the perpetrators of a horrible murder in his section, and at once recognized two of them as the murders for whom he sought. This at once settled their fate. Death was decreed and the sentence carried out immediately at the place and in the manner mentioned."

Few people who have had even the briefest residence in California but have heard of Hangtown, and, despite the coarse cognomen, its mention always brings with it the memory of the most romantic era of the modern El Dorado--the pioneer age--when the hardy sons of the Atlantic States, through danger and toil, had won their way to these canyons and gorges of the western slope of the Sierra Nevada, and turned up the earth of all these hills and ravines of the mountain's side, and moved hills as well as creeks and river beds, until it yielded the shining gold to their eager search. There was a day when Placerville was a solid mass of houses, a time when the "Emigrant ravine road" was lined night and day with the teams of the incoming pioneers.

For those that have seen the town of Placerville in those early days, as the beautiful but wild and romantic youth, radiant in her brilliant luxury, but criminally careless about her

Old Mountain Wickman House, Placerville

Steve Crardell Collection

My Dear Wife

I have delayed writing to you till this late date in the month, with the hope that I might receive something from your hand before being compelled to write you again: But I find this to be a delusion hope, for nothing, nothing, nothing, has been the answer to all my enquiries and messages from Sanfrancisco, Sacramento, and Weaver since I have been in the country. And I know not now whether I have a friend on Earth; for I have not received a solitary line from any person since leaving Independence

A year is destined to perform many changes, and especially where that fell disease the cholera has raged as I learn it has in the States during the past year, its changes are often those of the most saddening and gloomy character But I hope and trust that the merciful hand of God has spared that life on which depends so much of my Earthly happiness,

Remember me affectionately to Them All, and may I still be remembered by You all at the Throne of Grace

Believe me my Dearest one your most devoted and Affectionate Friend

E. A. Spooner, February 22 1850

Probably but few know that the Digger Indians burned their dead. Immediately in the rear of Ham Hawley's and Bob Shirley's stables at Diamond Springs, was the consecrated ground on which they paid the last funeral rites to their deceased warriors, wives, brothers, sisters, sweethearts and children by cremation. For hundreds of miles around were the dead transported on liters to this sacred spot. We witnessed one burning in 1852, of a chief, who had been brought from Georgetown. There ceremonies ran into the late hours of the night. It was a wild, weird, sickening, stinking operation. Hundreds of Diggers had collected, the bucks dressed in all manner of attire, with painted faces, the women and female children with tarred heads. The dead body of their chief was placed naked on the ground, then covered with pine splints and fired, when bucks and squaws set up as unearthly, maniacal a howl as ever came from mortal throats. Round and round they danced until there was nothing left of the corpse of poor "Digger Jim." At a late hour of the night the spectacle was a scene for an artist. Hundreds of rough dressed, uncouth, unshaven miners, storekeepers, visitors, etc., had collected and almost surrounded the Indians. The stench from the burning body was almost intolerable, the burning fagots kept up a bright light, but no one interfered with the ceremonies, for there were no hoodlums in those days.

Steve Crandell Collection

Grandpa Fairchild in his drug store on Main Street in Placerville.

future--the city of Placerville, now so quite and staid, her dress much too wide for her shrunken body--it must be a contrast of indescribably and saddening effect to look on so many deserted houses, left for dilapidation and decay, and offending the passer-by with the view of these modern ruins.

Even the most sanguine of the inhabitants of this place, in the spring of 1850, scarcely dared to hope that their village would ever attain a greater dignity than that of a temporary mining camp. All those that had mined here during 1849 asserted that the mines were worked out in this vicinity, and a sort of general stampede followed, so that the town during the early part of the summer of 1850, was well nigh deserted. Lots and houses on Main street, where now the center of the business place is concentrated, had been abandoned by their then owners as valueless. The coming of the immense overland immigration of that year gave a new and unlooked-for impetus to business. Lots which, a few months previously, could be had by the mere act of taking, became valuable and in demand for the sites of stores and residences. The town at once extended itself along the banks of the creek, and a perfect mania for building seems to possess the people; and as everybody calculated to profit from this emigration, the result, of course, was that more houses were built and more stores opened than the number of inhabitants required or the business of the place could support. Complaints of dull times and of tenantless houses followed, and again there were many who predicted that Placerville had seen her best days. Just then the South Fork canal was commenced, and many indulged again in the most extravagant expectations, on account of the opening of new mining fields, which had not been worked before on account of the lack of water; but now, with the water of the South Fork canal, Placerville had to expect the whole benefit and could not miss the future greatness. But that work was undertaken at a time when labor, as well as material, were so high and money demanded such high interest that, in the hands of the original projectors, the completion of the work was impracticable, and as the difficulties to its completion seemed insurmountable, again the public confidence in the permanent prosperity of Placerville was shaken. The great work passed into other hands, the difficulties were overcome and it was completed, to the incalculable advantage of the place and benefit of all pursuits. Notwithstanding the heavy disbursements consequent upon the agitation of the county seat question, the destruction of the most populous and valuable portion of the city by fire, and that depression in business and lack of confidence in California's career from which Placerville, in common with all other cities of the State, so long suffered, she steadily made improvement.

Prior to the great conflagration of 1856 there were only very few stores and hardly any of the residence buildings erected

JP Stevens Livery Stable in Placerville. The first stable burned in a 1856 fire. This 1860 photo shows its replacement.

Steve Crandell Collection

A report came to the mill that a party of Indians had decended to the camp of five white men on the North Fork, while the latter were engaged in labour, had broken the locks of their rifles which were in their tents, and then fallen upon and cruelly beaten and murdered them. A large party, headed by John Greenwood was immediately mustered at the mill, and tracked them to a large Indian *rancheria* on Weaver's Creek. This they attacked, and after killing about twenty of them, took thirty prisoners, and marched to the mill. Here they underwent trial, and six of them were sentenced to be shot. They were taken out, followed by a strong guard, and, as was anticipated, a little distance ahead being allowed them, they ran. They had no sooner started than the unerring aim of twenty mountaineers' rifles was upon them, and the next moment five of the six lay weltering in their blood.

Edward Gould Buffum, 1849

Steve Crandell Collection

Placerville – looking toward Big Cut, 1870

Whilst I was here [Cold Springs], an election for delegates to the convention, to organize a Territorial Government, was taking place in different parts of the country. As an evidence of the utilitarian spirit prevalent, I received a bullock, with a request that I would have him slaughtered on a certain day, and, at the same time, open polls for the election of two delegates from my district. Notice was given to the miners in all directions. The bullock was killed, the polls opened, but the attraction was not sufficient. Gold was more powerful, for no one attended. The beef spoiled and the election was defeated.

James L. Tyson, 1849

in other than the most combustible materials. The buildings that were built after that catastrophe have been constructed quite substantial, and show that they were not designed for the day or the season, as of old, but for this and coming generations.

It is possible that not all the citizens of Placerville do fully appreciate the advantages of the place or the beauties of its surroundings. Those of the pioneers, however, who have staid here for more than thirty years, and found, when coming, nothing but the spot, not dreaming then that they would remain here for nearly a lifetime, when looking back on all the changes that have taken place since in town and country; how the city was growing to its present proportions; how the barren or timber-covered but unproductive-looking hills did make place for vineyards and orchards, and, by the use of irrigation, were enforced to yield a crop of vegetables that cannot be surpassed anywhere. First it was tried as an experiment, but the final result was the present productiveness of the valley, just sufficient for the daily need.

The first theater was built and opened in the city of Placerville in 1852. This was the "Placer Theater," and it was used for theatrical performances, for concerts and for lectures, as well as for public meetings. The "Empire Theater" came next, and was quite successful in doing some opposition. But the big fire of July 6th, 1856, destroyed them, with many other buildings, and a new theater was built on the site of the former Empire by O'Donnell & Russell. It was arranged with a capacity for 1,500 people, and opened on October 30th, 1856, under the management of John S. Potter, with an address composed for the occasion and read by Miss Granice, and a play of the Risley Troupe. Mr. Schulz was the architect of the house.

THE PLACERVILLE FIRE DEPARTMENT organized a fire company in Placerville, although a number of unwieldy hooks had been purchased by contribution some time previous, which had for their depository the backyards or the allies of the embryo town.

On the evening of June 23d, 1853, a number of the young men of the town met together at White's Hall, with the intention to form a band that had for its purpose the protection of life and property from the ravages by fire. The first hose house of the company was situated on Maiden Lane, now Center street . . . authorities went on to purchase a house and lot for the use and benefit of the department on Main street. The fire of July 6th, 1856, that swept everything before it, rendered the company homeless.

The great damages by the fire of the year of 1856 had shown the citizens of Placerville that even the best organized fire company will be lost confronting a great fire without a fire engine.

This is one of the Blair mills. J. & J. Blair owned three mills, the Elkhorn, the Sportsman's Hall, and the Cedar Rock mill and they maintained a lumber yard at Placerville. They also had a box factory and manufactured a large quantity of boxes for the fruit trade.

Yesterday I returned to Salmon Falls, and am again encamped beneath the old oak upon the hill, Mr. C. and his friend being with me. They have slung their hammocks up among the branches, where they sleep comfortably, protected from the ants and vermin. My bed is, as usual, upon the ground, where even my night-bag does not guard me from the annoying attacks of the ants and lizards. Last night, after I had fallen asleep, my companions were aroused by hearing a ciote barking near us, and soon they saw him come and smell of my hands and face, seeming to doubt whether he could take a bite without being detected.

Daniel B. Woods,
Aug. 25th., 1849

These soldiers were part of the Placerville City Guard, which was part of the larger California National Guard Militia. They were formed during the Civil War; the 4th Infantry Regiment commanded by William Wiltse is marching toward the bell tower in 1871. Based on the number of flags and the dress uniforms the soldiers are wearing, this was likely part of an Independence Day celebration.

We fell into the error of taking more than was necessary to the mines. One strong suit, with a change of under-clothing, blankets, and the necessary tools for mining operations, are all that are requisite, as such provisions as the country affords can be obtained at any of the stores, established in every direction in the vicinity of the mines, and those who cannot put up with the privations and hardships incident to a life of this sort, had better stay at home. The mines of California are no places for them.

James L. Tyson, 1849

The Confidence Engine Company No. 1, after having kept up their organization for twelve years, with only very little assistance from the city, withdrew as an active company in the Placerville Fire Department, on June, 19, 1869, stating that the company had been forced to succumb on account of indebtedness on their building, and pretty heavy taxation to themselves in order to keep their property.

The citizens of Placerville, however, were not satisfied with the withdrawing of the engine company, and opened a subscription list; the ladies of Placerville also willing to participate in the interest and welfare of the city, gave a festival on July 13th, at the Pavilion, for the benefit of Confidence Engine Company No. 1, which proved a fine affair and financially an entire success. The receipts were $396.35, this, together with the amount subscribed by the citizens, aggregated a sufficient sum to pay off all the indebtedness of the company, and to make all the necessary repairs on their buildings. Thus, Confidence Engine Company No. 1 was reorganized on July 9, 1869, and with their new Jeffrey's Engine, they have been taking active part ever since. Confidence Engine house, after the old building had been partially destroyed by fire, on September 1860, was erected at the present site in the fall of 1860, the expenses were covered to a certain part by subscription.

INDUSTRY. A sawmill advertised the following prices for lumber: Scantling $35.00 per M. feet; Mercantable boards $35.00 per M feet; flooring six to eight inches wide, $44.00 per M feet; selected sluice lumber $40.00 per M feet; clear lumber $50.00 per M feet. Mr. J. H. Predmore & Co., in the spring of 1854, established the "Excelsior Mills," grist and saw mill, a 4-stamp mill of the Pacific Quartz Co. was connected.

Mr. S. Randall, in 1856 to '58, manufactured brick on an extensive scale at the old yard near the cemetery.

Another industry of Placerville is the slate quarry at Chili Bar, and the manufacturing of roofing slate, which business had been started by Placerville businessmen in 1875, in which year the first roofs in California had been covered with this domestic article.

Messrs. Rogers, Greely & Co., of Placerville, in the midsummer of 1855, were erecting large flouring mill on Weber creek, about three-fourths of a mile below the crossing of the Sacramento road and the creek. This mill was designed for waterpower, and a great business was done here for years.

Placerville locomotive, 1890s

Steve Crandell Collection

Early in June, 1852, I organized a mining company on Texas Bar.

It was only about two miles from Placerville, then generally known as Hangtown, from the fact that at that place five men had been hung the same day on one tree. As related to me by one who professed to have been an eye witness, there was in the village a saloon and gambling den known as the headquarters of a notorious gang of thugs. Men supposed to have gold were killed and robbed; others were murdered in their cabins. No one felt safe. The citizens resolved that every professional gambler must leave town within twenty-four hours.

The thugs became more bitter and defiant than ever, and a leading citizen who had obtained evidence involving four of them in the murder was shot and killed while passing their headquarters.

The enraged miners gathered, surrounded the saloon, and finding the four, seized and bound them and without further ceremony hung them to a tree.

The proprietor of the saloon became very angry, charged the crowd with murder, and threatened to avenge the death of his patrons. The mob, suspecting that he was an accomplice, quietly obtained a rope and he was hung up with the rest. The mob concluded to finish the business and get rid of the professional gamblers. But upon making search not one could be found; they had taken the hint and gone.

Rev. John Steele, 1850

A scene occurred that exhibits the summary manner in which "justice" is dispensed where there are no legal tribunals. We received a report on the afternoon of January 20th, that five men had been arrested at the dry diggings, and were under trial for a robbery.

A mexican gambler, named Lopez, having in his possession a large amount of money, retired to his room, and was surprised about midnight by five men rushing into his apratment, one of whom applied a pistol to his head, while the others barred the door and proceeded to rifle his trunk. An alarm being given, some of the citizens rushed in, and arrested the whole party. Next day they were tried by a jury and sentenced to receive thirty-nine lashes each. Never having witnessed a punishment inflicted by Lynch-law, I went over to the dry diggings, found a large crowd collected around an oak tree, to which was lashed a man with a bared back, while another was applying a raw cowhide to his already gored flesh. A guard of a dozen men, with loaded rifles pointed at the prisoners, stood ready to fire in case of an attempt being made to escape. After the whole had been flogged, some fresh charges were preferred against three of the men-- two Frenchmen, named Garcia and Bissi, and a Chileno, named Manuel. These were charged with a robbery and attempt to murder, on the Stanislaus River. The unhappy

continued in far right column

5 Mile House

After its destruction the whole county of El Dorado, for years were dependent on the neighboring country for their supply of flour and other mill-products; until in June, 1873, Mr. James Creighton's new flour mill was started. This mill is run by water power discharged by means of a Craig nuzzle against an eight foot hurdy gurdy wheel.

As an industry that was flourishing for a short time, being on high importance then, we have to mention the Hydraulic Hose factory of "Old Joe," at Coon hill. In 1854 and '55, when the hydraulic mining was introduced in the gravel mines of the surrounding country, a great amount of leather or double canvas hose was always demanded, until replaced by the iron pipes.

FIRES AT PLACERVILLE. Another fire broke out on July 6th [1856], the same year, and what had been feared only, on April 15th, became a reality for this time; the town was literally swept by the flames; the fire evidently of incendiary origin, spread with such an immense rapidity that all efforts to stop its progress proved fruitless and hopeless. The hungry flames devoured as well the houses rebuilt since the fire in April, as the remainder of the town, and hardly any of the shanties of old Hangtown had been spared, they all had to make space for more stately brick and stone buildings, better answering the character of the city of Placerville. And still for a third time in the same year, Placerville was visited by hungry flames on October 7, 1856, a fire broke out in the Pittsburg House of

Upper Placerville, destroying the greater part of that flourishing village. The fire was supposed to have been caused accidentally by a man John Murdock, who occupying a room in said hotel, went to bed in a state of intoxication only a short time before the fire was observed, and who was burned to death.

Twice after that Placerville has been visited by great and destructive fires; first on Sunday, November 6, 1864, between 3 and 4 o'clock A. M., and unoccupied house on Benham place was discovered on fire, and owing to the combustible material of the surrounding buildings it spread with fearful rapidity along Benham place, Quartz, Pacific and Sacramento streets, threatening at one time the whole town.

Before leaving the city of Placerville, may it be allowed to take a retrospective view far back into the time of old "Hangtown," passing a review of old faces: The very first store kept here in the fall of 1848, was by one Beaner; the following winter season there were, after a rough estimate, between four and five hundred Oregonians engaged here in mining; the spring of 1849 bringing the first Eastern people, and a lively business commenced. Col. A. W. Bee and brother were the leading storekeepers then, dealing in general provisions, etc. George Roth and James Bailey forming partnership kept a grocery store until 1854, when the partnership dissolved and George Roth continued storekeeping alone. Alex. Hunter opened the first Banking House and Express Office in con-

O'Keefe boys of Placerville, 1880s

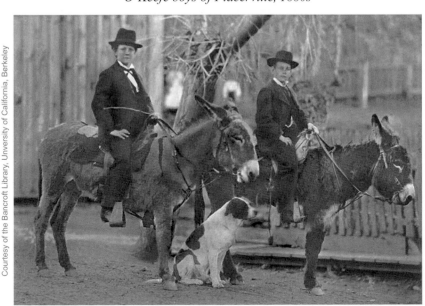

continued from far left column

men were removed to a neighbouring house, and being so weak from their punishment as to be unable to stand, were laid stretched upon the floor. As it was not possible for them to attend, they were tried, in their absence, by a crowd of some two hundred men. At the close of the trial, which lasted some thirty minutes, they had been proved guilty.

"Hang them." The proposition met with almost universal approbation. I mounted a stump, and in the name of God, humanity, and law, protested against such a cours of proceeding.

The prisoners were marched out, placed upon a wagon, and the ropes put around their necks. A black handkerchief was bound around the eyes of each. The wagon was drawn from under them, and they were launched into eternity.

This was the first execution I ever witnessed. God grant that it may be the last!

Edward Gould Buffum, 1849

To repress a system of thieving that was fast spreading; but the code of the famous Judge Lynch was unanimously adopted, and under its oral provisions any person caught "in flagrante delicto" was shot down without ceremony, or subjected to any other summary punishment the detector might prefer. I heard of several cases of instantaneous execution, and saw at the Weber one lad shorn of the rims of his ears, and seared deeply in the cheek with a red-hot iron, for the theft of a small coffee-tin. I never took part in any of those proceedings, nor did any of the company with which I was associated; but while disapproving of the modicum of punishment, and the manner of putting it in force, I must admit that some very stringent measures were necessary to keep in check the lawless and abandoned characters that flocked to the mines.

William Redmond Kelly, 1849

Adams and Company office, 1854

nection with Wells, Fargo & Co's office at Sacramento. Mr. R. G. Noyes was the resident agent of Adams and Co's Express Co., until July, 1855, when after the failure of Adams and Co., he became President of the Pacific Express Company. H. C. Hooker kept the first hardware store. Drs. Childes and Worthen opened the first drug store. Livery stable business was first started by George Condee & Co. and William Stevens & Co. M. R. Elstner kept the first hay yard, as well as brick yard. William M. Cary kept the Placer hotel, and after 1856, built the present structure of the Cary House, on Main street, corner of Quartz avenue, which was finished about August 1857. B. Herrick kept the Union Hotel, Mr. Levan kept the Orleans Hotel. Dud Humphreys was appointed first Alcalde of the district; when a Post office was first established; J. Q. A. Ballard was appointed first Postmaster, his place was at the round tent. J. B. Buker & Co. opened banking house in Upper Placerville, and were succeeded some time later by Read & Co. D. G. Weston, of Upper Placerville, started the first dairy on a larger scale, milking from 40 to 140 cows. The first white woman of Placerville was Mrs. Anna Cook, who died here on January 4th, 1879, at the advanced age of eighty-four years; she had been the first white person of her sex to arrive at Hangtown.

Benj. R. Nickerson, who threw the only law book, which there was in Hangtown at the Judge's head, because he decided a case against him, foreswore the practice of law, and got up a bull and bear fight on Sunday shortly afterwards, to get even on his client's fee, which was due but unpaid.

One day during the busy times of the 11th District Court, a case was on trial in which J. Hume and Silas W. Sanderson were engaged as attorneys on opposite sides. An angry controversy arose between these gentlemen, commencing with words, but ending in a clinch, each seizing the other by the throat, with many wild demonstrations. Before the mild calm face of Hume or the more pugnacious countenance of Sanderson was marred, or first blood claimed for either, the Sheriff, however, sprang between and parted them; each evidently pleased at this sudden cessation of hostilities, but ashamed of their display of temper. The cause proceeded as if nothing had occurred.

During the time of the secession war a cause being on trial in the County Court, and the Judge had charged the jury, who had retired to determine upon a verdict. The time being evening, they were left in the more comfortable court room. To beguile their time some of them sang and others joined in the chorus. The Judge was a staunch constitutional Democrat, and when he entered the Clerk's office, adjoining the court room, about 8 or 9 o'clock, they were lustily singing "John Brown," in which all had joined, and the old fellow's soul was boisterously "marching around." He hesitated a moment to satisfy himself that his sense of hearing did not deceive him, then he

This is the Slate Mine at Chili Bar that opened in 1875. It's easy to forget that there was more than gold in the area. In fact, marble, limestone, silicon, salt asbestos, chrome iron, iron, cinnabar, silver and copper were all mined in El Dorado County.

At daylight we tied light packs on all the loose animals, and drove them at the ascent, at which the horses stopped, as if they could not believe us in earnest; but when they saw the mules climbing, they also made the attempt, while we kept shouting and cracking whips below, not daring to follow them exactly, from the quantity of gravel and stones they rolled down in their efforts to get up, which eventually caused the death of one of the horses; a fragment of displaced rock coming tumbling down, hit him in the forehead, when he fell back and was killed.

William Redmond Kelly, 1849

Mining was hungry work. It may not seem as glamorous as "gold digging" but it was certainly as important, and frequently more profitable. This Mormon Island farmer played a key role in the area's survival and growth until the area was flooded by Folsom Dam's completion in 1955.

We entered the valley, through a deep gorge out of which the South Fork of the American River makes its way. Winding down the precipitous road we soon caught sight of tents like white specks among the trees, and in due time found ourselves in Saw Mill valley, now known as Marshall's or "Culoma Mills," where the gold discoveries were first made in 1848. The road to these mills was far better than we expected. Such had been the rush of adventurers, that it is a hard beaten track, and better than most mountain roads in the United States.

Theodore Taylor Johnson, 1849

rushed at the intervening door, nearly demolishing it with his thundering blows, and in a voice stifled with rage cried out: "If you don't stop singing, I will commit every one of you to the county jail for contempt. You were not sent there for any such purpose." And they didn't sing any more that night. The Judge had frightened John Brown's soul and very nearly the jurors also out of the court room.

RIVER MINING.

The greatest quantities of gold in most countries have been met with in the sand of rivers, and on the surface of the earth, in small grains or pieces of irregular form and size, called "placer gold," and California made no exception to this rule; the gold discovered by Marshall, on the 19th [24th] of January, 1848, in the Coloma mill-race, was placer gold, and all the mining done here during the next five or six years after the discovery was in the placers of the river and creek beds, and of the alluvial soil boarding these streams.

The discoverer, however, and his followers had not the remotest idea how to make the thing profitable, and up to the 7th of March, 1848, when Isaac Humphrey, from Georgia, went on to construct the first rocker, they had not proceeded further on the manner how to gather the precious metal; the instruments first in use were butcher-knives, iron spoons and small iron bars, to pick the gold out of the crevices. Very few of them were conversant with any kind of a method of extracting the gold from the ground where it had been embedded. But the greed of gain and the peculiarity of the American people to pick up and improve helped along. I. Humphrey had introduced the rocker, Baptiste Ruelle came to mine, as he had learned it from the Mexicans, using the batea, and soon hundreds of different vessels or bowls, resembling the Mexican implement--Indian baskets as well as any kind of a flat tin pan, was going to serve the purpose, and rockers were roughly made out of hollow trees or dug out of logs, or nailed together out of boards; everything of this shape from three to six feet in length, and set on an incline, suitable of being rocked back and forth while the gold-bearing gravel was filled in and water poured upon it.

The active mining, going out from Coloma, jumped right away down to Mormon Island, where one of the richest gold deposits was found, and from there the new-comers were up again along the banks of the American river, and every bar or place of deposited gravel inside the river-beds, was taken up by some parties.

The first improvement in the river mining was the introduction of the "long-tom," by some Georgia miners, early in 1850, working in Nevada county. This is a trough made of

This 1860s photo of Rattlesnake Bar shows miners working in the foreground and the Rattlesnake Bar Bridge in the background with wagons crossing it. Placer County is on the left side of the river and El Dorado County on the right. This area is now under Folsom Lake.

Placerville was the base of supplies for a large mining region. As in other mining camps, so on Texas Bar, provisions and mining implements were paid for by the miners and distributed by the merchants. And so it often happened that miners going to Placerville bought not only for their own, but for other companies, and thus often carried large quantities of gold.

Mr. Anderson, one of these agents from Chili Bar, on his way to Placerville in the early part of July, 1852, was murdered and robbed in Placer Cañon. A week later another miner met a similar fate near Placerville.

Rev. John Steele, 1850

Library of Congress, Lawrence & Houseworth Collection

We are located for the winter in the same place from whence I wrote you last, 40 miles N.E. of Sacramento

We have a very comfortable log House 12 by 16 feet inside, ocupid by five of us when all are here

Transportation from the Sacramento here is now worth $50.. pr hund pounds Flour is worth there $45.. pr bbb making it worth here at present prices $145.. pr bbb. rather dear eating, but this and hard bread and molasses, with pork and some venison, and coffee and tea constitutes our diet

We mourn for the vegetables but they are beyond our reach, indeed our health demand them, as their absence is what causes the scurvy, which has troubled many of the emigrants though our company have not felt any of its effects yet Potatoes onions and cabbage would be a great treat to us; things I have not tasted since I left the States Yes and a little milk now and then to go with our mush which we occasionally have would add much to its relish: and a little nice sweet butter, O what a luxury!!! would melt away before us, like snow before the summer sun.

Remember me to all the Family affectionately And believe me your most devoted Friend and Husband

E.A. Spooner, December 24th 1849

George Crooks ranch house on New York ravine in 1889. New York ravine, now under Folsom Lake, was located on the road between Folsom and Pilot Hill, now known as Salmon Falls Road. Since it is under water, New York Ravine is now called New York Creek Cove and is the closest one can get to this historic location today.

Folsom Historical Society

boards about 12 feet long, eight inches deep, and from twelve to fifteen inches wide at the head-end and double this dimension on the lower end; the wide portion terminates in a riddle of perforated sheet-iron, so curved that nothing goes over the end or sides. It requires a man to attend to it with hoe and shovel, to stir up the gravel and water as they enter, washing all that is possible through the riddle, with the shovel throwing the coarse gravel away. Beneath the sheet-iron is a box with riffles, where gold is retained with a small quantity of sand, from which it has to be separated by washing in a pan or rocker. A constant stream of water was running through the iron tom, which was provided with dirt by one or two men. To secure sufficient water for the use of the tom, wing-dams were built upward from the bar, and by their means and the thus built races, the water of a portion of the stream, or the whole of it, directed towards the head of the tom.

The tom, however, was but an intermediate step in the way of improvement in mining machinery, only proceeding the sluice. The size of the sluice-boxes are a twelve-inch board for the bottom, and two ten-inch boards for the sides. For catching the gold, cleats were nailed across the bottom-piece of the sluice, and numerous are the improvements that are in use still for this purpose, as "riffles," in the sluice-boxes of the hydraulic mines.

Starting from Mormon Island, and going up the American river, there were the following principal river bars, inside the line of El Dorado county:

Condemned Bar, where one of the first built bridges connected El Dorado with Placer County. A few miles further up the stream was Long Bar, and opposite Doton's Bar; during the summer months from 1849 to '52, there were not less the 500 miners engaged in working on both these bars. The afterwards grain-king, Isaac Friedlander, may be remembered here by old-timers; he occupied a little brush tent near the upper end of the bar, where he worked a single-handed digging and a rocker all by himself, and laid the first foundation of his future wealth. The following bars, with the exception of one, were all in Placer county: Beale's Bar, Horseshoe Bar, Whisky Bar, Beaver Bar, Dead Man's Bar, Milk Punch Bar and Rattlesnake Bar. Whiskey Bar was in El Dorado county; here a wire-rope bridge was built across the river, and finished in the fall of 1854, which circumstance may give to it the full right to the epithet of the *pioneer wire suspension bridge* in the State. On the Middle Fork of the American river, from the junction upwards, we have "Oregon Bar, Louisiana Bar, then New York Bar and Murderer's Bar, all in El Dorado county, the mines of both of the latter bars, together with those of Vermont, Buckner's Bar and Sailor's claim, on the opposite river bank, in the summer of 1850, consolidated for the purpose of a grand fluming operation, the united membership of the named five companies was over 500,

Church Gold Mining Company

El Dorado County Historical Society

I took the stage to Placerville, a journey of about seventy miles.

Of all public conveyances I ever encountered, the stages here take the lead, in discomfort and vulgarity. The carriage is either a lumbering, old-fashioned thing, constantly reminding one of that in which Sir Walter Scott places Lady Margaret Bellenden, or otherwise it is a waggon on springs; as many persons as can jam themselves in, do so; they have no regard for those who are already in possession of seats; the new passenger coolly gets into the vehicle, and placing himself between two others, sits down, and relies upon his own weight making the other two sufficiently uncomfortable, to aid him in establishing himself between them.

They all smoke, and unceremoniously discharge occasionally across you, and in every other respect are unusually dirty citizens; and, for some incomprehensible reason, when stages meet, the recognition of friends is announced by enormously swearing at each other, and in language that places blasphemy, if possible, as a light offence, comparatively.

Sir Henry Vere Huntley, 1856

Sugarman Mine

The monte and the faro tables were everywhere running flush. The gambling table indeed is the chief attraction in all new mining regions. The most pretentious and most elegantly furnished quarters, whether tents by the roadside or palaces in a city, are dedicated to this purpose. Such resorts are, in fact, about the only places in such regions where men can pass their leisure hours or find companionship and recreation.

David Leeper, 1849

and they had agreed to join flumes, covering more than a mile along the river. No saw-mill was in existence then in that part of the country, the nearest one being at Coloma, and it seemed a vast undertaking, but it is a well-known fact that the inventive genius always appears in the right time, in case of necessity; just so here, two men of Murderer's Bar, Stephen Tyler and Lefingwall made a proposition to build the flume for $6 per linear foot, the flume to be twelve feet wide and three feet high; provided the company would grade and prepare the way for laying the flume. The proposition accepted, the contractors went right on, procured an ordinary horsepower, connected it with a circular saw, and the saw-mill was improvised. A band of 150 horses were bought, as many as could be attached at one time were hitched up to the horse-power, and the mill was run as perfect as could be expected; nay, as could not be surpassed at that time. To the balance of the horses was given ample time to restore their strength by pasturing off the neighboring hill-sides, but these hill-sides were soon giving out, and the old horses and mules followed suit, until the hill-sides were scattered with the bleaching bones of the poor brutes as a memory of the pioneer saw-mill of the northern part of El Dorado county. When it became visible that the contractors would not complete their work that way it was proposed to use canvass for lining the flume, and here all the sailor-boys, and others that were able to use a palm, found there work and a half an ounce wages per day.

Meanwhile the grading of the flumeway went on, superintended by Otis T. Nichols; and in this company one could see men of all kinds of professions--doctors and lawyers and divines, just as the society of the mining districts at that time was made up. At the falls above, a dam was built for the purpose of turning the water from the river to the flume. But the work, where-upon months of labor of hundreds of men had been spent, just finished, sometime in September, 1850, was pitilessly destroyed a few days after the last nail had been driven, and swept away by the waters of an early rain-storm that had prevailed high up in the mountains. Thousands of men witnessed the march of the floating flume, that did not break up for miles, the canvass keeping it together as a whole for miles of travel.

Here, at Murderer's Bar, a ferry was carrying the travel from Sacramento by the road to Salmon Falls and Pilot Hill, through Cave valley into Placer county, to Yankee Jims, Iowa Hill, etc. Further up the river, there are: Rocky Point Slide, Mammoth Bar, Texas Bar, Quail Bar, Brown's Bar and Kennebec Bar, all on the opposite side of the stream; Wildcat Bar, Willow Bar, Hoosier Bar, Green Mountain Bar, Main Bar and Poverty Bar, however on the El Dorado county side. The population of some of these bars was quite large, at least large enough that the enterprising business firm like Lee & Marshall of the National Circus, found it profitable to visit the bars in the river-canyon, and give exhibitions at places like Rattlesnake Bar and Murderer's Bar.

Proceeding, we come to a number of bars named after the nationality of those who started the first work: there is first,

To-day we met several returning from the mines. They gave a dismal account of the state of affairs there, which none of our party were disposed to believe. It is a remarkable and probably a commendable trait in the character of our go-ahead countrymen, to admit no statement contrary to their preconceived opinions, till by personal observation they have proved its truth or falsity. On our first arrival in California, we were told to believe nothing we heard, and only half we saw!

James L. Tyson, 1849

Diamond Springs, Larkins Mine Crew, 1870s.

El Dorado County Historical Society

We went on the same evening, passing through a few miners' huts in a deep valley, which was called Weber Town. Here there was what are called, in professional phraseology, "dry diggins;" that is, where miners dig in the dry soil, picking out the particles from amongst the clay without the agency of water. Of course it must be plentiful, and in good sized grains, when the eye can detect them mixed with the red clay; and much that is in mere dust must necessarily escape in the first instance, but in the wet season many of them wash their heaps over that they dry picked before, and with very great success. I sat for half an hour by the side of a digger, watching how he worked, during which he frequently pointed me out particles in the earth, before he picked them out, that would certainly escape an unpractised eye. He admitted he averaged one and a half ounce per day, working only about six hours.

William Redmond Kelly, 1849

El Dorado County Historical Society

Druids in Placerville, 1899. The Druids were the Magi or philosopher-magicians of the early Celtic civilization. Druid history dates back to the migration of the Indo-European-speaking people in the second millennium B.C. Druids were generally tall and skilled horsemen, metalworkers and warriors. Several meanings are offered for the word Druid including: "a servant of truth," "all knowing or wise man," "an oak," or "equal in honor."

Buckeye Bar; next is the American Bar, Sardine Bar, Dutch Bar, Spanish Bar, African and Drunkard's Bars; only Spanish Bar is located in El Dorado county. Here the stage road from Georgetown to Todd's valley and Yankee Jim's crossed the river by means of one of the first built wooden bridges in this section of the country. Further up are: Ford's Bar, Volcano Bar, Sandy Bar and Grey Eagle Bar, Yankee Slide, Eureka and Boston, on the El Dorado side of the river, and Pleasant Bar on the opposite; Horseshoe Bar and Junction Bar, at the mouth of State ravine, and Alabama Bar on the El Dorado side. All these bars on the Middle Fork of the American river, from Oregon Bar upwards, after the lowest estimate in the summer of 1850 not less than 1,500 men.

One of the richest and most wonderful strikes in river mining was made in the Middle Fork of the American river, at a place known as "Big Crevice," crossing the river in a diagonal line at Murderer's Bar. J. D. Galbraith broke in here first in 1850, and worked the spot to the depth of twelve or fifteen feet, well back under the hill, on the El Dorado bank. The operations of 1851 enabled the working of the river bed, and disclosed the continuation of the crevice across the stream. A dyke of limestone here crosses the country, and this singular hole seems to have been a cavern which became filled with sediment rich in gold, perhaps before the present river system existed, as there is no gravel between the sediment.

But the work was dreadfully annoying; but four men could work in the excavation, two of whom were constantly bailing out water, one had to throw out the top gravel stratum as it fell in, while the fourth was grappling up the gold-bearing slum. During this operation the gold could be seen laying upon all sides of the pit in apparent handfuls.

The Hoosier Bar Gold Mining company have adopted a new invention in the line of hydraulic mining, by using the pressure of the water to elevate the gravel out of the pit, about forty feet below the water-level of the Middle Fork of the American river, to such a height as the sluice-boxes. One stream of water forces the gravel into the lower extremity of this pipe, whence it is driven upward with great force by another stream from a "Little Giant." By this means, for every 100 feet of pressure in the driving current a column of water and gravel can be driven upward forty feet. The Hoosier Bar elevator is giving eminent satisfaction and has opened up some very rich ground.

The dam built at Murderer's Bar, in 1853, was the largest and best at all the river bars, and was able to stand the high water of the flood of the following winter; at this bar the water,

A photo op for these Placerville miners in 1870.

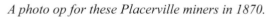

Steve Crandell Collection

I spent the night of the 28th at Mud Springs, in an hotel kept in a large canvas tent. They gave me a very fine bed to sleep in, and treated me most kindly.

During the day the wind commenced blowing briskly from the south. After we had all retired to bed, the rain began to fall heavily, and the storm became so severe that the fastenings of the tent gave way, and nothin was left of the frame but the main upright pole, about thirty feet high, that stood in the center, to the top of which the canvas was securely fastened, while it hung flapping around the pole at the bottom. The rain came down in torrents, and the only way we could keep dry was to stand around and hug the lower end of the pole until daylight. This was the first hard rain of that most rainy season of 1849-'50. I never passed a more cheerless and uncomfortable night than this. I was very tired and sleepy, and frequently found myself asleep on my feet, and in the act of sinking down with my arms around the pole.

Peter H. Burnett, 1849

California State Library

Skinner Winery – Zentgraf Home & Winery, Deer Valley Road, Green Valley

rocks and pay-dirt all had to be raised by steam and water-power.

On the South Fork of the American river, bars were not as numerous as on the sister stream, there were Dutch Bar, Kanaka Bar, Red Bar, Stony Bar, Ledge Bar, Missouri Bar and Michigan Bar.

On the Cosumnes river there were: Big Bar, Michigan Bar, Buck's Bar, Pittsburgh Bar, and Wisconsin Bar.

INTERNAL IMPROVEMENTS

BRIDGES. The many streams of perennial running water, having their sources high up in the Sierra Nevada mountains, only enable a fording at one spot, while for the greater part of the year the high stand and the rapid flow of their waters necessitate some other means to carry the travel across.

As the first device, to assist the traveling people on said roads across the natural waterways, ferries of the most primitive make up and clumsiest construction and shape were in use; old ship's boats of all sizes had been pressed into the service or an ingenious fellow had accomplished the same purpose by transforming some old emigrant wagon-beds that had come all the way across the continent, while the first were brought up the Sacramento river. Even the simple form of a raft not seldom had to fulfill the programme; until the owners of the place could afford to build a scow of sufficient capacity, to replace the former. Thus continuously laboring against perfecting the system not only as far as the ferryboat itself was concerned, but the better facilities in its motion and the arrangement of

The government of my country snubs honest simplicity but fondles artistic villainy, and I think I might have developed into a very capable pickpocket if I had remained in the public service a year or two.

Mark Twain, 1872

the cross-cable also. Such ferries existed from the earliest time at Coloma, at Uniontown, at Chili Bar on the South Fork of the American river, and at Condemned Bar, at Beal's Bar, at Rattlesnake Bar, at Oregon Bar and Murderer's Bar on the American river and the Middle Fork of the same stream. All these ferries had been built in private enterprise with considerable expense. The owner of the ferry was granted the undisputed right to levy a considerable toll on all who took the chance of this privilege. By that means some of the most traveled crossings became quite profitable business places of their owners.

The first bridge thus built in this county was

The Coloma Bridge, a wooden structure crossing the South fork of the American river from Coloma to the village of North Coloma, on the opposite bank of the river. John T. Little the proprietor of the ferry, sold his interest to E. T. Raun, who immediately, in February, 1851, went to work and put up here a common truss structure of three spans and sixteen feet breadth. This bridge, though rough, was quite substantialy built and stood the floods of several years; but anticipating that it would not stand a higher freshet without some larger repairing, Mr. Raun preferred to build a new bridge right away. This second structure was then erected in the Fall of 1855; was stronger and set up on a much higher foundation. The general belief was, that this bridge was safe against any flood; in spite

I soon came out on the margin of a prairie, some four miles in diameter, the road running through its center; I had but just entered upon it, when I discovered the track of a--not a grizzly bear, dear reader, but of a female. I did really discover the track of a female in California. It may seem a trivial circumstance to you, it was not so to me. A galvanic battery would not have created a more startling sensation.

John M. Letts, 1849

Coloma miners, 1885.

El Dorado County Historical Society

This is the first wire-rope suspension bridge at Folsom. As you look at various bridge pictures you'll find that many of them were very similiar. There were standard acceptable bridge plans and only a handful of bridge builders and owners (most were privately owned toll bridges in the early days). This bridge was built in 1855 and lost to the flood of 1862.

My share to-day is $1 25. These details may appear dull and uninteresting; but the reader will bear in mind that it is the writer's object to give a full and true description of a miner's life. He might pass by all the days and months of profitless labor, and record only the days of success; but those who have friends at the mines, and those who purpose going there, will certainly wish to know what are the trials and discouragements of such a life. They wish to know the truth.

Daniel B. Woods, July 5th, 1849

of this belief, however, it was destroyed by the Spring flood of 1862. A. H. Richards built another bridge on the same spot, which was finished in December the same year. This was swept away also, no more attempt has been made to span the river for the accommodation of wagons the travel has changed into other channels and at present the frail construction of a narrow wire suspension bridge or walk, only for footmen, is leading across the South fork from Coloma to the North side.

At Uniontown the first bridge was erected in 1851; it was built on a subscription of sixty shares and run in opposition to the ferry. This bridge was renewed by Hogue, Ingelsby and Roubant in 1855, and after the flood of 1862 washed away the approaches these latter have been renewed again. Tolls on this bridge ran as high as $600 and $800 a month; to collect $25, in a single hour, was not considered anything too extraordinary.

A few miles further down the stream was Rock Bridge, so-called on account of the natural abutments found there. Wm. Gaylord was the first man who fully recognized this opportunity and took advantage of it by building a bridge across, which together with the connecting road for a long while served as a thorough-fare between Georgetown and Sacramento. The travel on this road, together with the facilities offered for diggings in the river bed, started quite a lively mining camp here around the bridge. The village, however, has disappeared, the site of it makes now a part of Mr. G. Bassi's dairy ranch.

The main traveled road between Sacramento and Georgetown, by the way of Pilot Hill or Centerville, crossed the South Fork of the American river at Salmon Falls. The first bridge here was built in 1853, and changing hands became the property of E. T. Raun, the owner of the Coloma bridge. Early in 1855 this bridge was washed away by the flood, but was replaced the same year by a first-class structure with wooden girder trusses. It was carried away by the flood in 1862, not to be built up after that, and this road, once one of the most traveled in the county, is only passable in the latter part of the year, when the river can be forded.

E. and H. George, in 1853, undertook to build instead of their ferry a strong and substantial bridge, at Chili Bar, which became a very important improvement on the road from Placerville to Georgetown, by way of Kelsey and Spanish Flat. This bridge was open for foot and horsemen, as well as pack trains, on the 1st of December, of said year, while the grades up and down the mountains on both sides, for the passage of wagons, were not finished before May or June of 1854. With the opening of this bridge the Pioneer stage line, running between Placerville and Georgetown, had its stages running

Miner along the American River near Coloma.

Steve Crandell Collection

In the fall of '50 the camp was the scene of another hanging-bee. The subject was "Irish Dick," who killed a man across a gambling table in the "El Dorado." The crowd on the inside, in less time than it takes to tell it, seized the wretch and thrust him out the door to the quickly assembled crowd on the outside, when a noose was put about his neck and he was hurried off to the most convenient tree. The other end of the rope was thrown over a limb and grasped by a number of men, when the fellow was asked if he had anything to say. He coolly took a monte deck from his vest pocket, and began to shuffle the cards, saying, "If anybody wants to buck, I'll give him a lay-out." A quick haul upon the cord, and the graceless, conscienceless villian dangled in the air.

David Leeper, 1849

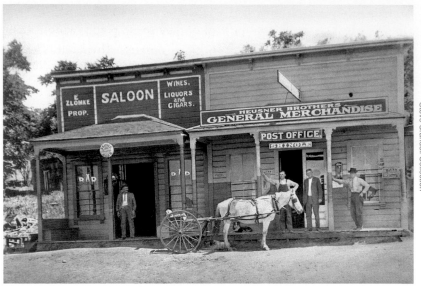

Shingle Springs Post Office and the Saloon of E. Zlomke, 1889. The sign in front of the Saloon advertises Rainier Beer which was created in 1883 by Seattle's Bay View Brewery.

As we rode into town, and passed in double file through the streets, Captain at the head, erect, and evidently feeling his dignity, the young men descried a billiard-saloon, became suddenly demoralized, broke ranks, incontinently dismounted, frantically rushed in, and immediately the click of the billiard-balls was heard.

Joseph Le Conte, 1870

over this route and bridge, and when the line was extended from Georgetown, across the Middle Fork of the American river at Spanish Bar to Paradise, North Star house, Todd's valley and Yankee Jim's, a bridge like the Coloma bridge was built across the Middle fork at Spanish Bar. On the road from Work's ranch to Mount Gregory, in Georgetown township, a toll bridge crossing the waters of Otter creek was built in the year of 1854 or 1855.

Besides those already mentioned bridges, at Condemned Bar. Whisky Bar and Oregon Bar, the river had one more crossing at Wild Goose flat; this bridge, together with the connecting turnpike road, was owned by the Horseshoe Bar and Pilot Hill Turnpike company.

The first "Wire-rope Suspension Bridge" that was ever built in this county, is said to have been the one erected by N. H. Smith, crossing the Middle Fork of the American river at Murderer's bar, built in 1854. The suspension bridge at Whisky Bar, below the junction on the same stream, was built the year after, in 1855 for the sum of $50,000. Mr. Bronk also contracted and superintended the wire-rope suspension bridge across the American river at Folsom.

At Mormon Island was the first bridge built in 1851, by J. W. Shaw; this was a wooden structure after the common American truss system, and after the high water, in the Spring of 1855, had washed it away, Mr. Shaw immediately decided to have a wire rope bridge put up on the same place, which was erected during the following summer . . . when the high flood in January [1862] swept it unmercifully away. Mr. Shaw re-built the bridge soon after, and took precaution to get it up on a higher point of the bank, where it stood the floods for more than twenty years.

Lyon's bridge, on the toll road from Auburn station to Cave valley, is a wire suspension bridge of about 85 yards span, swinging across the North Fork of the American river directly below the junction of the North and Middle forks. The con-struction of this bridge was accomplished during the summer of 1865. W. C. Lyon, the principal owner of this bridge, in 1856, had erected a suspension bridge across the same stream at Con-demned Bar, and when the travel at the latter place began to slack down, he took the bridge down and removed such parts as were practicable to the site of his present bridge. It is the most important link in the thoroughfare between El Dorado and Placer counties, connecting those towns in the northern part of the former county—Georgetown, Greenwood valley, Cave valley, Pilot Hill, Coloma, etc., with the railroad at Auburn sta-tion; forming one of the few outlets for market products of the county.

Patrick Gordon, in 1859, built another wire-rope suspen-sion bridge across the Middle fork of the American river at Volcano Bar. And still another bridge of the same construction crosses the South fork of the American river on the road from Placerville to Mosquito valley.

Hydraulic Mining at Michigan Bar

El Dorado County Historical Society

On the margin of the race and just below the mill, we pitched our tent under the shade of a scrub oak. We fixed upon this spot in the midst of the sand and dust of the settlement, as it was the best place to traffic and dispose of our merchandise and surplus articles; for like nearly all California adventurers we had long since rued our great error in bringing so much baggage with us, and determined to "tote" it about no longer. One of our party had brought merchandise, but though the remainder had come only for the purpose of gold digging, and were of course anxious to proceed in their enterprise, yet it was impossible either to store the baggage or carry it with us.

Taking our tent-fly we erected it in front of the tent, and placing a barrel under each of its four corners, laid boards upon them, thus having on each side a convenient counter for the display of our articles.

Theodore Taylor Johnson, 1849

Moving a hay press. Until the middle of the 19th century, hay was cut by hand with sickles and scythes. In the 1860s early cutting devices were developed. The stationary baler or hay press was invented in the 1850's but did not become popular until the 1870's.

There were some other kinds of diggings discovered different from the river mining, called cañons, one I know of, called the Oregon. It was described like a tunnel, deep down in the earth, where a party of three persons from near our locality went and returned in about three weeks and had from three to five thousand dollars apiece, which they showed me. It was not scale gold, but nuggets of all sizes. Of course, they had unusual luck.

Daniel Knower, 1849

STAGE LINES. The discovery of gold at Coloma and the rush of the gold-hunters of early days, who all had the idea that this new El Dorado was concentrated to the very spot of Coloma, turned the entire travel of 1848 and '49 from Sacramento up over the road that Capt. Sutter piloted to his sawmill; and periodically this road was perhaps the most traveled road in the United States, being crowded day and night in the periods that followed the arrival of each steamer or larger vessels in the harbor of San Francisco. But conveyances were scarce in California at that time, all traveling being made on horseback. The Oregonians were the first to bring their big wagons into California and El Dorado, and these became the first means and the material with which to undertake the first change in the transportation of passengers and freight from horseback to a wagon seat, a kind of fast-freight. The first regular stage line was established between Sacramento and Coloma, and about the same time Graham of Georgetown, ran a stage from Coloma to Georgetown, which was united, however, with the former line soon after. Another line of stages owned and managed by Dr. Thomas and James Burch, established as the "California Stage Company" in 1851, running from Georgetown by the way of Pilot Hill and Salmon Falls to Sacramento, with a branch line from Salmon Falls to Auburn. When the Sacramento Valley Railroad was finished to Folsom this stage line ran to connect with the railroad at Folsom. The United States Mail contract was then awarded to H. F. Page, now United States Senator, and Bart. Morgan, who sold to J. L. Lewis, who runs two lines of daily stages now from Auburn to Georgetown and Placerville both ways.

A stage line was established also in early days between Sacramento and Placerville via Diamond Springs, and soon after, in 1851, Stevens & Co. commenced to run an opposition line. Bill Williams set the fare down to $5.00; and kept up with the opposition for several years, but finally succumbed. Stevens' line, called the "Pioneer Stage Line," with Alex. Hunter as agent. In April, 1855, another branch line commenced running between Fiddletown and Mud Springs. With the activity of the railroad, this stage line had to accommodate itself to the terminus of the railroad, thus changing its course from Sacramento to Folsom, to Latrobe, to Shingle Springs.

Messrs. Condee & Co., the owners of a stage running between Placerville and Coloma since 1851 or '52, on August 1st, 1854, inaugurated a new tri-weekly stage from Placerville to Drytown, Amador county, by the way of Diamond Springs, Mud Springs, Logtown and the Forks of the Cosumnes, (Yoemet) connecting the stage lines running to the Southern

As forests at lower elevations were clear-cut the operations were moved farther up the Sierras. This 1889 photo shows the logging operation of the Smith Lumber Company in Union Valley, east of Georgetown in the El Dorado National Forest. There's a saw mill, powered by a steam donkey engine. This is believed to be Bill (Wild Bill) Calmaker's Crew.

The roads were so wretched that supplies could be got to the mines only by pack-animals. A dollar per pound was the customary rate to Coloma and to Hangtown, which were about the same distance from Sacramento. Gold dust was the universal currency, and the "blower" and the scales were a fixture in every place of business. The weights were often home-made, and of very dubious specific gravity.

David Leeper, 1849

Steve Crandell Collection

Main street in Greenwood.

 In the afternoon we rode fourteen miles, to Patterson's Tend House [El Dorado Hills]. We found this a delightful place. Mr. Patterson is really a very pleasant and courteous gentleman, and gave us a most excellent supper. This put us all in excellent humor. The young men got lively. One of them, Mr. Perkins, played on the piano, while the rest joined in a stag-dance. The clattering of heavy boots on the bare floor was not very harmonious, it is true, but then it was very enlivening. The host and all the guests in the house seemed to enjoy it hugely.

Joseph Le Conte, 1870

mines, and changed on April 1st, 1855, into a daily stage with very good result. The consequence of this result was that a party of Drytown denizens started an opposition stage line on the same route, which commenced running in the middle of March, 1856, tri-weekly.

OVERLAND MAIL LINE was established from the Atlantic to the Pacific States soon after. The first overland through mail coach from the East successfully arrived at Placerville on July 19, 1858, over this first continental mail route, and was continued regularly for nearly ten years, up to the time when the Central Pacific Railroad commenced to run regular trains to Cisco, when the stages were taken over there.

GREAT ATTRACTION
AT THE IOWA HILL
Amphitheatre
Panther!
AND
BEAR FIGHT

THE PROPRIETORS HAVE PROCURED

A LARGE AND FEROCIOUS PANTHER,

Caught near the summit of the Sierra Nevada Mountains, and purchased

THE CELEBRATED GRIZZLY BEAR, LOLA MONTES,

WHICH THEY WILL FIGHT

ON SUNDAY, NOVEMBER 5.

Rich and Rare Sport may be expected, as both animals are in fine condition. The Panther is one of the largest of the species, and the Bear unequalled for his weight. They have also procured

A NUMBER OF FINE GAME CHICKENS!

Which they will fight. Any persons having Game Chickens, and wishing to test them, can have an opportunity either for sport or wager

The whole to conclude with a Match Fight between the
FAVORITE DOGS, UNION AND STAR!

FISH & BROWN.

Mr STEVENS will enter the celebrated Dog, Major, with **$500** attached to his neck, challenging any Dog of his weight for a **Rough and Tumble Fight.**

GOOD NEWS

FOR

MINERS.

NEW GOODS,

PROVISIONS, TOOLS,

CLOTHING, &c. &c.

GREAT BARGAINS!

JUST RECEIVED BY THE SUBSCRIBERS, AT THE LARGE TENT ON THE HILL,

A superior Lot of New, Valuable and most DESIRABLE GOODS for Miners and for residents also.   Among them are the following:

STAPLE PROVISIONS AND STORES.

Pork, Flour, Bread, Beef, Hams, Mackerel, Sugar, Molasses, Coffee, Teas, Butter & Cheese, Pickles, Beans, Peas, Rice, Chocolate, Spices, Salt, Soap, Vinegar, &c.

EXTRA PROVISIONS AND STORES.

Every variety of Preserved Meats and Vegetables and Fruits, [more than eighty different kinds.]   Tongues and Sounds; Smoked Halibut; Dry Cod Fish; Eggs fresh and fine; Figs, Raisins, Almonds and Nuts; China Preserves; China Bread and Cakes; Butter Crackers, Boston Crackers, and many other very desirable and *choice bits.*

DESIRABLE GOODS FOR COMFORT AND HEALTH.

Patent Cot Bedsteads, Mattresses and Pillows, Blankets and Comforters. Also, in Clothing—Overcoats, Jackets, Miner's heavy Velvet Coats and Pantaloons, Woolen Pants, Guernsey Frocks, Flannel Shirts and Drawers, Stockings and Socks, Boots, Shoes; Rubber Waders, Coats, Blankets, &c.

MINING TOOLS, &c.; BUILDING MATERIALS, &c.

Cradles, Shovels, Spades, Hoes, Picks, Axes, Hatchets, Hammers; every variety of Workman's Tools, Nails, Screws, Brads, &c.

SUPERIOR GOLD SCALES.   MEDICINE CHESTS, &c.

Superior Medicine Chests, well assorted, together with the principal Important Medicines for Dysentery, Fever and Fever and Ague, Scurvy, &c.

N.B.—Important Express Arrangement for Miners.

The Subscribers will run an EXPRESS to and from every Steamer, carrying and returning Letters for the Post Office and Expresses to the States. Also, conveying "*GOLD DUST*" or Parcels, to and from the Mines to the Banking Houses, or the several Expresses for the States, insuring their safety.———The various *NEWSPAPERS*, from the Eastern, Western and Southern States, will also be found on sale at our stores, together with a large stock of *BOOKS* and *PAMPHLETS* constantly on hand.

Excelsior Tent, Mormon Island,
    January 1, 1850.

ALTA CALIFORNIA PRESS.

WARREN & CO.

This grandiose three-story Classic Revival building was completed in 1898 and constructed with local materials. The county's first courthouse on Court Street was built of wood and cloth with an adjacent log jail. A two story wooden courthouse with a bell tower was built on the hill in 1853. The log jail burned in 1855. In 1857, a new two story brick jail was built to the east of the courthouse on the hill. The two buildings were connected via an iron bridge running from the jail to a second story courtroom. This building is now listed on The National Register of Historic Places.

Chapter 2: Placer County — Auburn, Colfax and vicinity

In the general history of the county, the early discovery, the movements of individuals, the incidents of settlement, the success of miners, and in other references, nearly every town, river bar, and mining camp, of old and of modern times, have been mentioned, and in some instances quite full histories given. There are many localities whose history is full of interest, and upon which memory loves to linger in commune with the recollection of scenes of those bright and hopeful days when time seemed so laggard and the future at command. Then

The vices of gambling, drunkenness, and obscene oaths, were as prevalent here as elsewhere. Monte tables were constantly in operation about the little tent-stores and groggeries seated on the hill-side.

James L. Tyson, 1849

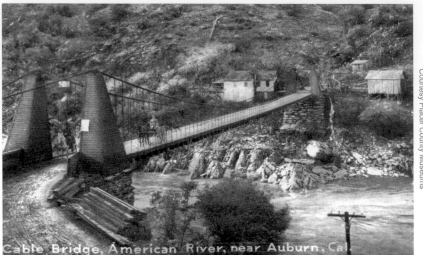

Cable Bridge, American River, near Auburn, Cal.

This cable bridge was built in 1865 and had a span of 85 yards, swinging across the North Fork of the American River just below the confluence of the North (on the left) and Middle Forks. It was a toll bridge, originally built by William Lyon who had erected a suspension bridge across the same stream at Condemned Bar. When the travel at the latter place began to slack off, he took the bridge down and moved it to the site shown. It was known as Lyon's Bridge for many years. It was ultimately taken over by the state and replaced with a modern bridge in 1951.

The scarcity of ladies in California, is the theme of much conversation. There is an anecdote almost universally told in connection with the subject; it is as follows: At a certain point in the mineral regions, part of a lady's hat was discovered, which caused so much excitement and joy, that it was immediately decided to have a ball on the spot, in honor of the event. Invitations were immediately distributed throughout the country, and, on the appointed day, three hundred miners assembled, each dressed in a red flannel shirt, and accompanied by a bottle of brandy. In the exact spot was driven a stick, five feet high, on the top of which was placed the hat, and around it was wrapped a flannel blanket. It was made to represent, as nearly as possible, a female form. By the side of this was placed a miner's cradle, or machine, in which was placed a smoked ham, also wrapped in a flannel blanket. At the close of each dance the president of the meeting would rock the cradle, while the secretary would pour a bottle of brandy down the back of the lady's neck. The ball lasted two days, at the end of which time the ground was surveyed into town-lots, and called Auburn.

John M. Letts, 1849

conventionalities and classes were unknown. Equality reigned supreme, and toil had no terrors, so that hope spread the inaccessible bed-rock with gold or directed the impracticable tunnel to the auriferous channel. These recollections may be preserved in the legends of the pioneers; aborted and exaggerated in the stories of the magazine and novel writers; or found in occasional sketches in the newspapers. Their aggregate would burst the volume covers.

AUBURN. Auburn the county seat and principal town of Placer County, is on the line of the Central Pacific Railroad, thirty-six miles northeast of Sacramento, the depot having an elevation of 1,360 feet above tide water, the principal portion of the village being forty or fifty feet lower.

The history of Placer County is so much the history of Auburn that a special reference may appear superfluous. The town antedates the county some years, the gold-digger having sought its hidden wealth as early as 1848. The first, however, that it bore a habitation and a name was early in 1849, when it was called the "North Fork Dry Diggings," the name of Auburn being given in the fall. Some have referred to Auburn as formerly bearing the name of "Wood's Dry Diggings," but of this we have no recollection nor contemporaneous record, and conclude that such appellation was not generally applied.

The existence of gold in the ravines had been proven in 1848, and the centrality of Auburn, its accessibility, and its proximity to the North Fork, pointed it out as a good trading-point and a good place to pass the winter.

The first stores were established about the middle of July, 1849, by Wm. Gwynn and H. M. House. Shortly after, Julius Wetzler, in company with Capt. John A. Sutter, started II. trading-post under the firm name of Wetzler & Co. George Willment and W. B. Disbrow, Joseph Walkup and Samuel B. Wyman, Wm. H. Parkinson and Wm. Leet, Bailey & Kerr, and Post & Ripley, were also store-keepers in 1849.

GREAT FIRES. The first and most destructive occurred on June 4, 1855. The fire originated in one of the Chinese houses on the side of the hill below the Methodist Church, spreading with fearful rapidity, and seeming fairly to lick up the buildings as it went. Those residing on the south side of the town were unable to secure much from the devouring element. The time occupied in the burning was one hour and twenty-five minutes.

From the American Hotel to Russel's orchard, on the west side of the street, and from the residence of Wm. McDaniel

The Auburn Volunteer Fire Department is testing water pressure at the firehouse on Railroad Street (later Lincoln Way). The building to the right is a bowling alley, next the Kennedy Hotel, and then the Union Stable (later Louie Armbruster's)

Courtesy Placer County Historical Society

On Monday, the 6th of October, 1856, [Tom] Bell's career was brought to a sudden termination by the noose of self-constituted hangmen. A few days before, he had been engaged in a terrible fight with Sheriff Henson, of Placer county, and a posse at the Franklin House, near Auburn. Bell was assisted by Texas and Ned Connor. On the fatal Monday, a party of nine men were scouring the country in search of the outlaw, and suddenly came upon him near the Merced River. Bell, unaware that he was being pursued, was sitting carelessly on his horse, his leg thrown over the pommel of his saddle, conversing with a Mexican. The first intimation he received that an enemy was near, was the summons to surrender, to which, backed as it was by nine rifles, he gracefully acceded. He was told to prepare for his final end, and after consuming four hours in writing two farewell letters to his family in Tennessee, he said he was ready to meet his doom. The night shades had gathered darkly around the forest trees that skirted the rushing waters of the Cowchilla and Merced; and there, with none but the omnipresent stars to witness the swift justice of his captors, his lamp of life went out forever. How many scenes of blood and pillage he had enacted, witnessed by the silent sentinels of the night, will never be known. They departed, and the sad winds sobbed a requiem over the last resting-place of Thomas J. Hodges.

Freeman Hotel fire, 1908

They were a mixed class, made up of various nations, representing every vice that morality, religion, or law hold in abhorrence, reminding me strongly in their turbulent demeanour of a parcel of convicts during the absence of the overseer. No doubt some good citizens were scattered amongst them, but they were like isolated grain-blades, smothered with noxious weeds.

William Redmond Kelly, 1849

to the banking house of Hall & Allen, on the east side, all the houses were destroyed. Before the embers had cooled, busy preparations began for re-building, and, before dark, lumber was on the ground ready for re-building. The loss was about $119,000.

[One of several fires] occurred October 28, 1863, in which nineteen buildings were destroyed, with a loss of about $60,000. These repeated losses had the effect of stimulating the erection of safer buildings, and those put up for business purposes in succeeding years have been mainly of brick and stone, and fireproof in their construction.

INCORPORATION OF AUBURN. During 1855, and for some years, the subject of a town incorporation was persistently advocated by the Whig and Herald, the two papers then guarding the interests of the place. As presenting the condition of the town, and reasons for the incorporation, an editorial upon the subject in the Herald of January 9, 1856, is here inserted:

During the month of April last, the subject of petitioning the County Court for a town incorporation, was somewhat discussed by our citizens, and a petition to that effect was put in circulation. For some reasons, the project was not carried into execution.

By reference to the files of the Auburn Whig, of the 18th of April and the 5th of May, 1855, we find the attention of our citizens called to the matter in two well-written articles, by the editor of that paper. The necessities of the move, the law upon the subject, and the entire question is so ably treated therein, that we will extract from those articles such portions as our space will permit, but would recommend those interested, and who have the files of those dates, to read every word he has there written.

The Chinese portion of the town is much more extensive now than it was then. Many more of that people are here now than then, and although we have, in re-building the town, erected some barriers calculated to stay an entire sweep of the town, in case of another fire, in the shape of some good fire-proof brick buildings, yet, we apprehend a fire in Chinatown would, in all likelihood, destroy as great an amount of property now as it did before, when the whole town was consumed. Perhaps if there had been a town corporation, the calamity might nevertheless have befallen us; certainly sufficient police arrangements can be instituted to lessen the danger fifty per cent.

Further: "The condition of our streets and alleys is not at all times such as we could desire, yet the obstruction existing, and the remedies required are not properly under the control of the Road Supervisor. "

The law provides that whenever the majority of the electors of any town or village shall petition the county court to that effect, the court shall proceed to incorporate the town, and order an election of a Board of Trustees, Assessor, Treasurer,

Railroad Street, now Lincoln Way, Bank of Auburn, Ann Arbor Bakery, Woods Lunch, Lee's, Louis Klumpp, Roelekenver Insurance and Conroy Hotel, 1906

Courtesy Placer County Museums

An American company put up a notice that their "valuable site was for sale," as they were going up to the Juba, and a lot of Germans, who had just come in, offered themselves as purchasers. The price asked was exorbitant. The following day was appointed for the Germans to come and see the fruits of an hour's working, the sellers going in the course of the night and secreting gold dust in the banks, so that it would come to light as the natural deposit during the course of the experiment, and getting their worthy countrymen to puff up the cheat in the mean time. The following morning the poor Germans were so charmed with the apparent richness of the place, they gave 500 dollars and two valuable gold watches for the property; and oh! what indecent laughing there was at the "stupid dupes." I felt for the strangers, who were neither strong enough to enforce a restoration of their property, or rebuke the unbecoming insolence they were exposed to. They stoically put up with jeers and taunts. It is unnecessary to say, that the proceeds of their first day's labour was not very encouraging; nevertheless, they persevered ... their perseverance rewarded by some very promising indications. The third day the indications led to veritable realities, enabling them to turn out the best day's work done in the diggings up to that period, and to proceed with an increasing daily average, which turned the laugh against Mr. Jonathan, who, with the most unprincipled impudence, sought to reclaim by force what he disposed of by a swindle.

William Redmond Kelly, 1849

There were many physicians among early California pioneers, as well as some who called themselves physicians with absolutely no medical training. This was no doubt a reputable doctor and dentist in early Auburn. This building housed the offices of Dr. J. Gordon Mackay and Dr. (dentist) Howell. Even though the sign says 1852 these doctors weren't in practice until much later.

At 3 o'clock, P.M., arrived at the "dry diggings," (now Auburn.) This was a place of three tents, situated on the main road leading to the Oregon trail, which it intersects twenty miles above. These mines were not being worked to any extent, owing to the scarcity of water. There were a few, however, engaged in carrying dirt, a mile on their backs, and washing it at a puddle, in town.

John M. Letts, 1849

and Marshal; said officers to hold for one year, and their pay to be fixed by the Board of Trustees. The powers of the Trustees, as fixed by law, are 'to prevent and remove nuisances; to provide for licensing public shows and lawful games; to prohibit disorderly conduct; to regulate and establish markets; to construct pumps, aqueducts, reservoirs, or other works for supplying the town with water; to keep in repair public wells; to layout, alter and keep open and repair the streets and alleys of the town; to provide such means as they may deem necessary to protect the town from injuries by fire, and to pass such other laws and ordinances for the regulation and police of the town as they may deem necessary.

Such, after an examination of the acts passed upon the subject, we find to be substantially the law in relation thereto, with this addition, that they may have a Recorder, with the powers of a Justice of the Peace in criminal and ordinance violations, within the limits of the corporations, if they desire it. It seems admirably adapted to our necessities; the expense of the administration can be gauged by the judgment of our citizens. Elect your Board of Trustees from among your property-holders, and they are not likely to produce a necessity for taxing themselves.

We are painfully sensible that the fire has crippled our citizens in their resources, and we incline to favor this move, from the fact that it will produce greater results, a more uniform improvement, and excellent police arrangements much cheaper than in any other way. The revenue from fines, the license from shows, etc., would of itself not be inconsiderable. Most of the officers, we have no doubt (as it would not require more than two hours a week), would serve gratis, and those it would be necessary to pay could draw it from the fees of office.

Aside from all other considerations, it is something of a favor that this is the county seat of a large and populous county, where our citizens come and spend their money, and we owe them something in the way of keeping up a comfortable, pleasant, orderly town.

We have been led to make these remarks at this time from the fact that a petition is again in circulation to effect this, as we think, desirable object. We hope it will not fall still-born again, but that our citizens will pursue the undertaking to the consummation so devoutly to be wished for.

The town of Auburn was incorporated by an Act of the Legislature approved March 29, 1861. The area of the town was fixed by the Act at one and one-fourth miles square, having the Court House as the centre. On the 30th of March, 1868, the Act of incorporation was repealed, and since that time the citizens of Auburn have got along as best they could without any town government.

FARE REDUCED. The coaches of the California Stage Company leave Auburn as follows: From Auburn to Sacramento,

There are almost as many thieves as honest men; one will murder the other for the sake of gold, they rob and steal whenever they can, and the only thing which preserves a semblance of justice is the Lynch Law. If a murderer is caught, his captors make short work with him, and hang him on the spot.

Herman Scharmann, 1849

Sam Putnam built the Putnam house (large white structure in back left) in 1880. It burned and was rebuilt in 1883. Bought and sold a couple of times, it ended up in the hands of ex-sheriff W.C. Conroy in 1899 and became the Conroy Hotel. Note the barber's striped pole near the front of the wagon. Next to it the sign advertises a "shaving saloon."

Courtesy Placer County Museums

Buggy on hill overlooking Auburn.

One evening of the previous winter a party of these roystering mountain blades were indulging in the bottle, when one of them unperceived emptied his canteen of pure alcohol on the head of another who was a famous bully, and seizing the candle, communicated the flame at the same moment. "Man on fire, man on fire, put him out, put him out," was the universal shout; and put him out they did with a vengeance, many embracing that opportunity to pay off old scores, and at the same time most effectually curing him of his bullying propensities.

Theodore Taylor Johnson, 1849

every day at 7,10, and 12 A. M.; from Auburn to Grass Valley, Nevada, and Forest City, 12 and 2 P. M.; from Auburn to Yankee Jim's, Todd's Valley, and Michigan Bluff, 2 P.M. from Auburn to Illinoistown, Iowa Hill, and Cold Springs, 2 P. M.; from Auburn to Marysville, Tuesdays, Thursdays, and Saturdays, at 1 o'clock P. M.

A BUSINESS VIEW. Auburn has a population of nearly 2,000 people. There is a good public school of four departments. There are several churches, and more projected.

The scenery in the vicinity of Auburn is grand, and the climate, though warmer in summer than that prevailing along the coast, is extremely healthful. Residences on the main streets are surrounded with the prettiest of gardens, filled with shade and fruit trees and flowers of every hue, which make the atmosphere fragrant with their odors. There is no healthier spot in the State. The main portion of the town is about 1,300 feet above the sea-level-an elevation sufficient to lift it above the fogs of the valley, and yet not high enough to bring it within the storm-area of the Sierra. Snow is seldom seen, and then only remains for a few hours. At the present time it is the center of a large and increasing trade. The numerous mines located in the immediate vicinity furnish employment to a large number of men. The towns and mining camps on the Forest Hill Divide also draw their supplies from this point. Considerable quantities of fruit and wine of excellent quality is produced by the farmers and fruit-growers of the slopes and fertile valleys; so that horticulture and wine-growing have become very important industries. Silkworms are raised to a limited extent, but sufficient to show that the industry, if properly managed, might be a remunerative one. Wood, coal, building-stone, and iron of fine quality are convenient, giving assurance of future importance as a manufacturing centre. The greatest period of depression appears to have been in 1873, as shown by statistics of business kept by the agency of Wells, Fargo & Co., since which time it has steadily increased. The total amount of golddust, coin, and currency shipped through Wells, Fargo & Co.'s Express from Auburn during the year 1881 was $434,634.65. Of the above amount $281,379 was gold-dust.

APPLEGATE. The region including Applegate was first settled upon in 1849 by Lisbon Applegate, and a village grew which bore the name of Lisbon, in honor of the pioneer settler. The locality was on the road from Auburn to Illinoistown. The precinct was first designated as the Bear River House, but in 1855 received the name of Lisbon, a post-office being then established under that name, with G. W. Applegate as postmaster. The voting population numbered from twenty-five to fifty, through a series of years, the majority being anti-Democratic-Whig, Know Nothing, and Republican, in their order-until the abolishing of the precinct, in 1871.

Here is one of the finest fruit regions of the State, as has been demonstrated by the success of Mr. Geo. W. Applegate and others of the locality. At an early day Mr. Applegate planted

The wolves Stole some meat from a neighbor's tent, taking it from within a foot or two of his head. We got 2 small loaves of bread baked at a Mormon family that arived overland. They charged $1. per loaf for baking & verry heavy hard bread at that.

Hiram Dwight Pierce, Thursday August 9th, 1849

Auburn Railroad Street, now Lincoln Way

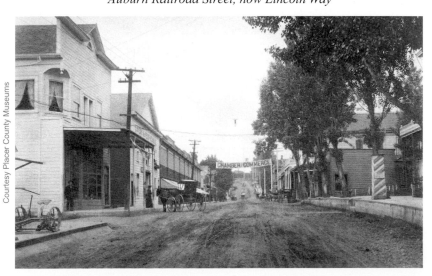

Courtesy Placer County Museums

Parlor of Charles Keena home

Phillips kept a wayside tavern, called the Mountaineer House, on the Folsom road, about three miles from Auburn. This place did not possess the best reputation in the world from the start. As time passed on, rumors of midnight gatherings at Phillips', of other characters besides honest teamsters and mule-drivers, began to gain ground, and the place was avoided by everyone who regarded his life or property. After events proved that the house was a rendezvous for most of the desperadoes that then cursed the country, the worst being Tom Bell's gang, a band of cut-throats and highway robbers that numbered several hundred, and who pillaged the State from the Oregon border to the southern lakes, rivaling Murietta and his horde in boldness and brutality. These men had a regular code of signals, signs, and passwords, by which they made themselves known to each other whenever they met.

a nursery, and also cultivated hay and grain, fencing in upwards of 1,100 acres of mountain land. From his nursery he has extended his vineyards and orchards until his trees are numbered in thousands and his grapevines in hundred thousands. Apple, pear, plum, peach, quince, fig, orange, and almond, are the principal trees; grapes of every variety, and berry bushes and vines in great number. In connection with this extensive vineyard are cider-mills, wine-presses and tanks, stills for brandy-making, wine cellar and store-houses, and all the appurtenances necessary to so extensive a business. Such is one of the mountain ranches and vineyards.

Applegate is the station on the Central Pacific Railroad contiguous to this region. It is ten miles northeast of Auburn, at an elevation of 2,014 feet above the sea, and is in Township No.4, of the political divisions of Placer County.

COLFAX. This place is situated on the Central Pacific Railroad, fifty-four miles from Sacramento and eighteen miles northeast of Auburn, and is another of the many towns that sprang into existence upon the completion of the great overland railroad. The rails reached Colfax September 1, 1865, and regular trains were running on the 4th of that month. The town of Colfax was laid out in 1865 by the Central Pacific Railroad Company. The site was subsequently sold to Messrs. Kohn & Kind, and a sale of lots took place July 29, 1865, which amounted to between $6,000 and $7,000.

Within half a mile of where Colfax now stands is the old settlement of Illinoistown, and when Colfax was laid out in 1865 it gathered to itself all that was left of this ancient place. Colfax has, since that time, steadily increased in population and importance, until now it is one of the leading towns in the county.

In 1874 a company was formed to build a narrow gauge railroad from Colfax to Nevada City. The work of construction began in 1875, and the road was completed and the last spike driven at Nevada on the 20th of May, 1876.

The Mineral Bar covered bridge was below Cape Horn (near Colfax). For some years Illinoistown was regarded as the "head of wagon navigation" on the Divide between Bear River and the North Fork of the American River. Pack mules carried the merchandise from Sacramento to the mining camps in the nearby canyons. One of these trails led via Rice's Ferry at Mineral Bar on the North Fork to Iowa Hill. At a later date one of the most important turnpike roads in the county was constructed, connecting these points with a substantial covered bridge over the river. This road and bridge was constructed by Charles Rice & Co., at a cost of about $75,000. For several years, while the Iowa Hill Divide was in its heyday, it was a very valuable property. Stages and teams traversed it from the railroad at Colfax to Iowa Hill and other points on the Divide. From the bridge, looking northeasterly, is the rocky area known as Cape Horn, around which rush the trains of the Central Pacific Railroad, 1,500 feet above the river, 1865.

My dear Wife

I feel much more safe with money in my pocket here than I should in the States. I have never known an instance of a man's being killed for his money in this country, and yet the miners when they leave the mines carry off their gold in bags as publicly as one would carry a grist of corn to mill in the States.

Horace Root,
June 18, 1850

Library of Congress

At the Middle Fork
the general average
at that time was two
ounces, the particles
a good size, with
numerous handsome specimens,
that fetched far above their intrinsic
value; there were several of the
dandy class in those diggings, but,
as might be expected, they were
not particularly successful; there
was also a very flash company
of that school, who regulated
their movements by sound of
trumpet, with tents, uniform, and
implements to match, whom it was
quite a treat to see turn out in the
morning, with military order and
precision, managing everything
with great system and success, save
and except the matter of getting
gold, which appeared to be repelled
by their polished tools and formal
appearance; for while ragged
fellows with rusty picks and clumsy
shovels carried home of evenings
their nice little pannikins of clear
glittering gold.

William Redmond Kelly, 1849

People weren't just digging for gold during California's early years. The Capitol Granite Quarry in Rocklin, shown here in about 1865, was one of many granite quarries in the area. There were also marble quarries, slate mines or quarries, and other "building materials" mines in the area.

Rich veins of quartz were discovered near Colfax in 1866. A test of the rock was made at Grass Valley, and found to be worth between $27 and $28 per ton. A company was organized and a mill constructed in 1869. The mine was christened the "Rising Sun." The gold is of a pure quality, being worth $18.50 per ounce. The mill had five stamps of 800 pounds each, and was capable of reducing ten tons per day. The mill was subsequently increased to twenty stamps, and still continues a paying mine. The Montana Mine has been worked to some extent, and numerous buildings have been erected. The Meda Mine is situated on the dividing ridge, three miles from town. The ore is rich and has yielded an average of $30 to the ton.

A destructive fire occurred in April, 1874, which swept away the main portion of the town. With undaunted energy the citizens have re-built, and now it is difficult to discover any traces of the fire, and the place is now handsomer and more substantially built than ever.

Library of Congress

The climate of Colfax is similar to that of the other towns on the western slope of the Sierra. Its altitude is 2,421 feet above the sea level, and with its salubrious and healthful location, its mountain breezes, laden with the spicy odors of pine forests, disease cannot linger. Fruits of all kinds that grow in temperate latitudes are raised on the ranches, and apples and peaches are much better flavored than similar productions in the valleys.

The population of Colfax is about 600. The business establishments consist of dry goods and grocery stores, two hotels, drug store, wagon and blacksmith shop, bakery and restaurant, saloons, lumber yard, meat market, shoemakers, etc.

FRYTOWN was located on the Auburn Ravine, about two miles below Ophir. It was first settled in 1849. Only a few houses were built, but the miners were in the habit of using the place as supply head-quarters. There was a general merchandise store, kept by Messrs. Fry & Bruce, which supplied the miners in the immediate vicinity with the necessaries of life. The town received its name from the senior partner in the firm. It was one of those mushroom towns which sprang into existence and soon died. But "twas lively while it lasted."

DUNCAN CAÑON. This stream is an important confluent of the Middle Fork of the Middle Fork of the American, and rises pretty well up toward the western summit of the Sierra, between

John Norton was murdered in the fall of 1877 on the public highway leading from Auburn to Forest Hill by two of the most desperate Indians, Indian Charlie and Indian Bill. It seems that when the Indians saw Norton coming alone down the road, they made up their minds to rob him. They demanded his money. Norton told them he had none, and started to run. At this Indian Charlie shot him, the ball striking his shoulder, but the shot, failing to have the desired effect, the other Indian fired and Norton fell to the ground. The Indians drew knives to complete the job their bullets had commenced. In their endeavor to cut his throat, Norton evidently grabbed the knives by the blade to ward them off, for, when found, his hands were shockingly cut. While engaged in their butchery another man came in sight, and the Indians, becoming alarmed, escaped in the brush. By excessive diligence Sheriff McCormick finally captured Charlie some ten miles above Auburn, near the North Fork of the American River.

After the capture of Charlie, he obtained information that his man, "Indian Bill," was at one of two camps in El Dorado County, either Volcanoville or Bottle Hill. Arrangements [were made] for making the search. [Once located] they surrounded the camp but the Indians refused to come out. The door of the cabin was then broken down...and discovered their man ... he immediately began to shoot. After some shooting on both sides they threatened to burn him out, and at once began to pile fuel against the side of the wigwam. Seeing this he finally gave himself up.

Auburn had its share of saloons like most communities. Conroy Hotel Bar is shown here at the turn of the century. William Conroy was sheriff from 1893-1905.

Courtesy Placer County Museums

When the Central Pacific Railroad was completed in the late 1860s, several towns that started out as mining communities quickly shifted into transportation related businesses. Illinoistown was the first settlement in the area now known as Colfax which sprang up and absorbed Illinoistown when the railroad came through. This is a late 1860s view of the depot at Colfax.

Being weary and worn out, I was unable to wield the pick and shovel, and so I left in a few days for Sacramento where I undertook to make a little money by painting, but it was a failure, both as to workmanship and as to financial gain. However, by this time I had gained some strength and left for Beal's Bar at the junction of the north and south forks of the American River. Here I mined through the winter with some success.

Lell Hawley Woolley, 1849

the main North Fork and Picayune Valley. It was never noted for its gold product, and to-day, by reason of its undisturbed condition, its clear, pellucid water, the tangled mat of undergrowth upon its flats, and noble forest trees growing adjacent to its unscarified banks, it reminds the "old-timer" more of the primitive days than almost any other stream of like magnitude in the mountains. James W. Marshall says that it derived its name from Thomas Duncan, who came to the country overland, in 1848, from Missouri, in the train of Captain Winter, and who entered California via the road, or mountain trail rather, diverging from American Valley, and following down the ridge south of the North Fork.

In the fall of 1850, Antoine and other cañons in that locality having been slightly worked, and considerable gold of a coarse character exhibited, which had been taken therefrom, naturally the attention of gold-seekers was directed thither, and persons who had been there were eagerly sought, and the oracular knowledge they dispensed was readily "taken in" by credulous inquirers. No tale was too extravagant; however palpable the canard, there were always more to believe than to doubt. The chronicler hereof remembers well how, in the spring of 1849, when one of the pioneer mail steamers of the Pacific Coast entered the harbor of Panama upon her first return trip, the city was thronged with Americans, who had only purchased tickets to the isthmus and were unable to get further. There were still doubts as to the reputed richness of the gold mines, and a thousand anxious and excited interviewers stood upon the shore, ready to make prisoners of those who landed. Two brave sailors becoming thus corraled, and finding escape impossible, edified the crowd with yarns that did credit to their imaginative powers, satisfied their listeners, and disillumined the brilliancy of Alladin's Lamp. Exhibiting a buckskin bag which evidently contained nuggets, one of them said: "Why, look here, it's no trouble to get gold anywhere in California; it's all over-every-where! Just after we left the port of San Francisco, the mate set me to cleaning the anchor which we had just hove up, and see! here's over $200 that I panned out from the mud I scraped off the flukes!" and the crowd believed him-for why should they doubt?

In like manner did Tom Duncan regale the senses of a crowd of miners who happened to be at work near him on Shirt-tail Cañon, late in the fall of 1850. He had, in coming into the country, traversed the region where Antoine Cañon flowed; more than that, he had found diggings in a creek, but never stopped to work them, nor had he ever been back to them

We found several tents pitched, and one or two tent-stores, around which persons were talking and swearing in the most approved California fashion. When I attempted to remonstrate with one of these, and pointed out to him not only its vice but its absurdity, and asked him why it was so general, "Oh," he replied, with an oath, "it's the nature of the country!"

James L. Tyson, 1849

Old Auburn. First train through town on the temporary track, 1909.

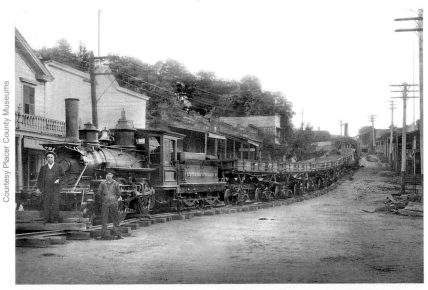

Courtesy Placer County Museums

Ogden Mallory Harness shop on Washington Street in Auburn, 1899

Wednesday, 22d.
1849 I felt verry tierd.
My back getting lame
in consequence as I
think, of getting my
feet wet days & sleeping on the
ground nights. I was provided with
a pair of boots that would have kept
my feet dry but had them stolen at
Sacramento Citty & am compelled
to wear thin Shoes.

Hiram Dwight Pierce 1849

since. Could he find them for a consideration? Most assuredly. Thereupon a company of select spirits entered into a compact with Tom, that he would pilot them to the spot. Furnishing him with a horse, the party started out in quest of the favorite spot, which Duncan declared he had been to two years before. Reaching the vicinity, the cañons all looked so much alike that Tom couldn't strike the right spot; members of the company canvassed the matter; the guide had either lied to them or was "throwing off" for a better thing-each offense deserving capital punishment. Tom was distrusted. At night he was placed under guard, and he roust soon show the place he had contracted to do, or be shot. While camped in the bed of a certain cañon, near its head, the guide led the party to the northern side of the ridge, overlooking the North Fork of the American River above Sailor Bar. Here were some small flats and ponds, where gold enough was found to induce a relaxation of vigilance, to the extent that no guard was placed over Duncan the following night. The next morning's sun rose in the cañon upon a decimated camp. Tom Duncan and a mule had gone! The party afterward found the mule at Todd's Valley, but Tom Duncan they never saw again. He had sought new diggings out of reach of his late companions-while as a remembrance, they christened the stream upon which they had camped, Duncan's Cañon and thus it goes down to history.

FORT TROJAN. This peculiarly-named town was located on the Auburn Ravine, about three miles from the present town of Lincoln. It does not date back in its history to the days of '49, but reaches only to the year 1858. It was lively until the starting of the town of Lincoln, when the business was transferred to that place. There was a hotel kept by Jerry Henderson, who was also postmaster for the town; Mills & Evans had a general merchandise store; Gray & Philipps had a meat market, and Peter Fritchard had a blacksmith shop. There were two saloons, one owned by Honeycut & Hoffman, and the other by E. A. Gibson. James Beck was Justice of the Peace, and James Berg was Constable. There is nothing left to denote the existence of this town, except the memories of the men who were familiar with the facts. The common appellation given the place by the miners was "Fort Trojan."

HUMBUG CAÑON. The above-named stream is one of the earliest placers worked, and empties into the South Branch of the North Fork of the American, from the south, a short distance above its junction with Blue Cañon at Euchre Bar. It heads at the base of the grand gravel ridge, upon which are located the Mountain Gate and adjoining mines, having several branches, and was first explored early in 1850. In February of that year L. P. Burnham, now a resident of Damascus; Robert E. Draper, who subsequently lived a long time in El Dorado County, and at Aurora, Nevada, at which latter place he figured in a duel with Dr. Eichelroth, and a man by the name of Kirkpatrick, were among the crowd who first rushed, during the pleasant weather which at that time prevailed and gave promise

It's unknown exactly where this miner and his cabin were, but it looks like the sad reality of his mining experience was displacing what probably started as optimism and hope.

Courtesy California State Library

December 19th.—A fiendish, heathenish murder and robbery was committed at Stewards Flat, below Newcastle. Booker Chambers, one of the oldest miners on the Flat, and a quiet and estimable gentleman, was the victim. A Chinaman had called at Chambers' cabin once or twice, trying to buy a mining claim, and it seems that he had gone there again, and that Chambers had ceased mixing bread (as the dough was still on his fingers when found), and taken his pick and pan and gone to show him how rich the claim would prospect. Chambers' position when found would show that he was on his right knee, bending over, and had struck one or two blows under the bank of the claim, when he was struck a heavy blow on the back of the head with a sharp hatchet, cutting through the coat-collar and partially severing the spinal bone; a second blow struck on the side of the neck, severing the jugular vein. He then fell or was pulled over backwards, and again struck on the right forehead, burying the bit of the hatchet in the brain, and a fourth just above the right ear, and a fifth below the right eye and ear. Chambers was known to have about $200 in gold coin on his person, and about the same or a greater amount of gold-dust, and a gold hunting-case watch. The watch-guard was cut and the watch taken, and his pockets were turned inside out, and empty. Chambers was the fourth or fifth victim of these brutal, heathenish man-butchers within a few years in the county, and the weapons and mode of slaughter and stealthy acts were almost identical in each case.

Freighting in Placer County

May 12th, 1855.—
The Indians in the
neighborhood of Gold
Hill were performing the
funeral rites upon a deceased
member of their tribe, when
a quarrel ensued between
a squaw and one of the males,
which resulted in a brutal murder.
The man took the woman's child
and deliberately cut its head off
throwing the body on the fire which
was consuming the body of the
dead squaw. The woman in revenge
took the child of her opponent
and threw it on the fire, but it
was rescued from the flames by
some of the spectators. The Indian
was arrested, but subsequently
discharged on a *nolle prosequi*.

of an early opening of spring, to the locality of Bird's Valley
and Michigan Bluff. Snow covered the ridges, and the water in
the main streams was so high that but little mining was done
there then, which circumstances caused a feeling of restlessness
to pervade the minds of the nomadic prospectors, and these
three men concluded to "strike out" in search of other diggings.
Therefore, the same month, they mounted snow-shoes, left
camp at the future-to-be Michigan City, and boldly turned their
footsteps toward the unknown region to the northeastward. Arriving at the head of a cañon which ran toward the North Fork,
after a weary journey of some eighteen or twenty miles, they
proceeded down it to where another branch came in, the two
forming quite a large stream within a deep gorge. Here they
camped, and, upon prospecting, found gold sufficient in quantity to induce them to locate claims. As it was of importance
enough to do this, a proposal was made that a name be given
it, and the throe pioneers having all emigrated to California
from Mississippi though none were natives of that State but
Kirkpatrick they bestowed upon the stream the name of Mississippi Cañon. A few days work, however, seems to have disgusted
them, for thereafter they shouldered their blankets and climbed
the hill, with the intention of returning to the place from
whence they started. After leaving their camp in the cañon, and
while toiling up the steep mountain side, Kirkpatrick, in an in-
terval while resting in the assent, gave expression to his disgust
by saying: "Pshaw, hasn't any gold of any account, it's a regular
humbug, and instead of Mississippi we'd better call it Humbug
Cañon."

Just as the three men had scaled the precipitous sides of the cañon, and were fairly setting out on their return journey down the ridge, human voices were heard, and soon after human forms descried approaching them. The new-comers proved to be a party of men following up their trail, supposing they had discovered rich diggings. No declarations upon the part of the three could deter the new party from going ahead; the more the three endeavored to persuade them that the cañon was a "humbug," the more determined were the interlopers that they were upon the portals leading to great wealth, and into the cañon they would descend. This determination on the part of the last party re-enthused the hopes of the first, and they, too, would return and define the boundaries of their claims. Consequently all went into the cañon, when the following day a mining district was organized, and rules and regulations were adopted. At the meeting held, Robert E. Draper was chosen to act as Secretary, and in his written minutes of the proceedings occurred the following words: "At a meeting of the miners of Humbug Cañon, held this - day of February, 1850," etc., which have ineffacably attached themselves to the place, to the entire obliteration of the primal cognomen of Mississippi. Subsequent workings have proven the banks and bed of the cañon to be rich -- no humbug-it having been washed over several times, and at each time producing large amounts of gold.

JOHNSON'S RANCH. Among the many camps that sprang into existence in this county during the few years subsequent to the discovery of gold in California, was the one known as

Early day Highway 49 bridge over the North Fork of the American River.

Courtesy Placer County Museums

A desperate attempt was made to rob the East-bound mail and express train on the Central Pacific Railroad, near Cape Horn Mills, on the night of September 1, 1881, but fortunately the would-be robbers obtained no booty. To stop the train the robbers had torn up one of the rails and the engine jumped the track. Alarmed at the shock, the clerk of the mail car appeared at the door, when he received a command to throw up his hands. This was the first intimation as to the cause of the stoppage. A similar demand was made on the express messenger; but instead of complying with their request, he dodged back at once and extinguished the lights. No further demands were made, but a few minutes later the robbers were heard halloing to each other as if collecting their forces for a retreat. A number of detectives were dispatched to the scene of the would-be robbery. On an inspection of the grounds after the departure of the robbers, there were found nine masks, fifteen or twenty giant-powder cartridges, a quantity of fuse, axes, sledges, etc., It was afterwards learned by Sheriff Boggs that three men were living in a cabin on the North Fork of the American River, who claimed to be miners, but who had neither mining tools to work with nor a claim to work. This suspicious circumstance furnished a clue, which being worked up, led to the capture of every one engaged in the attempt.

*This locomotive is crossing the Long Ravine Bridge near Colfax
probably in the late 1860s.*

This morning a
Mr Dwinell of Iowa
committed suicide
by shooting himself
in the head with a
revolver the bullet entering his
brain, he lived about 3 hours.
there was a coffin then made for
him and he was buried. He was
said to be well off at home, and
it was supposed he had money
buried there, as he was a miser.
And it was thought by many that
disappointment in getting gold
caused him to go deranged.

James Tolles, April 11th, 1850

Johnson's Crossing, or Johnson's Ranch. The spot where the
little town once stood is still there, but the inhabitants have all
sought other fields for their labors. There was a bridge across
Bear River at this place, and it was a stopping-place for the
many teams engaged in hauling freights from Sacramento to
the mines in the upper country. In 1852 there was a small hotel
kept by a man named John Shuster, and soon after that the
town commenced to flourish. It was located about twenty-five
miles northwest from Auburn, which was the principal town in
the county at that time. Mr. Young Dougherty, now a resident
of Sheridan, and from whom the information regarding the
place was received, pitched his tent there in 1852 and the next
year built his house. In 1856 there were about thirty dwelling-
houses and the usual number of business places. Wm. O'Rear
was the first postmaster, and was appointed in 1854. He also
kept a hotel.

The place at one time had a population of over 100, and
supported two blacksmith shop, two stores, and also a couple of
saloons. It was a voting precinct and often polled as high as 150
votes, though the voters came in from the surrounding country.

Among the earliest settlers were Claude Chana, who came
there as early as 1846. After him came John Shuster, Wm.

B. Campbell, John Swearer, A.H. Estell, Joseph Rears, Philip Tracy, Dr. Gray, Dr. Esmond, John Boone, Dennis Neugent, Harrison Kimball, Young Dougherty, and others.

In the year 1862 the floods nearly destroyed the place, and then came the debris from the hydraulic mines higher up on the river, and now there is not a vestige of this lively little town left visible. The deer and bear run wild over the site of the town. The real cause of the desertion of the place was the debris from up the river.

GOLD HILL. In the early history of Placer County Gold Hill was quite a conspicuous point, but as a village its glory has departed. It is situated in Auburn Ravine, seven and one-half miles west of the county seat. Here are the lower foot-hills of the Sierra, slight undulations distinguish it from the great valley that a few miles west stretches off a level plain, and at the present time orchards, fields, gardens, and vineyards occupy the places once devoted to mining. The first attempt at mining was in 1851, and in April, 1852, the village was organized and received its name. J. M. Bedford was Justice of the Peace; T. Taylor was Constable, and C. Langdon was Recorder of mining claims. The busy population of its early days may be estimated from the votes given. In 1852, Presidential election, the vote at Gold Hill numbered 444; in 1853 it was 304, and in 1854, 294. The diggings were in the surface, and almost everywhere, where water could be obtained, a miner could get some gold, and in some spots rich deposits were found. Gradually the village declined, until at present it is not distinguished as a voting precinct.

Freighting on the Foresthill Divide

Courtesy Placer County Museums

There came a big buck well calculated to create a sensation. Mrs. Rachael Griffith and two young men were sitting under the booth when in marched the gentleman alluded to. He had procured a plug hat; a cavalryman's jacket—all blue with gorgeous stripes of red and yellow. These he had donned—and nothing more—and now appeared before a civilized assemblage in civilized costume, sans shirt, sans pants, sans everything, save the tall plug hat and the short jacket of a U. S. dragoon. It was a frontier scene which no artist could correctly transfer upon canvas. It was decidedly comical. There was no escape for either the young men or women. Stoically and with statue-like rigidity stood the Indian, no doubt supposing himself the admired of all beholders.

This was too much for human risibilities. A glance from one white man to the other caused the of opening the safety-valves of the entire quartette of throats, and a loud guff-haw broke forth as the women scampered laughing with all their might. The noble red man, divining that his appearance had brought him ridicule rather than admiration, without even saying a word or changing his immobile features, contemptuously turned upon his heel and sought the cover of the adjacent forest.

Mining operation along the American River, late 1800s.

Morning warm. The rest & quiet of the Sabbath was verry agreeable. All in this place so far observe the Sabbath as to cease work at gold digging though many go ahunting & attend to other things. Attended meeting 3 times. It would not be entirely uninteresting to see a company of grisley long bearded Men sitting flat on the ground under an Evergreen, listning to the Word & many of them Joining in the Singing.

Hiram Dwight Pierce,
Sunday, August 26th, 1849

NEWCASTLE. The present village of Newcastle is on the line of the Central Pacific Railroad, five miles southwest of Auburn, in Township No.2, having an elevation of 956 feet above the sea. Here was a mining town of the early days, but now it is the center of one of the most important fruit-growing districts of the State.

ILLINOISTOWN. Let vagrant memory plume her pinions and take flight backward over time's unending course, to linger for a while where lie the embers of a neglected past, buried by the rubbish of more than three decades; let truant thought unloose to wander as it lists, and call up the scenes and transactions of a third part of a century gone; let the grave be invaded and those who have long lain dead be awakened, brought forth and rehabilitated with life once more; let the thin, gray locks of wrinkled old men with piping voice assume the gloss, and color, and luxuriance of that which is wont to adorn the form of fresh, hopeful, and noisy adolescence; let grown men and matrons, as in that long ago, be turned over again, "infants mewling and puking in the nurse's arms;" ... rummaging thought invades, digs up the heap, and now and then drops a scintillating spark which at length kindles into a flame of recollecting light; and lo! obliterating all the ravages made by time's progressing strides!

SITE OF ILLINOISTOWN. The site of Illinoistown is a little valley which lies just below Colfax, on the southern side of the Central Pacific Railroad. People began to rendezvous there early in 1849, and as it was the uppermost point upon the dividing ridge between Bear River and the North Fork of the American that wagons reached, it became the distributing point of supplies for all of the mining camps at the north, south, and east of it. Many of the first inhabitants who went to the Deer Creek (now Nevada City) mines, either bought their provisions for the trip there or had then brought to the place from Sacramento by wagon. As a business locality it ranked the Dry Diggings (Auburn) until late in the fall of 1849, when the emigration, and people who supposed they could not exist in the river cañons during the winter, congregated in great numbers at the latter place, attracted by its more genial, winter climate, as well as the shallow surface placers where an occasional large lump of gold could be found, making it at once the business center of the predestined County of Placer, as well as its future shire town.

ALDER GROVE. At a bend in the valley about half a mile below Colfax, in a narrow place, a fine large spring flowed to the surface; and about a quarter of a mile below that was another, which had caused the formation of quite a plat of boggy meadow land, on the lower side of which grew many thrifty alder trees, which became a favorite camping place. At that time— the early part of '49—the North Fork of the American was thronged with men from Kelley's Bar to the Giant's Gap, mainly from Oregon. They at first called the place Alder Grove. Subsequently, when wagons reached there, a corral was built in the upper portion of the valley, and some of the Oregonians designated it as the Upper Corral. Early that summer three log buildings were erected for trading-posts, one by Sears & Miller at the extreme lower end of the valley; one by John W. Piersons at the spring at the narrows, and another about a quarter of a mile above, upon the eastern side of the valley, by a Mr. Neall.

MINING ON THE RIVER. The rush to the river had been too early—in April and May—at a time when the water was high,

Jarvis Mine, dump house tunnel in Placer County around 1900.

Courtesy Placer County Museums

The victims were Mr. H. N. Sargent... the murderers were Chinamen, headed by a young viper named Ah Sam, who served as cook in different families in Auburn. Mr. Sargent had sold these Chinamen a mining claim for $120, and the only known provocation for the murder was the desire of the Chinamen to repossess the money. Mr. Oder and his wife told him [Sargent] they wanted to purchase more mining ground, and wished him to go with them to the claim for that purpose. While on the way the Chinamen walking in the rear shot Mr. Sargent in the back; a Chinaman in advance shot him again. Five times he was shot before he fell, and then, for fear he might survive, he was shot again in the head. The murderous wretches rushed back to the house and completed their bloody work on Mr. and Mrs. Oder, before hunting for the money. Mrs. Oder, shot with a pistol and her head cut open with an axe, was found lying in a pool of blood on the floor, and in an adjoining room, trunks, broken open with the same bloody axe that had served to scatter the brains of Mrs. Oder, were found, rummaged of their contents. The body of Mr. Oder, was lying senseless on his face, and pierced with three bullets.

A neighbor, seeing the mangled and gory form of Mrs. Oder, at once started for Rocklin to give the alarm. Officers began at once a search for the murderers. Mr. Sargent was taken to Rocklin, he revived sufficiently ... he gave the information that his assailants were Penryn Chinamen.

Fifteen Chinamen were taken into custody ... a heavy guard was required to keep the enraged citizens from taking possession of the prisoners and lynching them.

Freight wagon hauling donkey steam engine boiler across the original Georgetown Swinging Bridge. Note the warning bell on the lead mule.

May 25th, 1860. — The stage from. Iowa Hill to Illinois-town was stopped within a mile and a half of the, former place, before daylight, and the treasure-box of Wells, Fargo & Co. was robbed of $11,000 by a party of five or six highwaymen. After the stage had been stopped one of them held the horses while the others brought their pistols to bear upon the driver and passengers, and one mounted the boot and took out the treasure-box. At the time of the robbery there were six passengers in the stage, not one of whom was armed.

and therefore all the gold that could be got, came either from the higher bars or from pits, to work which required bailing of water. The consequence was that before the water in the river became low enough to work advantageously, most of the men left in search of other diggings, leaving alone the stream on the bars, in their abandoned camps, everything they had taken in there but the clothing they wore (generally of buckskin), and their blankets. August 1, 1849, there were not more than twenty white men from Barnes' Bar to Green Valley working upon the North Fork, and six of these were former Hudson Bay Company employees, at work in the bed of the stream just above the Giant's Gap. Some very fair stocks of goods had been put in store at Alder Grove about the time the exodus of the miners from the river began, and the traders were disappointed at the turn that affairs had taken. Sears & Miller, who had a large assortment of goods suited only for the Indian trade, immediately began to hire them to work, and from about July 1st to the middle of September employed an average of fifty Indians a day, whom they kept panning out upon the river bars, and in this way accumulated a great deal of gold.

THE PIONEER SETTLERS. Among the Oregonians who came to Alder Grove in May, 1849, was B. T. Mendenhall, who had left a young wife and babe encamped among the sand dunes of Happy Valley, San Francisco, while he went mountainward to spy out a home for himself and them. He learned from experience that the mines upon the North Fork were good, and at the same time looked with very favorable eyes upon the pristine beauties of the valley in which were located Alder Grove and the Upper Corral. Here he determined to set up his altar, gather around him his household gods, and establish a home in the wilderness of California. With this laudable intention, about the middle of the summer he proceeded to San Francisco, and soon thereafter had his wife, infant, and what few articles of indispensable household material were at hand en route for the mountains.

Thus, on the 28th of July, 1849, on the deck of the little schooner Sea Witch, in the harbor of San Francisco, did the writer first encounter them. With the other passengers were two more Oregonians, a Mr. McLeod (an old-time Hudson Bay employee) and a Mr. Atwood, both of whom were "old miners," having worked on the Stanislaus in 1848, and having been back to Oregon, were now just on their return to remain during the season of '49. How natural it was for the young novice to listen to the tales of these "old miners," and become captivated to ingratiate himself into their esteem, to that extent that they would allow him to accompany them to the diggings, where, profiting by their large experience, fortune might soon be accumulated.

Mining operation at Mammoth Bar on the North Fork of the American River

Courtesy Placer County Museums

Three drunken, worthless fellows, deserters from the army, with the uniform of "Uncle Sam" on their backs, happened on one of these rich "gulches" within a few yards of where other and more deserving men, with severe toil, scarcely realized any thing; so fickle is the blind goddess, and often so prosperous and apparently favored by fortune, are the dissolute and abandoned! These unworthy characters were nearly always intoxicated, and yet dug out their hundreds with hardly an effort.

James L. Tyson, 1849

Auburn stage.

A man drowned just below here to day. 3 men started down the River in a large canoe, and one was draged out by a bush, and was not able to swim ashore and was lost. This is the last day of the year 1849 which is now rolling into eternity

James Tolles, Dec 31st, 1849

LANDING AT SACRAMENTO. The *Sea Witch* made her landing under a big sycamore tree in front of the future city of Sacramento, on the morning of July 29th, having had a remarkably quick passage, and preparations were immediately made for transportation to the mines. Without remarkable incident the place was reached on the 3d of August. He put up his little tent, built a booth of poles with cross pieces covered with brush, and forthwith the first hotel of the place was established, where, for one dollar and a half, the wayfarer would be served with bacon and beans, bread, and pie made of dried fruit—all the delicacies then obtainable— from the hand of the pioneer white woman of that whole region, Mrs. Mendenhall.

FIRST PROSPECTING EXPERIENCE. Atwood and McLeod, with their protegé, meanwhile prospected every bar upon the North Fork, from Barnes to the forks of the river above Green Valley. The two first-named, during the previous summer, had luckily been possessed of big diggings, from which, inexperienced as they were they had realized $20,000 to $25,000 each. Consequently their ideas were quite exalted, and no common diggings would suit them.

The river banks were almost untouched and were rich everywhere, but with the heavy, deep tin pans supplied by the Hudson Bay Company, these men would pan out in the presence of their companion, and obtaining no more than twenty-five cents to one dollar and a half a pan, would in variably say "wake kloshe, kultus," hit the bottom of the vessel a kick with their toe and consign the gold again to the stream. They didn't want the fine dust; they were seeking chunks which were doubtless higher up in the mountains. McLeod and Atwood concluded they would go over to Feather River, which they did.

THE MINING LESSON LEARNED. The novice who had thus far followed the fortunes of the two "old miners," concluded that he had learned all they had to impart; he was footsore and fagged out by much travel… he would revisit his ideal spot to mine, and there attempt his virgin effort at digging for gold.

The place was on the North Fork of the American, nearly opposite Cold (now Mountain) Spring, upon the southern side of the river. There he picked up a rocker dug out of a log, with no apron, and with a riddle made of rawhide, and some other rude tools that had been left by the earlier Oregon men.

As the winter of 1849 approached, men began to leave the river, as at other points, and gather at the settlements on the ridges, and Alder Grove became quite populous. Before the rains had fairly set in, Mr. Mendenhall had completed a double log house—he occupying one part as a hotel and Charles L. King and Horatio Hoskins the other portion as a store. In September John D. Egbert, Roberts. Egbert, and Oliver Egbert had arrived and located in the vicinity, the two latter settling down to mining, making shakes, and doing all sorts of work, while the former, having a commercial turn, devoted his time to teaming and trading. It was not long before the Egbert Brothers had a cabin filled with miners' supplies, and were ready to trade in

Miners were continually coming in from different diggins, to expend a part or all of their gold on what they term "a burst;" which is a constant revel, day and night for three or four days, and often a week at a time. Drinking brandy at half an ounce, and champaigne at an ounce a bottle as freely as water, they wandered and roved about from groggery to store, and store to tent, wild with intoxication; brandishing bowie knives in sport, or shooting with the rifle at any mark they fancied, with the ball often but half home and the rammer in.

Theodore Taylor Johnson, 1849

Teaming from Cash Rock, taken on November 29, 1910

Courtesy Placer County Museums

Newcastle Plaza around the turn of the century.

February 12th, 1864.—The community of Auburn was startled by the announcement that Samuel McDonald, the night-watchman, had been found dead, having been shot through the heart with a pistol-ball sometime during the night. The deceased was found lying in the rear of Steiner's brick store, and upon examination, it was found that an attempt had been made to break into the store by forcing away the brick wall next to one of the iron doors. He was shot through the upper part of the heart, the ball ranging from the left side in a direction slightly downward—showing that he must have been shot by some person standing in the street above, on the ascending ground.

those or any other article going. Pierson, meantime, had been busy laying in stores, and had several ox-teams running over the road freighting from Sacramento.

INDIANS. As there were many beautiful little valleys upon the divide between Auburn and Illinoistown, and as the locality reached the altitude where grew the sugar-pine, as well as being the home of the black oak, and there being an abundance of game, it was a favorite abiding-place of the Indians, and scores of little knolls overlooking the small valleys spoken of were covered with the circular-shaped huts, constructed mainly of bark. Cords of the long cones of the sugar-pine were stacked up near these villages, with the seed, or nut, still in them, which were only shelled when required—their natural cell affording better protection from the effects of rain by the closing up of the scales of the bur by dampness upon the outside, than any method the Indians had adopted for their preservation. Immense caches of manzanita were also made. Large cribs were built of small-sized logs, filled with acorns and covered with bark. These were the main winter stores of the aborigines, and were then an adjunct to every cluster of wigwams, and the quantities gathered and stored were astonishing.

Toward the end of November the Indians began to get impudent and saucy. They were more numerous than the whites; they were, of right, no doubt, the natural lords of the heritage; the country had been occupied by their ancestors away back to a time beyond the memory of the oldest among them, and they soon began to look upon the interloping gold-diggers as legitimate subjects of plunder. A slight castigation for a few instances of palpable theft made them avoid the settlement. When any would come, it would only be an old man or two, accompanied, perhaps, by several urchins of the tribe, but "signs" of a great many could be seen at any time just at the outskirts of the place, which circumstance was looked upon as an unfavorable indication of their good feeling and intentions.

DASTARDLY ROBBERY AND BLOODLESS BATTLE. Finally, about the second week of December, during the temporary absence of the proprietors, who had gone to Auburn, the Indians broke into the store and carried off or destroyed nearly everything that was portable, except liquors, which at that time they never drank. For several nights they continued these visits, and no one came to make them afraid. But just at dusk on the evening of the 15th of December, 1849, during the prevalence of a heavy storm, which had been incessant during the day, the proprietors of the store approached the place with five pack-animals laden with additional supplies. A smoke issuing from a hole in the shake roof, instead of coming through the chimney, first attracted their attention. A bar was spiked to the logs on the outside, across the door, as they had left it six days before.

Listening for a moment, suppressed sounds of merriment were heard in the Indian dialect. It was no time for parleying, but one for action. The howling storm without, and the darkening pall of night had more terrors to the fatigued and hungry white men than the arrow points of the exuberant savages within. The barricade was wrenched from off the door, which was suddenly thrown open, and two drenched and storm-chilled angry white men confronted more than a score of comfortably conditioned Indians, surprised at their feast. The fire they had made under the place they had entered prevented escape in that way, and their only opportunity was to flee through the door.

Team in Volcano Canyon

Courtesy Placer County Museums

On a Sunday morning soon after my arrival, I was called to see an Indian whose head was shockingly cut by an Oregonian, a white man, whom he had accompanied into California. The man's tent was a short distance from mine, and I heard the shriek when the blow was struck. Some one had persuaded the Indian to leave his employer, and he was about doing so. To compel him to remain, the Oregonian, who had incurred expense on his account, struck him with some heavy weapon and felled him to the earth. On the following day the man went in pursuit of another Indian, to shoot him, whom he charged with stealing his horse. The Oregonians, and an immense number were in California, were severe on all Indians, wherever they met a naked or wild one, unhesitatingly shooting him down

James L. Tyson, 1849

Covered bridge at Kelley Bar on the North Fork of the American River, 1850s

There was a question raised there amongst the Americans themselves, which led to much angry feeling, being an objection on the part of one class, that large companies should have the privilege of employing Indians or any other labour, taking advantage of their capital to engage a great number, staking off a space for each hand, whether an employer or not, and thus establishing a system of monopoly.

William Redmond Kelly, 1849

A rifle barrel was poised before them, its aim directed at the most prominent one, and the trigger sprung. The hammer struck a cap rendered harmless by the dampness, and a savage life was prolonged. A pistol was then jerked from a scabbard underneath the outer garments, levelled and attempted to be fired, but the damp had penetrated to the percussion upon that, too, and made ineffective. The fist was next tried, and several fleeing Indians rolled upon the sleet-covered ground as they came in a body over the threshhold of the door. Their bows were all unstrung, and the suddenness and fierceness of the attack had frightened the Indians so that they were glad to escape.

The mules were unpacked and tethered for the night, the fire removed to the ample hearth, and the hole in the roof patched up. Supper got and eaten, and clothing dried, the two occupants of the cabin sought the repose of their blankets.

PURSUIT OF THE INDIANS. Morning came, and not a mule was found where the previous night they had been securely fastened, and the tell-tale tracks showed but too plainly where they had gone. The Indians had taken them. Following up their trail, a couple of miles brought the pursuer to a place where one of them had been killed, though not a particle of the animal remained, only the offal emptied from the entrails. Returning to the town, the citizens were informed, and several men volunteered to follow up the trail and attempt the recovery of those yet alive.

Of this party Mr. Pierson was one, and the trail had not been long followed before it became apparent that the Indians had taken some oxen as well as mules, and if so they were cattle belonging to Pierson. Though the animals at first had been driven, or led, singly and circuitously, upon nearing the strong-holds of the Indians the tracks augmented and the trail became more marked. Places were found where other animals had been slaughtered, and the flesh packed away on the backs of Indians. Pierson was furious over his loss.

FIRST MILITARY COMPANY ORGANIZED. It was unsafe for the small party in pursuit to go further. They therefore decided to return to Illinoistown, report the situation to the inhabit-ants, and obtain reinforcements. This was done. A public meeting was called and held at Pierson's store, which resulted in the formation of the pioneer military organization of Placer County, under the euphoneous title of "California Blades."

CAMPAIGN AGAINST THE SAVAGES. Arming themselves as each member best could—some with United States yag-ers, others with old-fashioned muzzle-loading rifles, swords of curious pattern, conceived by some fertile brain in the far East and fashioned for the use of some mining company that came across the plains, old cutlasses, single-barreled cavalry pistols glittering with much brass, Allen's "pepper-boxes," and such other incongruous weapons.

The day following the organization this company went upon the war-path. Some four or five miles westerly from Il-linoistown—the evidences of Indian depredations accumulating as they traveled—while following up a trail, the company came suddenly upon a ridge and surprised and captured an Indian who was evidently there as an outlook to warn the tribe of any

A few weeks after Mendenhall established his place at Alder Grove, there being nothing more than a tent where his wife and child slept and the booth under which the table was spread, and while Mrs. M. happened to be alone, there suddenly appeared before her six stalwart savages in puris naturalibus demanding "bishkit," and thinking her unprotected were quite impertinent. Becoming a little alarmed she approached the tent, looked in and began talking to an imaginary person therein. Upon this the Indians desired to look in also, but she, thinking her only salvation from harm depended upon their not being allowed to do so, seized an old rifle which stood there unloaded and presenting it, drove them off.

Miners with lunch pails and candles at a Placer County mine.

Courtesy Placer County Museums

Newcastle Hotel, late 1800s

April llth, 1855 — — — Smith was shot and killed by — — Woodward, in a negro dance-house in Dutch Ravine. Both men were gamblers, and the trouble grew out of the favors shown Smith by one of the negro women.

approaching enemy. Silently the whites proceeded, and not long after, unheralded, they entered the Indian village, but fired no shots. Alarmed, the Indians vanished in a moment—all but the prisoner and several decrepit ones unable to escape.

Here were undoubted evidences of their thefts; mules and cattle hides fresh from the animals were used to cover the bark huts; the meat and bones were found; many goods stolen from the store were in the wigwams, and there were even other articles seen which gave rise to suspicions that they had not been obtained without the murder of their original owner. Besides these were large cribs of acorns, piles of pine cones, and supplies of manzanita. The capture having been effected, the question was then mooted as to what disposition should be made of the captured material. Some argued that there would be no security from Indian raids until they were all driven across Bear River, and to do this their huts and stores must be destroyed; while others, who had lost nothing, thought it would be too inhuman to deprive the savages of their huts so cunningly contrived, and their food so carefully garnered. But the evidences of their raids were palpable; men out alone in the woods had been shot at with arrows, and if not punished, the Indians might construe an act of clemency into cowardice.

The advocates pro and con seemed to be about evenly divided in the ranks of the "Blades," and they would put the question to vote. The destructionists won by a single vote; and an hour or two later all that remained about that Indian village besides piles of ashes and glowing embers were the stone mortars and pestles used by the squaws in pounding into flour the acorns and manzanita, or something equally incombustible— the stolen plunder found there as well as the Indian property.

The same day another camp was attacked, two men killed, several children taken prisoners, and the village and stores destroyed. From that time on until the following June it was not safe for an Indian to be seen upon that divide. One after another did the "Blades" seek out these villages, destroy them as found, and drive the Indians across Bear River; and the Bear River Indians were rated as the most fierce of all the Digger Tribe.

During the month of January a party of them went down to Auburn, and just about daylight one morning stampeded and drove away over fifty head of oxen from a place in sight of the village, and they were never recovered. About fifty men organized for the pursuit, but dared not attempt it without the co-operation of the "Blades," and therefore came up to Illinois-town and the two companies went out together.

The result was fruitless, for the Auburn Company had fully half its members disabled by sore feet from traveling in snow, and the number being so great that the Indians were forewarned and got out of reach long before the party in pursuit could get at them. Several villages, however, were destroyed, the huts of which were covered with the hides of the stolen cattle. But a single Indian was seen on the whole scout, and he out of reach of gunshot, whooping derisively at the whites.

Returning to Illinoistown, Pierson was informed of his loss, when he called together the "Blades," with others who vol-

We soon saw three men mounted on mules, coming toward us, who appeared to be returning from the mines. They were in high spirits, galloping along a little off the main track. One of them, in order, probably, to show a proper respect, pulled out his revolver and fired. His mule, taking the cue from his master, wishing to make a proper demonstration in the presence of his fellow mules, gave a few peculiar gyrations with his tail, threw his head up, then threw it down, and threw his heels up, and at this particular time his master threw his heels up, and they parted company. It would be difficult to imagine a position more humble than the one assumed by the above mentioned master.

John M. Letts, 1849

Broad Street, East Auburn, late 1800s.

Courtesy Placer County Museums

Towle Brothers Co. Railroad, "Heavy" Ketchen Engineer, Ben Billings, fireman, and "Big Dip" Dependener on tender, while hunting escaped convicts.

January 18th, 1876.—S. R. Kidder, a prominent mine owner of Iowa Hill, was shot and almost instantly killed. He had employed a man to watch his sluices, and becoming suspicious that his watchman was not doing his duty, he set out to watch for himself, and was mistaken for a robber and shot. He had given his watchman orders to shoot any one he found about the mine.

unteered, and went into the last scout of the campaign. Some twenty or more Indians were killed and scalped, and a month later at nearly all of the wayside houses on the road from Illinoistown were scalps on exhibition. Several men (one named James Doane) and quite a number of team animals were shot by the Indians about that time on the wagon road between Auburn and Illinoistown; but practically the trouble was by this time ended.

A FRONTIER PICTURE. The foot-hill Indians at that time were a peculiar people. But few of them had ever visited the Missions, though many of the male adults had been to Sutter's Fort. While the females were but sparingly robed, many of the males in summer time went entirely naked.

THE CAMP RECEIVES ITS NAME. How the name Illinoistown stuck to the little settlement is past comprehension. Any of the other names which it bore were more euphoneous. Pierson's store was the place where the "boys" most did congregate and where "speculation" in cards was a predominating feature. Here a meeting was held in December, 1849, and the name fastened upon the locality, though there were probably not to exceed a half-dozen emigrant residents from the State of Illinois. It assumed a business importance second only to Auburn, which it maintained for fully fifteen years, or until the completion of the Central Pacific Railroad to Colfax, which place has now completely absorbed it.

HOUSES OF ENTERTAINMENT. Every house, nearly, at Illinoistown became a public stopping-place for wandering miners at the approach of spring, and from the middle of February there were but few nights when they were not all crowded to the utmost capacity. One dollar and a half a meal was cheerfully paid for the pork, beans and bread set before the wayfarer, and at times a dollar would be given for the privilege of spreading blankets down upon the floor and sleeping for a night. The floor of every house was generally thus occupied until the rains were over and the ground dried out, and men of all conditions would be stowed thickly, side by side, thus seeking the repose of sleep. The unavoidable result of such promiscuous contact was the generation of enormous quantities of parasitic pests, from which for a time there seemed to be no permanent escape.

Three men by this time were permanent occupants. A mysterious disease attacked these men; they itched, and scratching, itched and scratched and itched again. Some times at night, while in their bunks, they would fancy they felt some creeping thing upon them, which they would ever fail to catch.

This peculiar condition existed for several weeks; when a discovery was made. One of the trio, an old man and pious—a godly Presbyterian—in making his Sabbath toilet, was the astonished discoverer, and with tears in his eyes, came rushing into the pressence of the other two, exclaiming: "By George ! I know now what's given us the itch; we're lousy !— lousy, by

We had occasion to blast some boulders that were in our way. We had a blacksmith to sharpen the picks and drills who had a portable forge on the point of land between the two rivers. When we were ready to blast the rock we gave him timely warning, he paid no heed, the blast went off, and a portion of a boulder weighing about 500 pounds went directly for his forge and within about six inches of his legs and went on over into the North Fork. The man turned about and hollered to the boys in the canal "I surrender."

Lell Hawley Woolley, 1849

Rattlesnake Bar School, 1888. Mabel McKay teacher.

Courtesy Placer County Museums

A twelve horse team hauling a boiler up the grade to its destination.

T[Rattlesnake] Dick was not immediately concerned in every robbery perpetrated by his gang, but probably instigated and planned most of them. There was one, however, worthy of mention, that he was not at all cognizant of. This was the robbery of the stage running between Rattlesnake Bar and Folsom, by Jim Driseoli and ''Cherokee Bob." The two highwaymen concealed themselves in a ditch above the road, and when the stage came within proper distance they leaped upon the "boot," and before the bewildered driver knew that he had two unwelcome passengers on board, Wells & Fargo's treasure box, containing $6,000, was in their possession. They buried the money and separated, Cherokee Bob crossing the mountains to Carson, and Driscoll, making his way through Dick Fuller's to Vernon.

George !" And he piloted his companions to the spot where he had pitched his discarded garments, and there pointed out and exhibited in the seams of the cast off clothing innumerable body-lice, the first that either of them had ever beheld. Examinations speedily made disclosed that all undergarments were alike, and what was the proper thing to do? The fat and nasty-looking parasites were under the cover of every seam, while nits were strung upon every thread more thickly than scales upon a fish. There was but one road out of such a difficulty, and that was by the crematory route. A bonfire was soon blazing; good honest flannels, made in the far-off East were stripped from off the wearer and foolishly consigned to the flames, and with them countless parasites—victims immolated upon the altar of man's fastidiousness.

RESCUED FROM THE SNOW. Deeper snow prevailed in the winter of 1849-50 at Illinoistown than there has been at any time since, and several men came near losing their lives by attempting to travel in it, owing to inexperience.

Two men—Sharp and Murrey—remained during the winter at Barnes' Bar, being the only residents there. From time to time they came to Illinoistown for supplies, which was not a formidable trip when the ground was bare of snow. A prolonged storm in January, which at the Bar was rain, deposited upon the ridge from two to four feet of snow.

At this time, their provisions being exhausted, these two men started up the hill for Illinoistown early one morning. Before reaching the top of the hill they got into snow which, upon arriving at the crest of the divide, was four feet deep, soft and wet. There was nothing then to mark the road to be traveled; all being covered with a white pall, looking similar, they could only guess the route from the general course traveled by them often before. Floundering on in this, first one man in advance for a few rods until well blown, and then the other, they were soon wet to the skin from the waist down. This severe exercise made them perspire freely, and they therefore would not suffer from cold unless compelled to lie out through the long and prospectively clear, cold night before them.

The distance to be made, all told, was not more than eight miles, but often they wished they had braved the pangs of hunger and delayed starting, or taken the way toward Auburn. Noontime found them in still deeper snow, and but little over half way to the coveted goal. Wearily they floundered on, becoming more and more exhausted as the moments lengthened into hours, and the sun sank out of sight below the western horizon.

One, who had a single-barreled pistol, struggled onward in advance of his companion, who had succumbed to drowsiness and fatigue, and, disheartened, was prone upon the snow. The avant courier at length reached a point in advance of his companion, a distance of perhaps a quarter of a mile, when he, too, gave up and fell limp and completely blown into the yielding snow, and gazed upward to the glittering stars, which now were

Mineral Bar Bridge on the North Fork of the American River on Iowa Hill Road. The house in the background belonged to Frank Vennewitz Sr. The bridge collapsed in the early 1930s.

Courtesy Placer County Museums

"I came to the place where you stayed last night, yesterday morning, and was told that there were a number of bears in the neighborhood, and that no one dared to hunt them. I remarked that that was my business, and I would take a hand at it; I strapped on my revolvers and knife, shouldered my Kentucky rifle and started out. I had not gone more than half a mile, when I discovered one of the animals I was in search of, and away my bullet sped striking him in the hip. I made for a tree and he made for me! I won the race by stopping on the topmost branch, while he howled at the base; while reloading my rifle I heard an answer to his wailing for me or for his companion it didn't matter which. Very soon a second cry came from another direction, and still one more from the third point of the compass. By this time one had reached the tree and I fired killing him. Hastily reloading, I was just in time to fire as the second one responded to the first one's howl; he fell dead; then the third arrived and shared the same fate. Having allowed the first one to live as a decoy, his turn came last; then I descended and looked over my work--four full-grown bears lay dead at my feet."

Unknown Kentucky hunter, 1849

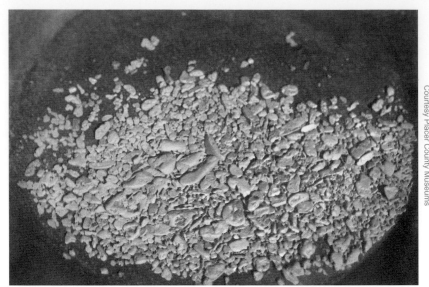

What was the fuss all about anyhow? This pan full of gold might have been a good day's haul for lucky miners. The unlucky ones were happy to earn enough for the bare essentials of their hard life.

There is much drinking and gambling done here, many will die next summer from the effects of drinking too much liquor, which is very injurious in this climate.

James Tolles, March 21, 1850

fast appearing in the blue sky overhead. He was a tough old whaleman, and many a cruise had he made in the Arctic seas, and would make one final effort to extricate himself and friend from the certain fate which must follow further apathy. Raising himself, he yet continued the struggle for life, but exhausted nature could do but little; only a few yards were gained. Then it was that he bethought of the pistol in his belt. By firing it off, the echoing sounds might reach the ears of some one who would come to his relief. Lucky thought!

The sharp report of the weapon rang out upon the chilling air of fast gathering night, and the weary man who fired it again fell fainting upon the fleecy snow! A young man who happened to be out of the door of the lower cabin at Illinoistown, preparing wood for the night, heard the unusual sound and divined its meaning. Fresh, impulsive, and athletic, he started down the valley in the direction whence the sound had come. The progress was slow, and the work tedious, as there was no track, but finally Murrey was reached, and by encouragement and assistance was dragged nearly dead into the house.

Aid was then procured and Sharpe was sought, and with difficulty at length got in. Before the huge fire upon the ample hearth, with hot punch and mulled wine, did the two men soon recover, and years afterward, when the shifting scenes of life casually brought them in contact with their rescuer, would they recall the event with tear-beglistened eyes.

AN EXHAUSTED TRAVELER. Upon another occasion during that historic winter were the inmates of the lower cabin in the valley aroused in the night by a knocking upon the door. The first thought on being awakened was the "Indians!" but to the question of "Who's there?" came the response of "Me," from the lips of a white man. Recognizing the voice of a young man named White, the door was speedily unbarred and he was admitted. A brisk storm had raged all the day, and now the snow twirled in thickly falling flakes, and the wind soughed with ominous portent through the surrounding forest trees. Snow lay at a depth of two feet, and was fast augmenting; it was a night in which he with shelter might thank his lucky star that no compulsory incident could send him forth to breast its dire inclemencies.

White, who was usually bright and jovial, seemed now somewhat dazed, and evasively answered questions asked him. That he had been out in the storm some hours was evidenced by his drenched clothing and his wearied air. The ruddy fire, a hot brandy punch, and a bottle of mulled wine, with other good cheer tendered him, brought revival to his waning mind, and he told how he and a companion had that day left Auburn, and that the latter had been left on the way in the snow!

It was fully an hour after the arrival of White at the cabin before this fact became apparent from his incoherent utterances. Something must be done to rescue the man. The same

I never saw more broken-down constitutions than I witnessed during my stay in California, and few who work in the mines, ever carry home their usual full health. . . . On the 26th of August, I saw my last patient mount his horse and start for home, anxious to be out of a country that had nearly cost him his life.

James L. Tyson, 1849

Freeman Hotel with a 13 star flag. What's wrong with this picture? You can count the 13 stars, but they're simply not where flag historians say they should be. If you look at the pattern below you'll see that they were a little off kilter.

Courtesy Placer County Museums

This miner was pretty well off with his powerful three donkey engine providing the latest 12 hoof traction for those steep grades.

There were some queer characters here. One man, whom I had bled at his request, thought he derived so much benefit from the operation, that he brought up his little Indian boy, and induced many other to submit to the same process. Sunday morning was usually the time selected by them for this purpose, so as not to interfere with their labors through the week. Though perfectly well, they would take no refusal, but insist on its performance, and as the charge was an ounce for each, I generally gratified them, and sometimes would have two or three bleeding around my tent at one time.

James L. Tyson, 1849

young man who had brought in Murrey and Sharpe immediately set out after aid, the two companions in the cabin being both advanced in years. Going to King & Hoskins' store, he there found a person about his own age, named Henry Close, who unhesitatingly agreed to start out with him when the situation was explained. At Pierson's place was a powerful horse… Pierson loaned the horse to the young men, who, about 12 o'clock, got started upon White's back trail. The tracks were well nigh obliterated by falling snow; the little streams running in the canons were all full; the snow was slumpy and wet, and a person in walking would sink down into it fully a foot at every step. Alternately riding the horse and walking, the two young men searched out the way by following the tracks.

About five miles below Illinoistown, lying beside a prostrate tree, the lost man was found, groaning piteously, chilled to the marrow, foot-sore and exhausted. Had he lain there a few hours longer, most likely he would have been done for. A stiff horn of brandy from a flask brought by the rescuers for the purpose, and the presence of those who would save him, aroused him to effort. He was placed upon the animal, plied with another horn from the flagot, the horse's head turned homeward, and he given instructions to not direct the animal's course, when off they were started, leaving the two men to themselves. Anxious to reach shelter, the horse, within two hours from the time of leaving the place where the perishing man was found, reached the house with him in safety. Close and his companion did not get in until 11 o'clock the following day. The man rescued was from Kentucky, then aged about twenty-eight years.

Miners in Waukesha Mine at Relief Hill, 1895.

CHAPTER 3: Nevada County — Nevada City, Grass Valley, Rough & Ready and vicinity

SETTLEMENT AND DEVELOPMENT OF THE COUNTY. The first settlement in Nevada county was made by John Rose, whose name was given to the celebrated Rose Bar, near Smartsville, Yuba county. Rose and Reynolds were engaged in trading with the miners and Indians, their store being at Rose Bar. They also supplied the mines with meat, being the owners of a large Mexican grant, on the south bank of the Yuba river, just above Marysville. Their cattle roamed the grassy plains from Bear river to the Honcut. Rose, who attended to this branch of the business, built a cattle corral at Pleasant Valley, between Bridgeport and the Anthony House, early in 1849. Later he established a trading post there, and built a small adobe house. Rose and Reynolds had been engaged in ship carpentering at Yerba Buena since 1842, and came to this region after the discovery of gold at Coloma.

Nevada was situated in a valley, surrounded by hills and creeks. Deer Creek was the most important stream, and even this beautiful transparent river was turned from its natural course; in truth the very heart of the city was dug up, and there was no telling where the digging would end.

Luther Melanchthon Schaeffer, 1849

"Brigadier General A. M. Winn has received a letter from Major General Thomas J. Green, First Division California Militia, and enclosing one to his Excellency, Peter H. Burnett, Governor of California.

Indian troubles are announced on that frontier. A volunteer company had prepared to march against the savages. The Indians are reported to number several hundred and to be headed by white men and some Chilians. An engagement is said to have taken place on Deer creek in which four whites and fifteen Indians were killed. General Green has very wisely determined to take the field, both for the protection of the citizens and to prevent excesses on their part. He recommends that the Adjutant General should be ordered to his head quarters with instructions and authority to make a further call upon the militia, and U. S. troops, should the emergencies require it.

We are further advised that some two hundred Indians were seen near Johnson's ranch, on Friday. A party of thirty went out from Nicolaus, and killed four of them, one of the party being slightly wounded in the forehead. A teamster from Nicolaus was found dead in the neighborhood, with fourteen arrows in him. His wagon and merchandise had been burnt up, and four pair of oxen killed. The repeated outrages in every direction will induce a more general militia organization throughout this part of the State. We learn that

continued in far right column

Searls Historical Library

This huge slip-tongue wagon made moving large logs easier. Logging began as soon as the early miners and settlers started to arrive in 1848. Along with the muscle of these hardy loggers, they harnessed power from mules, oxen, and steam engines.

Following the establishment of Rose's trading post at Pleasant Valley, a man named Findlay, from Oregon, opened a trading post on Bear river near the mouth of Greenhorn creek. David Bovyer also opened a store at White Oak Springs, in Rough and Ready township, in September. The Rough and Ready company settled at the town of that name. Boston Ravine, and Badger Hill in Grass Valley were settled the same fall. Work was commenced on Gold Run and Dr. Caldwell built a store on the site of Nevada City. A party of Oregonians settled at Jefferson, and an Indiana company at Washington. The Holt Brothers and Judge Walsh erected saw mills about four miles below Grass Valley. A mule corral was built by a Frenchman at French Corral. During the fall of 1849, miners spread themselves all along the Middle and South Yuba, Deer creek, Bear river and along some of the principal tributaries of those streams.

In this spring of 1850 considerable trouble was experienced with the Indians, who committed a number of depredations, and were severely punished. Among other acts was the attack upon the Holt brothers at their saw mill about four miles below Grass Valley. During the preceding winter Samuel and George Holt and James Walsh and Zenas Wheeler had erected two saw mills and were busy sawing lumber on May 3, 1850, when the Holts were attacked in their mill by a party of Indians. Samuel Holt, the elder brother, fell at once, his body filled with arrows. George Holt, with a small pocket-knife fought his way through eight or ten Indians up the hill to where the mill of Walsh Wheeler stood, where he fell bleeding and faint from thirteen wounds, into the arms of the proprietor. During the night the mill and property of the Holts were burned, and Walsh's camp was threatened. A few friendly Indians, Captain Day and another man came in during the night and gave their assistance. The body of Samuel Holt was brought in by old Chief Wemeh. The next morning Captain Day and his friend went to Camp Far West, near Johnson's Crossing, on Bear river, and the next day returned with twenty-four United States troops, supplied by Major Day, in charge of the station. Mr. George Holt was removed to Stocking's store, on Deer creek, and soon recovered. A hundred miners from Deer creek came to the scene, and in a few days they and the soldiers punished the Indians severely and drove them from the neighborhood. This was but one of a number of depredations and outrages committed at this time.

NEVADA CITY. Nevada City was at first the most important settlement in the region, and when the county was organized in the spring of 1851, became the seat of justice. The reason for the more rapid growth of Nevada City was the discovery of hill diggings and the "Coyote claims." It became for the time the commercial center of the county. In 1851 Grass Valley began to acquire considerable prominence; the discovery

The following was attached to this image and looks like a clipping from an 1850s newspaper. It is a good example of how newspapers would create or sensationalize stories or half-truths in that era. "The Digger Indians of the Pacific slope have an unpleasant custom of burying young infants alive with the bodies of their dead mother. Recently, a young squaw of one of their bands died, leaving a papoose about four months old, and it is authentically asserted that the child, 'alive and kicking,' was placed on the body of its dead parent, and they were buried together."

continued from far left column

a volunteer company of young men is being now formed in Sacramento City. They will be the first to tender their aid should future developments require the further call upon the militia."

I sent the following note, with a flag of truce, to the chiefs, by an old woman who had been taken prisoner: —

Wolf creek camp, May 20, 1850.

To the Indian Chiefs Weima, Buckler, Poollel, and others:— Your people have been murdering ours, robbing their wagons and burning their houses. We have made war upon you, killed your men and taken prisoners your women and children. We send you this plain talk by one of your grandmothers. When you cease to rob and murder our people we will cease to make war upon you, and then you can come in and get your women and children, who will be taken care of in the meantime. If you wish peace come down to Johnson's old ranch, on Bear river, and report yourselves to Captain Charles Hoyt, who will protect you until your Great Father shall speak.

Thos. J. Green, Major General, First Division, California Militia.

Placer Times, of Sacramento, May 20, 1850.

As if endowed with the wonderful properties of the "seven league boots" the county made enormous strides towards settlement and prosperity. The State census, taken in 1852, within two years after the organization of the first city, showed the population to be as follows:

White, Males	12,418
" Females	920
Negroes	103
Foreigners, Males	721
Females	61
Indians	3,220
Chinese	3,886
Total	21,329

The population was estimated in 1856 to be about 20,000, exclusive of Indians.

The Frazer river excitement in 1858, and the Washoe exodus in 1859 and 1860, materially reduced the population of Nevada county. The latter became almost a hegira, so great was the excitement and the eagerness to secure a claim in the fabulously rich silver districts.

The result upon the population of Nevada county can be plainly seen in the returns of the United States census, taken in the summer of 1860:

Nevada Township	4,040
Grass Valley Township	3,940
Bridgeport Township	2,720
Eureka and	
Washington Townships	2,100
Rough and Ready	
Township	1,782
Little York Township	1,048
Bloomfield Township	784
Total	16,414

Early view of Martin Marsh's sawmill on Rock Creek

of quartz ledges in the vicinity and the consequent excitement giving that city an impulse forward that soon made it rank second to Nevada City. The town of Rough and Ready, also, became a large and prosperous one. Moore's Flat, Woolsey's Flat, Orleans Flat, Cherokee, French Corral, Sweetland, and many smaller places became thriving mining camps. The year 1852 saw the opening up of the hill claims in Little York township. Little York, Walloupa, Red Dog, Hunt's Hill, You Bet, Lowell Hill, Remington Hill, Omega, Alpha, Humbug (Bloomfield), and a great many smaller places sprang up as if by magic within the next two years.

Others may have come and passed away, leaving no trace of their presence, but the first-settlers in the vicinity were Captain John Pennington, Thomas Cross and William McCaig, who prospected in Gold Run in September 1849 and built a cabin there. But a month later Dr. A. B. Caldwell opened a store, from which he supplied goods to the miners who had begun to settle in the vicinity. The locality became known as Caldwell's Upper Store. During the same month a Mr. Stamps, with a family consisting of his wife, her sister and several children, came to the locality and built a cabin on the fork of the ravine back of Coyote street. This was the first family and these the first ladies to settle here.

By March, 1850, the collection of tents, brush shanties and a very few board houses began to assume the appearance of a town. The people recognized the fact that a government was necessary, and as the new courts had not yet opened their doors, the election of an Alcalde, a judicial officer under the Mexican laws, was determined upon. At this election some 250 votes were cast, and Mr. Stamps was elected Alcalde. A better and more stable name was desired for the growing town, and a meeting of leading citizens was called at the store of Truex & Blackman, for the purpose of selecting one that would suit all parties and be a credit to the place. Among the names presented were, Sierra, Aurora, Nevada, Deer Creek and Gold Run. The name selected was suggested by O. P. Blackman, and the little town was christened Nevada.

A letter from Benjamin P. Avery, a well-known newspaper man of the Coast, published in Bean's History and Directory of Nevada County, California, is so interesting in its description of early mining life, and of the birth of Nevada City, that the following extract is given.

"I started from Mormon Island on a prospecting trip to Reading Springs (Shasta), in October, 1849. Rode a little white mule along with pork and hard bread and blankets packed behind me. On the way from Sacramento to Vernon, a trading station just started at the

The railroad cut at Gold Run, mid-1860s.

Some time in the summer of 1867 a notorious negro named George Washington attempted to rob some Chinamen on Deer creek, but was set upon by his intended victims and terribly beaten. They then tied the hands and feet of the would-be robber and slipped a bamboo pole through them, the ends of which were lifted upon the shoulders of two muscular Celestials. In this way they carried him like a dead pig a distance of two miles to deliver him into the custody of the law. The ground was rough and rocky, and the pole bearers trotted along, the pendent Washington being unmercifully jolted and his body scratched by the chaparral through which he was carelessly drawn; and as they stopped to rest the Mongolian bearers dropped their burden with a thud. A formidable procession of Chinamen, armed with guns, revolvers, knives and clubs, escorted the prisoner, their discordant jabberings heralding the approach of the train. The Celestial in charge of the procession said, "He lobber man. Chinaman fixee him alle samee one hog; takee him to ollee man Ogee."

My dear Wife,

I have worked harder here than I ever worked at home. I have been repeatedly disappointed in making the amount of money I expected to make here. I knew that you were very anxious to see me and I could hardly bear the thought of telling you that I must be so long away from you. So you must excuse me for writing to you so seldom. I have never taken any comfort since I left you, no my dear for more than two long years I have never known what it was to lay down upon any bed at night contented and happy. Your image is ever before my central vision, and the only ray of earthly happiness that dispells the gloom from my heart proceeds from the thought of meeting you again in this world.

Horace Root,
October 11, 1851,
Nevada City

Miners working a mine in the Grass Valley area.

junction of the Sacramento and Feather rivers, I encountered a party on horse back who were coming from Deer creek, and who told me big stories about 'pound digging'! in Gold Run. As 'pound diggings,' i. e. claims that would yield twelve ounces of gold per day to the man, were just what I was in search of, I inquired the direction of this El Dorado, followed the old Emigrant road up Bear river to Johnson's ranch, at the edge of the foothills, and there took a trail for the creek, missing the road, or thinking I could take a shorter course. The first night in the foothills I had company, Caldwell, who was after a winter stock for his store on the creek, at a point seven miles below the site of Nevada, and several southern and western men.

"Arrived at Caldwell's store, the only trading post on Deer creek at that time. I found it a square canvas shanty, stocked with whiskey, pork, mouldy biscuit and gingerbread; the whiskey four bits a drink, the biscuit a dollar a pound. A few tents were scattered over the little flat and about a dozen parties were working the bars with dug-out cradles and wire or rawhide hoppers, only one or two persons having cradles made of board *and sheet iron. I prospected with good success in a claim that had just been abandoned by the notorious Greenwood, carrying dirt in a pan to a dug-out cradle. Went with shovel and pan seven or eight miles up the creek, testing several ravines as high up as the top of the ridges, seldom, in my ignorance, going deeper than a few inches, and always trotting gold. A preacher, whose name I forget, was then haul-in dirt from one big ravine back of Caldwell's on an ox cart, and washing it at the creek with good success. A few other men were carry-ing dirt from other ravines on their own backs or those of mules. All were close mouthed about yields, and regarded me as an interloper. They were Southwestern men, apparently, and mixed with their jealousy was a bit of contempt for the smoothed-faced 'Yorker,' whose long brown hair lying on his shoulders ought to have conciliated their prejudice, since it looked like following a fashion set by themselves. In my prospecting I some-how failed to get on the Gold Run side of the creek, and so missed my objective point, but I struck the conjunc-tion of ravines in the little flat known afterwards as the*

The large building in the background is the Union Hotel, built after a fire in 1863. These lovely young ladies look like they enjoyed this photo opportunity around 1870.

This Nevada City was a curious sight, not easily described. On account of the gold feve all business dealings were conducted on a fraudulent basis. The streets swarmed with horse and gold thieves, traders and speculators, gamblers and rascals. There were saloons in abundance where a few drops of brandy were sold for twenty-five cents to the men who were waiting for some gold dust to turn up. The gold diggers ran about, searching, hacking, picking, digging, scooping and washing from morning till night until they looked like animals who had been wallowing in the mud. Expressions of vexation and discontent were stamped on their faces because their profits had not been satisfactory and because the treasure which they had so laboriously taken from the earth was not sufficient for their needs.

All this drove me away from the place. A German baker who visited me in my tent told me that a few days ago he had been robbed of twelve mules. I took the precaution to fasten my mule by means of a locked chain to the ironbound wheels of my cart so that no one could steal him without making a noise.

Herman Scharmann, 1849

John Barrett was drummed out of camp and branded with the letter "R," as a rogue, for thievery. About the first of April, 1852 he stole a pistol from the store of Abbott & Edwards on Commercial street, Nevada City. He was forced to return the weapon, but was not prosecuted for the theft. He then went down Deer creek and stole two hundred dollars worth of gold dust, and coins to the total amount of $357 from a miner's cabin on Stocking Flat. He was tracked to Newtown and caught in Schardin's store. Upon his person was found the exact amount of dust and money that had been stolen. A miner's court was instantly organized and Barrett placed on trial and found guilty. The man laid on the stripes unmercifully.

Nevada City had been so overrun by thieves and dangerous characters that a protective organization had been formed. A few nights before, Miss Carrie Bowers had been assaulted in her house by a villain, the excitement was at fever heat.

The night after his whipping at Newtown, Barrett appeared in Coyoteville and robbed several miners' cabins, and was captured by the night patrol of Nevada City.

He was indicted by the Grand Jury for larceny, the first one being for the theft of the $357 of dust and coin. The jury found him guilty and attached the death penalty.

The gallows had been erected ... the unfortunate man was conducted, and in the presence of a large concourse of people, and surrounded by the citizen guard, he suffered the severest penalty the law can inflict.

Searls Historical Library

Milk delivery was common in most communities well into the 1960s. This Nevada City Dairy wagon was loaded for morning rounds, sitting in front of New York Hotel on Broad Street in Nevada City in the late 1800s.

site of Dyer's store; and in Rich Ravine, winding about American Hill, got a prospect that satisfied me to return immediately to Mormon Island for my companions. That locality was then completely unworked; I saw no 'prospect holes' anywhere in the vicinity."

"To my intense disgust I found that my ravine was occupied from one end to another by long-haired Missourians, who were taking out their 'piles.' They worked in the stormiest weather, standing in the yellow mud to shovel dirt into cradle or tom; one of them had stretched a canvas awning over their claims, which were only thirty feet along the ravine. All the other ravines leading into the flat at the foot of American Hill were occupied almost as thickly. Dyer had a log cabin in the midst, where whiskey and brandy were sold at six and eight dollars a bottle, molasses at eight dollars a gallon, flour one dollar a pound, and pork two dollars. Caldwell's new, or upper store was on the high bank of the ravine, above the little flat where the city of Nevada afterwards sprung into existence. It appears there had been great discoveries in this locality after my visit, the first of October, and as the streams rose in November the miners flocked in from the rivers. American Hill was covered with their tents and brush houses, while a few had put up log cabins. At night the tents shone through the pines like great transparencies, and the sound of laughter, shouting, fiddling and singing startled those old primeval solitudes strangely. It was a wild, wonderful scene. Gambling, of course, was common and fatal affrays were frequent.

"We pitched our tent by a big pine, using its trunk for a fireplace and cooking our pork and coffee out of doors. The woods looked grand when white with snow. Sometimes we had to rap it off the canvas roof at night to keep it from pressing upon our faces, or breaking down the tent.

"Other considerable settlements had gathered at Gold Run, Grass Valley and Rough and Ready, on the other side of the creek.

"We worked with rather poor success, in the vicinity, until the ravines began to dry in April, and then laid the beginning of that extensive and costly system of mining ditches that has since made Nevada pre-eminent in this, as in every other department of mining industry and invention. Small ditches were dug to bring the water from springs and brooks into the rich ravines about Dyer's, and were gradually extended as the water supplies retreated. The mines yielded wonderfully. From an

On a little island just below Broad street bridge stood a house occupied by a woman. When the creek began to assert itself the house was surrounded with water that soon began to make itself too familiar, and entered the house. The woman shrieked for help, and was carried to not dry but high land, on the back of a sympathizing miner, who waded through the turbulent stream.

This homestead is believed to be in Gold Run, probably in the late 1800s.

Courtesy of the Bancroft Library, University of California, Berkely

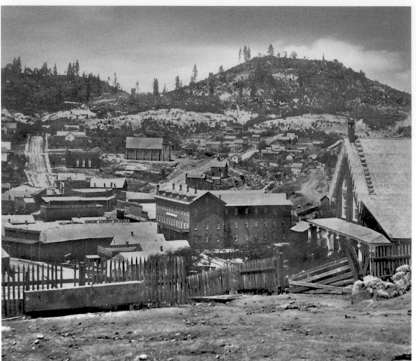

Nevada City in the late 1860s, from the South. You see the Catholic Church, Union Hotel, and Sugarloaf Mountain. What you don't see are forests. The hillsides were stripped to provide lumber for the buildings, mine timbers, and miles of flumes.

"Nevada city—This must be a fast place. Mr. Davis, of the firm of Brown, Davis & Co., has been in town, making arrangements for the opening of a reading room over their store, where they intend to have the latest advices from all parts. We find also numerous jobs from merchants, in every line, coming to our office; drug stores, hotels, livery stables and all the other concomitant pursuits of a veritable city, are represented upon 'posters' of every size and style. These are sure signs of business, and of the good sense of those who are engaged in its various branches. The population of Nevada City is estimated at about 2,000, but there are supposed to be four times that number within a circuit of four miles. A tri-weekly line of stages runs from Nicolaus through in one day, a distance of fifty miles, connecting with the steamer *Dana*."

The *Placer Times* of Sacramento in August, 1850

ounce to twelve ounces a day was common, with cradles; while many a long tom party took home to their cabin at night a quart tin pail full of gold, much of which was as coarse as wheat grains. Many a lucky fellow left with a fortune in the spring, and at the same time the embargo of mud and snow was lifted, so that teamsters and packers arrived with supplies from the lower country, and flour fell to thirty cents a pound, while boots that had been worth six ounces a pair could be had for one. It was not long before wagon loads of provisions sold for freight. With this rush of goods, accompanied by fresh crowds of fortune hunters, Nevada City sprang into being. My first sight of the embryo place was a surprise. I had been camping and working some distance lower down the creek, coming over to Caldwell's about once a fortnight for supplies we did not have, say for pipes, tobacco and molasses, or to pay an expressman two dollars to inquire if there was a letter for me at Sacramento.

"One Sunday on rounding the point of a ravine running down to the creek from American Hill, I saw a big round tent on the little flat, with a flag streaming

above it, muffled music resounding within, while around were several canvas stores, and wagons loaded with flour and other supplies, and, in fact all the signs of a brand new mining town. Franchere and I christened it Mushroom City on the spot. It was afterwards called Nevada, and when the first election for local officers was held we were importuned at our cradles, by genteel looking gamblers, who were the 'leading men,' to vote for their candidates. The population would have scattered rapidly but for the discovery of the famous cayote or drift diggings, which were first opened by a drift run in from Rich ravine, by miners who supposed they were following a ravine lead for a short distance. I sank a shallow shaft on the slope of American Hill, towards the ravine, during the winter, believing that the gravel bed might be rich, but struck water, and was obliged to desist, though I got a 'good color,' all the way down. You know how the entire hill has since been stripped to the bed rock. It was at Nevada that I saw the first ground sluicing in the State, which led by insensible degrees to hydraulic mining."

The term of Alcalde Stamps' office expired . . . the successful candidate was a man named Olney. A few months after his election he died of consumption. His will bequeathed all his ready cash to the "boys," who were to have "a jolly good time with it." The sum amounted to about $6,000, none of which

Idaho & Maryland quartz mine in Grass Valley, 1895 with the Nevada Narrow gauge railroad and a horse-drawn wagon along the tracks.

Michael Brennan, a man of liberal education and refined sensibilities, an Irishman by birth, was sent here to superintend the operations of the Mount Hope Mining Co., on Massachusetts Hill. At first successful, his operations began to prove disastrous, and his investments and ventures failures. Seeing no way in which to provide for the wants of the family dependent upon him, his reason became dethroned and in a fit of melancholy and dejection he administered prussic acid to his wife and three small children and finally to himself. On the morning of Sunday, February 22, 1858, the bodies were found cold and rigid in death. The children, the oldest but five years of age, were found in different rooms. He left a letter fully explaining the causes that had led him to the commission of the horrible deed, saying that he could not bear to see his family living in poverty and disgrace.

Nevada City from Washington Road, late 1860s.

Two Sacramento stages left Nevada City early on the morning of Monday, May 3, 1858, one some distance behind the other. On the first stage were eight or ten passengers including I. N. Dawley, who was riding on the outside with the driver, and had charge of $20,000, which were in a carpet sack in the boot. The last stage had Wells, Fargo & Co.'s treasure box, containing $20,000. When about half a mile from Nevada City the first stage was stopped by four or five men who handled guns as if they were familiar with their use. Dawley told them that the specie box was in the other stage and that there was nothing in the boot but some carpet sacks. The stage was allowed to drive on while the robbers lay in wait for the other one. The second stage was stopped in the same manner as the first and the specie box obtained.

Officers were immediately upon the alert, and the next morning arrested D. Ludington and Thomas Williams, alias One Eyed Tom, in their cabin near Grass Valley. The indignant miners who lived in the vicinity burned the cabin to the ground.

was allowed to be paid out for funeral expenses, everything being furnished and the grave being dug free of expense, but all was faithfully devoted to the object expressed in the will, and a "jolly good time" they had of it for several days.

About a dozen shake houses graced the town site on the first of May, most of them on Main and Commercial streets. These were all business buildings, and lots were staked off to the end of Commercial street, although not yet occupied. May 1, 1850, the first frame hotel was opened by J. N. Turner, on Main street, near the site of the present Union Hotel. It was called the Nevada Hotel, and entertained guests for the moderate sum of $25 per week. The house was 38x48 feet, and was built of rifted pine boards, all the boards, beams, floors, etc., being taken from one tree.

The first store on Broad street was that of Hamlet Davis, kept in a tent, in the month of May, 1850 Mr. Davis, Captain G. W. Kidd and Mr. Bedford extended the limits of the town in July, 1850, by laying out Broad street as far as the M. E. Church and Pine street from Commercial to Spring street.

Mr. Davis erected a two story frame building on the corner of Broad and Pine streets. In the second story a reading room was established where were kept Eastern papers from all the chief cities. These were obtained at the Sacramento post office, where thousands of them, sent by friends at home, were left uncalled for by the miners.

In August, 1850, Spring and Cedar streets were laid out. A bridge had been built across Deer creek a quarter of a mile below the Broad street crossing, and Bridge street was laid out to connect this structure with Broad street. This bridge lasted two or three years, and was then washed away. The next bridge built was on Pine street, to take the place of the old one.

Several small ditches were dug during the year, small now but for those times large enterprises. The Coyote diggings were discovered and the town of Coyoteville sprang up just back of Nevada City. As winter approached the merchants began to lay in enormous stocks of goods. The winter before had been so severe that transportation was impossible, and goods had been extremely high priced. The population to be supplied being now eight or ten times as great as during the previous winter and the season being expected to be as severe, the merchants made their calculations accordingly. The reverse of their anticipations was the result. But little rain fell, no water could be had to work the mines, hundreds of miners abandoned the place in disgust, the prices of goods sank down to the lowest ebb, merchants failed and closed their doors, and Nevada City seemed to be in the last stages of the ordinary mining camp of mushroom growth.

The mournful predictions of the croakers and the obituaries of the newspapers failed to terminate the career of Nevada City. The year 1851 opened with no less than two hundred and fifty buildings in the town, and scores of tents and cabins spread all over the surrounding hills for a radius of two miles.

Two men were killed on September 3, 1893 when a circus train fell off the tracks. All the animals stayed in their cars and were unharmed.

Searls Historical Library

Nevada city—This has been the great inland mining town of California, containing at one time from six to eight thousand inhabitants (in the vicinity). It grew up rapidly, its location being in what was considered the most productive portion of California, but of late it has gone back almost as fast as it advanced. The "growth of Nevada has been one of those wonders in California, which have astonished the beholder, but it shows the uncertainty of all business which depends upon the mines in any particular location. It may be good to-day, but disappear to-morrow. The mines may be productive in one locality for this month, but other mines may be better next. New discoveries are being made continually which entirely modifies the aspect of things."

Placer Times, 1850

Washington Hotel, 1890.

Among the amusements of 1851, and for a few years thereafter, were bull and bear fights. These took place on Broad street, in Nevada City. A bear, more or less tame and more or less lazy, was chained to a post, so as not to be able to beat an inglorious retreat or to charge upon the spectators. A bull was then turned into the arena and the two animals were provoked into a fight. Sometimes the bull was of a retiring disposition and the bear a jolly, good natured one, and a fight could not be forced upon them. Then the audience had to depart disappointed, sometimes almost creating a riot by their demonstrations of dissatisfaction.

It is related that at an entertainment of this kind, a large bear became loosened from his fastenings and made things lively for the keepers, until they escaped from the arena, barely having time to secure the doors to prevent bruin from following them.

Mining operations were active and business began to revive. While merchants were just recovering from their severe losses and the town was assuming again the lively appearance of the previous year, a fire swept away the board shanties that comprised the business portion of the town. This was on March 11, 1851, and within a month from that date, so active and energetic were the business men in repairing their losses, that new buildings had taken the places of the burned ones and scarcely a trace of the fire could be seen.

When rebuilt the city contained the Nevada Hotel, Gregory House, Washington Hotel and Phelps' Hotel on the south side of the creek. Some of the leading business houses were Hurst & Russell, Beard & Co., Davis & Hurst, O. P. Blackman & Co., Dr. John Locke, Truex & Co., and R. J. Oglesby. Main street was built up solid, but Broad street was only built in places here and there, and the residences and buildings throughout the town were very much scattered.

Several citizens, filled with a little too highly inflated opinion of the present and future greatness of Nevada City, prepared a charter, in the spring of 1851, for its incorporation on a most magnificent scale. Some thought better order could be preserved and some desired one of the many offices provided for by the charter, and the accompanying substantial salary. The charter was presented to the Legislature, and upon a report of its passage being brought to town an election was held and Hamlet Davis was chosen Mayor. Before he became fully invested with his new dignity, it was discovered that the election had been premature, the bill not having become a law when the election was called. Another election was therefore necessary, and Moses F. Hoyt was chosen Mayor. A few weeks later, Mr. Crandall moved away and Dr. Gardner died, and Niles Searls and one other were elected to fill the vacancies. Judge Searls was elected President of the Council. The government was conducted on as magnificent a scale as that on which the charter had been framed.

No taxes and but few licenses were collected, the expenses ran up to over $8,000, and ruin and bankruptcy began to stare the young city in the face. In September, 1851, a public meeting was called to discuss the situation. At this meeting, over which Judge Searls presided, all the Aldermen agreed to discharge all the city employees and suspend operations. Although this course was opposed by the salaried officials, it received the approbation of the people and was adopted. The Legislature was petitioned to repeal the charter, which it did early in 1852.

The Recorder, although a police judge, was mistaken by the miners to be a mining recorder and to him they brought their mining notices, which he accepted with the gravity of an owl, duly recorded and charged therefore a fee that would astonish us in these degenerate days. Business was lively, and when the government came to an end he had enough to retire upon.

Mine at Kohler Ranch

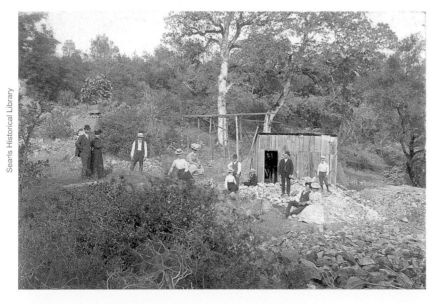

Searls Historical Library

Between the hours of eight and nine o'clock, Saturday evening, April 21, 1866, a man stationed himself at a convenient place on the road from You Bet to Neece's, and waited for some one to turn up. It was not long before the figure of a Chinaman was outlined against the stars, and the robber, after depriving him of a lonely half dollar, ordered him to sit down by the roadside. The next victim was a German, who was directed to sit by the member from China. Another Mongolian appeared and was added to the silent band, as were also an American and a wandering Swede. Two Chinamen, a German, an American and a Swede all sitting like statues by the roadside, each one convinced that the others were all robbers and that to resist or attempt to escape was certain death. The last victim was George Hilton, who saw the shadowy forms by the side of the road and, in view of such hopeless odds, cheerfully handed the robber sixty dollars. Aware that the deception must soon be discovered, and observing another man approaching, the ingenious thief gave his victims the command to "get up and dust," while he vanished amid the darkness of the night. The congress of nations that he had assembled gazed each into the others' faces, on which the expressions of astonishment and chagrin struggled for the mastery, and each thought what fools the others were to be deceived by a little game like that and then departed their several ways in silence.

Miners at a station in the Empire Mine

"Within the past year we have had several beautiful churches erected in our city. The general character of the city has improved. There is much less gambling carried on, less drunkenness, less fighting, and a higher tone in society generally. We have had also many families settling down in our midst, and, perhaps, to the humanizing influences of correct female society are to be attributed many of the beneficial results in morals we have named. The improvements at Nevada, generally, are not of a superficial character. They bear the stamp of enterprise and are destined to continue. The new developments in quartz leads of surprising richness make room for still move mills; and it requires little prophetic power to anticipate that before ten years are over, with a Sacramento railroad, a Yuba ditch, the influx of farmers, operations in quartz, new discoveries in placer diggings, and the consequent growth of mercantile and mechanic business, with the influx of families, Nevada will be second in importance and wealth to few cities in California."

Nevada Journal, January 3d, 1852

On the third of March, 1852, a severe storm of wind, snow and rain set in, that raged with fury for several days. The rivers and creeks began to rise and send their water in a rushing torrent down the mountains. Deer creek was "booming," drift wood and logs came rushing with irresistible force down the surging stream. Extending over the stream and resting upon supports was the Jenny Lind Theater, erected the year before, when the peaceful character of Deer creek gave no warning of such a scene as this. Early on the morning of the sixth the Broad street bridge was carried away, and about noon the crowd of spectators, who were watching the developments with great interest, saw a heavy log strike Main street bridge and drive it from its foundation, sweeping away the remaining props that sustained the theater. Amid yells of "There she goes," the building swayed and toppled into the stream, to be soon resolved into its component boards by the whirling and eddying waters. The Illinois Boarding House adjoining the theater accompanied it in its journey down the stream. The loss was about $10,000, and since then no one has been anxious to build over Deer creek.

As an evidence that the influences of "correct female society" were working for good, and that the people desired to approach more nearly to the conditions of the society to which they were accustomed before the alurements of gold drew them from home to embark in the wild excitements of mining life, is the fact that a public meeting was held on Sunday, August 8, 1852, to adopt means for the better observance of the Sabbath. Resolutions were passed requesting merchants to close their places of business on Sundays, and binding the signers to patronize only those who did so. Since then the majority of business houses have observed the Sabbath.

Another attempt was made at a city government in 1853. For two years the government plodded peacefully along, and then its vital spark was extinguished by the Supreme Court.

An Act passed the Legislature, approved, April 19, 1856, incorporating Nevada City, which was endowed with sufficient vitality to serve the purpose for which it, was intended. The city embraced one square mile, the center being the junction of Broad and Pine streets. The expenses of the first six months of this new government were exceedingly large, owing to the damage wrought by the fire, and it looked as if this was also to be a bankrupt government, but by economy the debt was soon extinguished.

Railroad construction and operation drastically changed the landscape in the late 1860s. Mule- or ox-drawn freight haulers worried that the railroad would kill their business. Instead they soon found more business, many operating profitably into the early 1900s. Pictured here is the Secretown Tressel on the Central Pacific Railroad at Gold Run in the late 1860s.

Courtsey of the Bancroft Library, University of California, Berkley

In June, 1859, the discovery of the Comstock lead was announced and crowds began to rush to the Washoe region. By this hegira Nevada City suffered a serious depopulation, which lasted for two or three years. Business was so dull that the merchants became quite skillful in pitching quoits. One saloon keeper went to the extent of advertising his wants and desires as follows:— "One hundred thousand square drinkers wanted at Blaze's, corner of Pine and Commercial. No drunkards tolerated on the place."

Madam Mustache. The first known of her was in Nevada City in 1854, where she one day arrived upon the stage coach, "pretty, dark-eyed, fresh-faced, and stylish, apparently about twenty years of age." Her advent naturally created a commotion among the rough miners, which was increased when she opened a gambling establishment on Broad street, and dealt the well known game of *vingt et un*, or twenty-one. The novelty of a pretty woman dealing at a gambling table ensured the success of her enterprise, and in a short time she had amassed considerable capital. Shortly afterward she formed a co-partnership with one David Tobin, a professional gambler, and together they opened a large establishment, where he attended to the larger games of faro and keno, and Madam to the smaller, such as twenty-one, chuck-a-luck, etc., etc., The house was kept open day and night, and Madam was a great favorite, paying all losses with a smiling countenance, and raking in gains with the stoical indifference of the true gambler. She commanded not only the admiration, but also the respect of the miners; and notwithstanding her strange mode of life her chastity was unquestioned. Her partnership with Tobin continued one year, when he went East and died in

continued in far right column

In a shaft of the Idaho Maryland Mine this miner was faced with the daunting task of reducing the quartz veins, those white streaks in the rock behind him, into small enough pieces to get out to the stamp mill in order to unlock the gold from its quartz prison.

In June, 1856, Amos T. Laird & Co., the most extensive gravel miners of Nevada City, entered upon the construction of a dam six miles above the city for the purpose of making a reservoir. The contract was let to Moore & Foss who had nearly completed the work, when the winter rains so filled the reservoir that the dam began to indicate symptoms of giving way. The contractors sent word to Mr. Laird, but as he had not accepted it he declined to exercise any authority that would render him liable in case of accident. The dam was forty feet high and the water was thirty feet deep and backed up over an area of 200 acres. An attempt was made on Saturday, February 11. 1857, to draw the water gradually off, but between four and five o'clock on Sunday morning the water burst out and came foaming and roaring down Deer creek in an irresistible wave fifteen feet above high water mark. Main and Broad street bridges were washed away and even Pine street bridge, high above the stream, was so badly injured as to be rendered impassable for some time.

The damage to flumes, mining claims, cabins, etc. made the total losses amount to about the sum of $100,000. Several suits for damages were instituted, but as Laird & Co. were held not liable and Moore & Foss were irresponsible parties, nothing was ever recovered.

On the morning of November 8, 1863, the city was again laid in ruins by flames, but it quickly recuperated. Companies were formed who immediately built the Union Hotel and National Exchange Hotel, new business houses were erected and a new court house.

On the night of Sunday, July 28, 1867, the Indian Rancheria, about two miles from the city, was destroyed by fire. It consisted of about forty or fifty miserably built huts and two or three wooden shanties. This place had been occupied by them ever since the settlement of the county by the whites. The Indians were all absent on a pow-wow at Brown's Valley, and were surprised upon their return to find their homes destroyed by a fire they had probably left burning when they went away.

FIRES AND FIRE DEPARTMENT. Nevada's baptisms of fire have been often and severe. Four times has she been nearly blotted from existence, the whole business portion being laid in ruins, and yet from the smouldering ashes, Phoenix like, she has arisen, a better and more substantial city.

While in the pride of her youth, with the soft flush of virginity still upon her brow, she received the first visitation of the Fire King. At two o'clock on the morning of Wednesday, March

Courtsey of the Bancroft Library, University of California, Berkely

This photograph is labeled "Digger Indian." The term Digger was commonly used to label nearly any Indian encountered in the area, probably because area tribes were hunter-gatherers and would be seen digging for roots or other edibles. Digger is now considered a derogatory term.

continued from far left column

New York in 1865, leaving a large fortune.

After this Madam wandered from camp to camp, always gambling and always a favorite. It became a saying among the miners that there was more satisfaction in losing money to her, than in winning from any one else. She was generous to the unfortunate, and no luckless miner ever "struck her for a stake" without getting it. She exercised considerable influence over her rough associates, and it is related, that once, at Pioche, the room in which she conducted her game was filled by a noisy and quarrelsome crowd, maddened by drink, and flourishing revolvers, bound on a free fight. The bar keepers and others strove in vain to avert the impending row, when Madam Dumont, observing their dismay, quietly approached the nosiest of the crowd, and laughingly reproving him and the rest for their ungallant conduct, succeeded in clearing the room and averting the threatened fight.

She obtained her sobriquet of "Madam Moustache," from the abnormal development of that appendage in her latter life.

On the morning of September 8, 1879, her dead body was found, about two miles south of Bodie, a bottle of poison lying near. Let her many good qualities invoke leniency in criticising her failings.

Hallidie's Pine Street Bridge in 1862 after its towers were enclosed

"Mr. William B. Pearson, one of our partners, together with A. J. Hagan, S. W. Fletcher and J. Johnson, all young men of unblemished character and integrity perished in the late conflagration. For two years they had had their offices and places of business under the same roof as ourselves, and in the vain attempt to save the building from the devouring element, they lost their lives. They had no intention of remaining in the building, but before they were aware of their danger, the wooden buildings around them had taken fire, and the brick walls in which they were enclosed proved but a feeble barrier to the intense heat from without. What their feelings must have been, when they found the roof above them on fire and the certainty of a horrible death staring them in the face, can better be imagined than described."

The *Nevada Democrat*

11, 1851, a fire originated in a saloon on Main street near Commercial, and so combustible were the closely packed shake and board shanties and canvas structures, that all thought of arresting the flames seemed futile. Here and there were quantities of powder stored, and these exploded.

Going a distance beyond the limits of the fire, the people quickly tore down buildings and with buckets of water and wet blankets combated successfully the passage of the flames across the narrow lane thus made.

At three o'clock on the morning of September 7, 1852 an alarm of fire was raised at the National Hotel. It was an accidental fire, originating in the kitchen of the hotel. The flames spread with great rapidity, and seized upon Adam's & Co.'s building on one side of Deer creek and the old Deer Creek Hotel upon the other.

Wednesday, November 28, 1854, a fire ravaged Main street, originating in a boarding house just above the junction of Commercial street. Great exertions coupled with a liberal supply of water in consequence of the pipes subdued the flames after nine buildings, valued at $6,000, were burned.

The next fire started in the kitchen of the Virginia House, on the West side of Broad street, February 20, 1855.

Every house between the two M. E. churches, sixteen in all, was burned. The flames were arrested by the pulling down of a house and the formation of a bucket line. It was a narrow escape from a conflagration. The loss was about $40,000, including the Virginia House, Hotel de France, Dr. Hillersheit's Hospital and Dr. Holdridge's Hospital.

It was not until July 10, 1856 that the people of the now busy and prosperous city learned what dreadful power lies in the combined force of wind and flame. About four o'clock on the afternoon of that memorable day, a fire was accidentally started in Hughes' blacksmith shop on Pine street; it rapidly spread, igniting a brewery that adjoined the shop, and then leaped across the street to the United States Hotel and the livery stable of Kidd & Knox. From here, impelled by a strong west wind, it made vapid headway, lapping up the frail buildings with its scorching tongue, and twining its long, red arms of flame about the brick structures, until, clasped in their warm embrace, they fell crumbling to the earth. It was estimated that the total loss of $1,050,700.

More than the destruction of their property, more than the sudden plunge from prosperity to ruin, the city mourned the loss of the brave spirits who became victims of their own heroic efforts to battle with the destroyer. Ten were known to have perished in the flames, and it was feared that still others met the same terrible fate.

These gentlemen entered the building, which stood on Broad street, was owned by Kidd & Knox and was the first trick

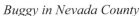

Buggy in Nevada County

Early Thursday evening, March 5, 1857, some men who entered the store of Isaac Rich, at Alpha, were horrified to find that gentleman lying upon the floor in a pool of fresh blood, apparently dead. Upon examination, his face and arms were found to be terribly cut and mutilated with a knife, while from his broken skull small pieces of brain were oozing out upon the floor. The wounds upon his arms were supposed to have been given while endeavoring to ward off blows aimed at his head. No robbery had been committed, and the appearances indicated that the deed had but just been perpetrated by some one who had entered by the rear door, and who had escaped in the same way, being frightened away by the men who found their unconscious victim before time had been given to secure any plunder. Mr. Rich was so severely injured that no physician was sent for until the following morning, and twenty-four hours had elapsed ere a surgeon arrived from Nevada City. The unfortunate man's wounds were dressed, and after hanging on the brink of eternity for a number of days, he began to improve, and finally recovered,

Prospectors in Nevada City on English Mountain near Summit City (Meadow Lake).

Upon the nights of August 4 and 5, 1877, a dastardly attempt was made by unknown incendiaries to destroy Nevada City. Packages of matches and gun powder, saturated with kerosene, were laid in many places throughout the city; but the project was discovered and frustrated before any damage had been done. A meeting of citizens was called for the purpose of organizing a vigilance committee. A night patrol established. Several suspicious characters were "warned," and straightway shook the dust of the city from off their feet.

building erected in the city, to close the iron shutters. With them was T. E. Beans, who with Mr. Fletcher went up to the second floor to close the shutters there. The fire by this time was burning fiercely on both, sides of the building, and Mr. Beans, who feared that retreat was cut off below, calling upon Fletcher to follow him, made a hazardous leap from the window upon a shed, and escaped. Mr. Fletcher either feared to take the leap or thought the building would withstand the flames, and closed the shutters. The friends of the imprisoned young men made strenuous efforts to save the building and rescue them, but all hope was ended by the explosion of a number of kegs of powder, that sent the building toppling in ruins to the ground. Several days after the bodies of the unfortunate victims were found in the cellar, buried under the ruins, whither they had probably retreated upon finding all hope of escape cut off from above.

A relief committee was immediately organized by the citizens to relieve the necessities and ameliorate the sufferings of the hundreds so suddenly deprived of both house and clothing. Those who had been so fortunate as to live beyond the reach of the flames generously threw open their houses for the reception of the houseless, while many in the city and sympathizing friends from without contributed to a relief fund, which the committee wisely and judiciously expended.

Spurred on to some protective measures by the great calamity so recently experienced by the city, the business men formed an organization, in August, 1856, for the protection of the city from fire. A detail of six persons was made each night to patrol the city and guard against fire. J. C. Malbon (King of Pungo) was appointed captain of this watch and devoted his entire attention to it. As freedom from fires instilled into the minds of the citizens a false sense of security, this excellent organization was allowed to die out from apathy. From this state of lethargy the people were again violently aroused by the dread alarm of fire.

After this lesson the people aroused themselves and did considerable able-bodied talking about a fire department. They even went so far as to informally organize a company. The ladies of Nevada gave a ball at the court house a year later, December 26, 1859, during a temporary revival of interest in this subject, the proceeds of which were to be devoted to the protection of the city from fire.

Notwithstanding this sum of money lay idle, no fire company was formed.

The advantages of a hose company soon led to the formation of a fire department. Nevada Hose Company, No. 1, was organized June 12, 1860

The next day, June 13, 1860, Eureka Hose Company, No. 2, was organized. Thirty-four members composed the company. Company No. 1 raised a subscription among the merchants of Main street, and purchased a four-wheel hose carriage of a Sacramento company for $400. Company No. 2 raised $1,000 by subscription on Broad street, and purchased a hose cart. Wil-

I reached the celebrated ''Nevada Dry Diggings.'' Here I pitched my tent and remained a considerable time and lived very pleasantly, although I had many hardships to endure, and was deprived of many of the comforts of life.

An old gentleman, I met here, with whom I had traveled to California, who was anxiously awaiting the arrival of his party, that were to mine and live with him. As he had no tent or mining tools, I invited him to stay with me until his party arrived. I found my friend very useful; I know I could not so easily have erected my tent, or put my mining tools in such complete order, had I not met my obliging acquaintance.

Luther Melanchthon Schaeffer, 1849

Nevada City, 1856

Searls Historical Library

This Idaho mine is an extension of the famous Eureka. The original length of the Eureka lode was 1,680 feet, but by purchase of an adjoining claim it is increased to 3,680 feet. The old Eureka yielded in 1869 $361,211 net profits to its owners.

There is a mournful history in connection with this mine. The original owner, after working it without success, and having exhausted all his money, was obliged to abandon it. He came to San Francisco, where he lived in indigence for some time, finally cutting his wife's throat and those of his two children, and then blowing out his own brains. Those who re-opened the mine struck the ledge only twelve feet beyond the spot where the poor fellow had ceased working.

J. G. Player-Frowd, 1870

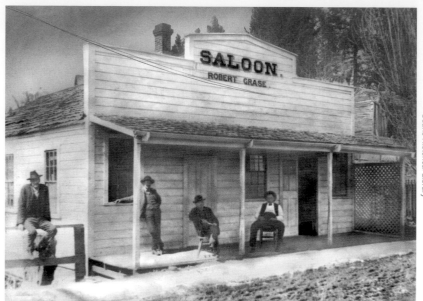

There was a whole lot of drinking and gambling going on and Robert Grase's Saloon in Grass Valley saw its fair share.

liam Barton was elected Chief Engineer, June 26, 1860, and one thousand feet of hose were purchased.

Notwithstanding the fact that the city had three well organized fire companies and an inexhaustible supply of water with a pressure of 150 feet, it again suffered a total destruction of its business houses and public buildings on Sunday, November 8, 1863.

Nevada City as it is seen to-day presents a most wonderful contrast with the collection of shake shanties and canvas buildings that were huddled together on the little flat thirty years ago. Handsome brick structures have taken the places of those temporary stores; large hotels open their hospitable doors to far different appearing guests than those who thronged the canvas and rude frame hotels and boarding houses of the '50s.

Nevada City [1880] contains two large and four small hotels, twenty-three saloons, nine grocery stores, four dry goods stores, three clothing stores, four drug stores, one boot and shoe store, two furniture stores, two books and stationery stores, four variety stores, one hardware store, one crockery store, three tobacco stores, three jewelry stores, five restaurants, one harness shop, one undertaker's establishment, one harness and saddlery dealer, two photograph galleries, three livery stables, four breweries, one foundry, six blacksmith and wagon shops, four meat markets, one hydraulic pipe manufacturer, one sash and door factory, two lumber yards, one bank, one post office, one Wells, Fargo & Co. express office, two newspapers, one gas works, one water works, six physicians, eleven attorneys, two dentists, two engine houses, two school houses, one theater, one hall, one military company, six churches, one city hall, one court house, one suspension bridge and a great many mining interests that will be enumerated in another place.

PINE STREET SUSPENSION BRIDGE. This large and expensive structure has had quite an interesting history. Could it speak, strange tales would it tell of friendships made and broken, of plans for business or amusement, and of hundreds of troths plighted by youth and maiden, while gazing at the play of the mellow moonlight upon the rushing waters beneath.

In 1850, a bridge was built across Deer creek, about one-quarter of a mile below Broad street. From this a new street was laid out, called Bridge street. This structure rendered service for about three years, when, with the help of the county, a suspension bridge was constructed at Pine street. When Laird's dam broke, February 15, 1857, the suspension bridge was consider-

A murder and suicide occurred on Squirrel creek, between Grass Valley and Rough and Ready, May 28, 1855. Three Frenchmen were working on the creek and living together in a cabin, one of them being employed by his two companions. They saw fit to discharge him, and the act so galled his soul that he procured a revolver and proceeded to the claims where the others were at work, and shot one of them fatally and wounded the other; he then put a bullet in his own brain and quietly subsided.

This is the second iteration of the Deer Creek suspension bridge. Completed in 1862, it partially collapsed in July of that year killing two men and several oxen. Repaired, it was back in service later that year. This photo was taken in the late 1860s, a couple of years after the repair.

Library of Congress, Lawrence & Houseworth Collection

South side of Broad Street, Nevada City, 1857

Auriferous quartz lodes are often found by accident. While miners are out walking or hunding, they will occasionally come upon lodes in which the gold is seen sparkling. Some good leads have been found by men employed in making roads and cutting ditches. In Nevada county, several years ago, a couple of unfortunate miners who had prepared to leave California, and were out on a drunken frolic, started a large boulder down a steep hill. On its way down it struck a brown rock and broke a portion of it off--exposing a vein of white quartz which proved to be auriferous, induced the dissappointed miners to remain some months longer in the State, and paid them well for remaining.

ably damaged; and, as both Broad and Main street bridges were carried away, great inconvenience resulted until the damage could be repaired.

A few years later, the bridge having become demoralized by service, it was deemed necessary to construct a new one. The contract was let October 2, 1861, to A. S. Hallidie & Co., of San Francisco, for $9,000; of this sum $4,000 were raised by the tax and the balance by subscription. The summer had been wasted in useless litigation, and the contractors pushed the work as rapidly as possible, so as to be well advanced before the winter rains set in. The season was an unusually wet and rainy one, and seriously delayed the work on the bridge. The towers and cables were in place, the latter being fastened to logs, as the roads were so bad it was impossible to haul the cast iron anchors. The incessant rains so softened the ground that the logs were moved, and the cables sagged in the center. The contractor then procured wrought iron rods with screws at the ends by which he raised and tightened the cables. These rods were three and one-half inches in diameter, and would have been amply sufficient had not one of them proven defective.

The bridge was completed in May, 1862, and on the eleventh of the following July was the scene of a terrible accident, caused by the defective rod. A heavy load of hay, drawn by an ox-team was on the bridge, and another ox-team was just passing upon the structure, when the bridge fell with a resounding crash, precipitating both teams and three men upon the

Searls Historical Library

barren rocks more than fifty feet below. Two of the men were killed, while the other, with a fourth who was not thrown into the chasm, was severely wounded. The oxen were terribly cut and mangled and fifteen of the twenty that fell were killed. The contractors immediately repaired the loss, and by September teams again began to cross. The bridge was thoroughly tested and finally accepted November 14, 1862. The bridge cost the contractors altogether about $15,000.

The history of Pine street bridge would be incomplete without a relation of the thrilling tragedy enacted there a few years ago. It was night; the everlengthening shadows had long since faded away and mingled with the universal gloom of night. The moon had risen from her horizon couch and shed her mellow light upon a scene of quiet loveliness and peace. The countless stars, attendants of fair Luna's train, gazed wistfully down upon the slumbering city. Like a peal of thunder from a laughing sky, a pistol shot rang out clear and sharp upon the still night air, and the dread cry of murder, echoed and re-echoed

Miles of flumes could be seen in most mining communities like this one in Gold Run. Between flumes, houses, stores and mining timbers, many of the area's vast forests were clear cut.

My dear Wife,

I have just returned from a prospecting tour for gold bearing quartz in the mountains. I was gone about two days about 30 miles north of this between the North and Middle Yuba. I found a ledge that had every appearance of being rich. I broke off some of the rock and found the gold in many places plainly visible to the naked eye.

I brought some of the poorer parts of this rock to Nevada and had it essayed by a regular Chemist and it payed nine cents of pure gold per one pound of rock. One man can quarry a Ton of this Rock per day which according to the above rate would yield one hundred and eighty dollars.

Horace Root,
November 4, 1851,
Nevada City

The stage was near Dry creek, on its way to Marysville, the treasure-box containing $100,000. Six mounted men confronted it and ordered the driver to stop, threatening to kill any who resisted. Dobson, messenger for Langton's Express, fired on them, and an indiscriminate shooting immediately commenced between the passengers and robbers, in which some forty shots were fired. All except [Tom] Bell and Gristy ran at the first shot, and they soon found that nothing but bullets could be expected from the stage and retreated. When the stage was ready to proceed, a mounted Mexican began firing upon them from the other side of the road. His fire was returned by Mr. Dobson, and the Mexican was unhorsed, whereupon he beat a precipitate retreat with two others who had been concealed in the thicket. One of the occupants of the stage, a lady, was killed, three others were wounded, and the stage itself completely riddled with bullets.

Gold Run was known for its "the pound diggings." Supposedly miners could reap a pound of gold a day. Photo c. 1870.

along the street, sent an agonizing thrill through many a stout heart. Lights flashed from windows that had before been dark; half clothed forms rushed hurriedly into the street and hastened to where the bridge was swinging by its wire cables across Deer creek's rocky bed. What a sight was there for pitying eyes to see? Scattered about upon the bridge were a valise, hat and cane, while streaks of fresh blood upon the railing spoke volumes to the eyes of hundreds now assembled. But a sight that made strong men shudder and turn pale, was a human form on the cold unfeeling rocks below, plainly outlined in the soft rays of the grieving moon.

All had heard the shot and the agonizing cry, but none had seen the deed committed. Who was the victim or who the murderer none could say and no one knew. All was confusion; those who assayed to gather up the scattered articles were advised to leave them until the officer arrived. But where was he? When the death cry was borne upon the air his ear was quick to hear, but his feet were slow to answer, for, alas, he was lame. Hastening as best he could to the stable he procured his horse and flew to the scene of action. As yet none had dared to approach that form lying so still and deathlike upon the relentless rocks below, but the officer supported on either hand by shuddering citizens, boldly advanced to see if life was yet extinct. He kneeled by the inanimate object, and murmuring from the fullness of his tender heart, "It's a pity, it's a pity," lifted the pulseless form in his arms. But why did he drop it like lead and gaze around with such a ferocious glare? It was stuffed with sawdust, and the fresh blood upon the bridge was that of a luckless feline, who had yielded up her precious life that the boys might deceive a confiding people, and harrow the tender feelings of a too vigilant officer. The crowd dispersed, and once more the calm visage of the moon beamed with a peaceful smile, and the merry stars winked knowingly at each other, as they heard the clink of convivial glasses far into the stillness of the night.

A PIONEER PRINTER. Among the strange characters of Nevada City, of whose eccentricities much can be said in a kindly spirit, was the well-known printer, Alexander Hunt. "Alex.," as he was familiarly known, was, in truth, an odd genius. He was early taught the mysteries of the "art preservative," and became an excellent job printer, and for a long time worked in the office of the New York Herald, when that influential journal was printed on a hand press. To manipulate this machine was the duty of Alex., and he pulled the handle with great dexterity. The most excellent papers that were early published on this coast bear witness that printers were not proof against the seduction of the gold excitement, and Hunt became one of those anomalies, a "forty-niner."

In Nevada county, several years ago, a couple of unfortuate miners who had prepared to leave California, and were out on a drunken frolic, started a large boulder down a steep hill. On its way down it struck a brown rock and broke a portion of it off-- exposing a vein of white quartz which proved to be auriferous, induced the disappointed miners to remain some months longer in the State, and paid them well for remaining.

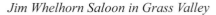

Jim Whelhorn Saloon in Grass Valley

Searls Historical Library

Interior of the Idaho Maryland Mill showing a section of the hoisting works.

In the fall of 1866 a boarder at one of the leading hotels of Nevada City, having exhausted both his credit and money and being firmly convinced that it was much cheaper to move than to pay his board, conceived a brilliant and strategic plan for effecting his purpose. His wardrobe was too extensive to be removed in the ordinary way without attracting attention, and he therefore secured the services of a friend to stand beneath his window, when night had enfolded the city in her dusky mantle, and receive the articles he would lower to him from above. When the time arrived the strategist peered down into the gloom from his third story window and cautiously inquired, "Are you there?" "All right," came in muffled tones from below. Article after article was swiftly and silently lowered, and the owner chuckled softly to himself. At last all had been safely lowered, and the exultant boarder descended the stairs to find that his effects were in the possession of the landlord, who had in person manipulated the lower end of the transportation line, and whose voice had uttered the laconic "All right" as each article fell into his clutch.

He first worked in the office of the Placer Times, at Sacramento, when T. H. Rolfe was editing that spicy little sheet. Alex. was a strong, powerful man, brave and generous, but he would get drunk, as other good printers have done before and since. It was his duty to work the press, and when drunk it was impossible to do this satisfactorily. One day he came in quite overcome with too great a flow of spirits, and Mr. Rolfe told him to make a still hunt for some secluded retreat, where he might sober off, but not to return until he had accomplished that end. Alex. was grieved—was wounded to the heart at the prospect of an edition of the paper being worked off without the press feeling the touch of his skillful hand. In his desperation he decided upon a scheme that would assure a due appreciation of the value of his services. When Mr. Rolfe had closed his eyes in refreshing slumber, and was just in the midst of his third and soundest nap, the man who was to do the press work awoke him and informed him that the handle to the press was missing. The handle was as important to the press as a clown is to a circus, and a diligent search was commenced, first for the handle, and then for Alex. After scouring the infant city, the object of their search was discovered curled up in a corner, with the coveted handle safe in his loving grasp. Both the man and the handle were hurried to the office, and the paper was run off in due season. Alex. many a time chuckled to himself over the success of his strategy.

Alex., a short time later, came to Nevada City, which he made his headquarters, working at times on nearly all of the papers that have flourished here. He procured a coffin of suitable dimensions, and used it as a bed, sleeping in it at night.

His home was wherever he could find room to store his funeral habitation.

Frequently he would engage four pall bearers to carry him through the streets in funeral procession. During these expeditions he would sometimes lie down in the coffin with all the gravity becoming the chief actor of a funeral, and at other times he would sit bolt upright and gaze upon the curious spectators. One night he found a hearse that had been left in the street, and into it he stowed his sepulchral dwelling and retired to rest. In the morning some boys, who caught sight of the coffin in the hearse, were very much agitated upon finding that it contained what they supposed to be a dead body.

A favorite habit was that of blacking one boot and whitewashing the other. It was his style of war paint, and when he appeared in that costume it was well understood that he was on the war path and would be thoroughly drunk before night.

Notwithstanding his peculiarities, he was kind hearted and generous, well liked by everyone, and there was none who had not a kind word for Alex. For a number of years before his death, which occurred in 1874 he was perfectly temperate, and although scarcely able to do any work, lived at the Union Hotel, where a few duties performed earned his board and clothing.

TOMLINSON'S CELEBRATION. During the exciting Presidential campaign of 1860, Bell and Everett had no more enthusiastic supporter than O. M. Tomlinson, of Nevada City. Tomlin-

At eight, the stage called for me to go to Nevada. The distance is but four miles, over a mountain of the Sierra Navada range, Nevada being situated on the other side of it. We toiled up the mountain and through the old woods, by a road which this sudden torrent of rain had cut up, so that our vehicle rocked from side to side, and constant orders were given for all to lean to the right or left, to prevent it from going over. All this was sadly to the terror of the only lady passenger, who most earnestly wished herself in San Francisco.

William Ingrahm Kip, 1854

Gold bars at the Idaho Maryland Mine.

*This woman is perhaps bringing lunch to her husband at the terminal of the
Independence Mine in Grass Valley, 1860s.*

During the year
1848 there were
very few, if any,
thefts committed in
California. The honest
miners kept their sacks of gold-dust
in their tents, without fear of loss.
Men were then too well off to steal.
Toward the close of that year some
few murders and robberies were
committed. But in 1849 crimes
multiplied rapidly. The immigrants
from Australia consisted in part of
very bad characters, called "Sydney
Ducks." These men soon began to
steal gold-dust from the miners,
and the latter showed them no
mercy.

Peter H. Burnett, 1849

son was an eccentric genius who owned some water power near
Sugar Loaf, that he had used in elevating and washing dirt.
When his claim was exhausted he commenced the erection of
a flour mill. As the fourth of July began to draw nigh the idea
of a celebration suggested itself to Tomlinson. He wrote four
verses of a campaign song, and each noon drilled his workmen
in its execution. Schmidt Schneider, a violinist, was engaged
to play the air for the men, while A. W. Potter acted as leader
of the choir. The untuneful voices of the workmen grated so
harshly upon the musician's ear that he would add his German imprecations to the general discord. At last came the long
expected fourth and the dedicatory service of the flour mill was
witnessed by a crowd of people. Judge Colburn read the Declara-
tion of Independence, and then Tomlinson marshaled his host,
before whom stood Potter with his baton and Schneider with his
fiddle, for the crowning effort of the day. With many dexterous
flourishes Schneider executed the well known air, "Oh! Wil-
lie We Have Missed You," after which was sung with majestic
wavings of the baton and ear-piercing discords of the choir four
verses.

THE BIG SCARE. The following occurrence on the night of January 17, 1865, is so well related in Bean's History, that we feel compelled to copy it:—

"Sheriff K. had received information during the day, from one of his attaches, who had visited the famous locality of Allison Ranch, that the secessionists of that place and Grass Valley contemplated a raid on Nevada. The direful news was whispered about among the brave and faithful, and the stifled cry of "to arms" passed from mouth to mouth. The Sheriff was sure his information was correct. The city was to be sacked, the banks were to be robbed, the arms of the Nevada Light Guard were a prize for lawless men intent on raising the standard of insurrection on the Pacific Coast.

Some families were removed to other quarters. It is said a few women and children were urged to flee to the fastnesses

Searls Historical Library

The poster in back advertises the Grand Ball that was to be held on Saturday, Sept 17, 1904 at Kohler's Hall in Washington. Carroll's Orchestra, pictured here, entertained the crowd.

On the night of January 1, 1851, a New Year's ball was given at the Grass Valley House which was attended by ladies and gentlemen from all sections of the county. The gentlemen were well educated, refined and polished. There was one man, however, John Allen, a member of the famous Stevenson Regiment, a rough, burly fellow, who made himself very disagreeable, by becoming drunk and thrusting himself upon those who did not desire to cultivate his acquaintance. Allen had a "hankerin" after a young lady from Cold Spring Valley, and who had declined the pleasure of his escort to the ball, an act which had filled his heart with bitterness and his stomach with whisky. He insisted upon seeing the young lady for whom his heart yearned so tenderly, and walked unannounced into the ladies' dressing room from which he was partly coaxed and partly pulled by Mr. Ross and others. He became violently angry at Ross, and threatened to kill him, but was finally taken away by his friends. Ross said "This man has been threatening my life all the night, and if he comes back here again I'll kill him." The dance went on and just as the time had come for merriment to cease, a voice shouted "Look out, Ross! Here he comes!" A score of pistol shots rang out in rapid succession. Allen staggered and moved up the street. A Dr. Vaughn then rushed out and fired a shot gun loaded with buckshot at Allen. The poor drunken fellow fell dead.

One donkey power was used in this section of the Empire Mine. Although the ledge yielded liberally, the owners failed in 1852 because of mismanagement. There were a couple of new owners through the years. Ultimately the mine yielded $1,056,234 by 1864.

Early miners and business men turned eagerly to the amusements of the day for the needed relaxation. Saloons, with their clinking glasses, convivial songs and inviting music, were among the first adjuncts of a new town. The miner, when his day's work was done, the merchant, when released from the busy cares of trade, the happy delver who had "struck it rich" and come to town to spend his "pile," as well as the penniless "bummer," all sought the cheerful rooms where music and liquor were plenty and where the games of chance formed an attraction even to him who simply watched the fitful changes of fortune.

of the Sugar Loaf, and complied in the greatest consternation. The Sheriff was indefatigable in mustering forces to defend the city to the last extremity. He proceeded without hesitation to fortify himself with old Democratic whisky. The Nevada Light Guard assembled at their armory, and the Sheriff attempted to take supreme command, by not allowing a soldier the privilege of going out to bid his wife the last adieu. He informed the warriors assembled that, like Jackson at New Orleans, he was going to make the property of the city defend it. It was expected the bugle blast for a charge would be heard at any moment. The Court House was surrounded by a cordon of braves, some prepared for the most desperate encounters with sixteen shooters, revolvers, hatchets and knives. The night slowly wore away. No enemy appeared. Judge B——, a distinguished lawyer, took the attache of the Sheriff, who had been in the camp of the enemy, and gave him a searching cross examination in private. He returned, shook his head ominously, and looked unhappy. Scouts, armed to the teeth, were sent out by authority, to examine every foot of ground on the way to Grass Valley, to reconoiter the enemy and return, if possible, to give warning to the beleaguered city. The weary guards, chilly with night watching, paced to and fro, the points of their bayonets gleaming in the starlight over their heads.

'Blaze' was kind hearted and considerate, as he always is when his race is in distress. He sent up to the Court House a bottle of cock-tails. 'Who comes there,' said Joe K__, the Senator, on guard. 'Friend, with a bottle of cock-tails.' was the answer. 'Advance, friend, with the cock-tails,' said Joe, promptly, 'd—n the countersign!'

The 'wee small hours ayont the twal' came and went, but no enemy. And thus ended the 'Big Scare.' "

COLD FLAT. The early mining of Deer creek and Gold Run has been detailed in the history of Nevada City, commencing in 1849. In 1850 the diggings on the flat were discovered, the run having by that time been pretty well exhausted. In August, 1850, there were four cabins in the run and two on the flat. In April, 1851, there was quite a mining camp on the flat, and by July the miners had come so rapidly that the place became a busy village, with two stores, a butcher shop, four boarding houses, six saloons, the Round Tent gambling house, about thirty cabins and a population of 300. In 1852 the flat was almost abandoned, the miners having gone to seek better places. In the fall of 1852 the claims were consolidated into large tracts, and companies began to sluice off the dirt. Amos T. Laird and J. G. Fordyce each brought in a ditch and the ground was worked off from six to twenty-six feet deep. The old tailings were also worked over. The chief miners were Laird, Allen, Monroe and Head. The town was all gone in 1853, and some

A Chinaman named Ah Look murdered a brother Celestial in Grass Valley in 1874, and was imprisoned at Nevada City awaiting his trial, when, on Sunday night, July 5, 1874, he ended "life's fitful fever" by hanging himself. There was a tier of bunks in the cell, and he removed the bottom of the lower ones and fastened the cord to the upper one, and when the jailer opened the cell in the morning his lifeless body hung cold and stiff between the posts. The following day was the one set for the trial, and it is supposed that he was overcome with dread of the dangers of a proceeding so mysterious to him.

Blaze's saloon and the courthouse behind it in the 1860s.

U. S. Gregory, well known as a hotel man in the city, had brought with him to California a number of Negroes, and one of these, a large woman, was abusing Mrs. Gregory, on the day in question, as Alexander Brown, usually called Sandy Brown, was passing. Sandy was enraged at the sight of a Negro abusing a white woman, entered the house and administered a severe chastisement to her. Sandy was a sporting character, and passed down to a saloon, taking no further thought of the occurrence. He was met in the saloon a short time after by a man named Smith, who began to abuse him and threatened to whip him for striking a woman. In the fight which ensued, Sandy was overpowered by his opponent, and just as Smith raised him in his arms to dash him to the floor, he drew a revolver and shot his antagonist in the hip. Immediately there was great excitement, and Sandy hastened to Gregory's Hotel, and delivered himself to the newly elected Sheriff, John Gallagher, claiming protection from the mob. Men were mounted upon horses and dispatched to the mining camps in the vicinity with the intelligence that a gambler had shot a miner. Miners began to hasten into the city, crying vengeance, and the prospects for a hanging were at high tide. The County Judge elect, Thomas H. Caswell, was lying ill in his room, when he received word from the Sheriff that a mob threatened to hang a man, and asking his assistance. Judge Caswell instantly arose and went to the hotel, and taking

continued in far right column

Searls Historical Library

Hotel de Paris at Broad and Bridge Streets, Nevada City, 1857

of the houses were hauled to Marysville, and the flat was again nearly deserted. A few houses remained, and as the quartz leads began to be discovered and developed, permanent settlements were slowly made, until now there are about sixty houses scattered about upon the flat. Most of the settlers are working in the quartz mines, many of whom own promising ledges.

COYOTEVILLE. Upon the discovery of the Coyote diggings in 1850 a bustling mining camp made its appearance on the lead, just above the old cemetery, which rejoiced in the name of Coyoteville. For several months the population was nearly equal to that of Nevada City, which was in danger of being outstripped by her vigorous neighbor. The consolidation of claims soon reduced the population of Coyoteville, and when the ground was worked out, the once extensive camp became but a suburb of Nevada City, of which it is now a corporate part.

"NOW, YOU GIT!" In the first year of Nevada's infancy, society was considerably mixed; gamblers and ministers, what few there were of the latter, were the only vain creatures who boasted of the luxury of a "biled shirt," and by this distinguishing mark were they known; but as to which of the two classes they belonged was always doubtful, and frequently ludicrous mistakes were made. But few families had at this time settled in the city, and the representatives of the gentler sex were chiefly single ladies and of none too good a character. One of these who blessed the city with her presence in 1850 was Mary Mahaffey, who was living with a since prominent violinist.

Mary went to Sacramento and there by her fascinating graces so enslaved the heart of a young man who had embarked in the then speculative business of ranching on Bear river, that he followed her to this city and laid his hand, heart and purse at her feet. After due deliberation a plan was hit upon to secure the purse without the other incumbrances.

It was the day before the dawning of the new year, and it was decided to have the ceremony that evening. The unsophisticated rancher was conducted to a saloon on Commercial street and introduced to the Rev. John White, who was a no less individual than Jack White, a prominent gambler. White had on a collar and "biled shirt," and these evidences of respectability, accompanied as they were by the fact that he had in some mysterious way secured possession of a bible, convinced the rancher that a regularly built minister stood before him. And when, upon interrogation as to the denomination he represented, White assured him that he was a regularly ordained minister of the Episcopal church, his heart beat with joy.

Tom Marsh, proprietor of the saloon, assumed the duties of County Clerk, and issued the candidate for matrimonial bliss a license, for which he charged him an ounce of dust. The party then repaired to the faro rooms in the Dawson house, and Tom Henry and Bill Robinson, who tended bar in Barker's

This is Main Street in Grass Valley in the late 1860s. With the numerous flags flying it is probably a 4th of July celebration.

continued from far left column

the prisoner by one arm, while the Sheriff grasped the other, started to convey him to the "Old Red Court House." Passing out of the hotel in which they had been surrounded by the angry mob, they forced their way through the crowd. The crowd permitted them to pass and became more and more demonstrative as new arrivals swelled their numbers.

Judge Buckner appeared advising them to remain quiet, as Sandy would receive a trial, and if found guilty would be punished and turning to one of the leading spirits, a large and powerful man, he continued, "Valentine Butsch, I hold you responsible for the safe keeping of the prisoner and his delivery for trial." At this juncture there was a cry of "He wants to get him off," followed by yells to "Hang the Judge!"

The next week the Grand Jury met and indicted Brown, who was safely delivered for trial by his guards. Judge Caswell had been requested by friends not to try the case in person, as it had been threatened that if the man was acquitted the Judge would not live twenty-four hours. He declined to be intimidated, opened his court with a speech in which he alluded to the threat and assured the people that any attempt at lawlessness would be put down with a strong arm, and called the case. The evidence showed so plainly that Brown had acted in self-defense, that the jury of miners, actuated as they always were by the spirit of justice, brought in a verdict of acquittal and Sandy Brown was discharged to walk the streets unmolested.

Library of Congress, Lawrence & Houseworth Collection

Planks made travel down Mill Street in Grass Valley in the late 1860s pretty easy compared to the rutted roads found elsewhere.

The mines of Nevada county are chiefly indebted to the famous Grass Valley district for their reputation. Grass Valley was the first to be worked for its quartz mines.

The nucleus of the miners is composed of Cornishmen, the best underground miners in the world, but the hardest men to manage, as the recent strike, which has diminished last year's returns one-half, fully proves.

The system of mining here is called 'the Grass Valley system,' which is acknowledged to be the most perfect at present in use.

J. G. Player-Frowd, 1870

Exchange, were selected as a committee of invitation. They evolved the following formula, a copy of which was sent to the choice spirits of the town. The uniformity of title shows the equality that then existed in social circles:—

"Dear Colonel—A rancher from Bear river will be spliced to Mary Mahaffey this evening. The business will be transacted over at Dawson's Castle, Parson Jack White bossing the affair. You are wanted for to be there, for Mary would feel bad if you wasn't.

Committee of inviters.

P. S.—No guest will have to kiss the bride if he don't want to. Parties will please leave their firearms and cutting implements at home."

About two hundred men responded to the invitation, and the ceremony was performed with due dignity by the mock parson, the bride being given away by her musical friend. After these solemnities they all passed out into the bar-room to "liquor up." A fine supper was spread and the merry wine went around, for which the deluded husband paid $800 with-out a sigh. With a few choice spirits the happy pair adjourned to the musician's house. While the serene benedict was enjoy-ing himself in sweet conversation with his dear one, and as the clock was just trembling on the stroke of twelve, the lovely siren took a shot-gun from the corner and said, "Now you git." He did, and his "love's young dream" went out with the dying year forever.

GRASS VALLEY. This beautiful mining city, for a long time the second but now the first in size and importance in Nevada county, lies in a lovely little valley, surrounded by gracefully sloping hills, whose sides are dotted with the hundreds of quartz mines that have made the city so famous and prosperous.

The place was known to them as the grassy valley from which the road was direct and easy to the name Grass Valley.

In speaking of this valley Boston Ravine and Grass Valley will be considered as one place, as they practically are, adjoining so closely that a stranger would be at a loss to say where Grass Valley ends and Boston Ravine begins.

The earliest actual settlers within the limits of the city appear to have been a party of five emigrants who crossed the plains in 1849 and built a cabin on Badger Hill near the east line of the corporation, some time in the month of August. The party consisted of Benjamin Taylor, who still resides here, Dr. Saunders, Captain Broughton and his two sons Greenbury and Alexander. Zenas H. Denman arrived August 12, and remained in the city nearly twenty years. John Little, John Barry and the Fowler brothers also built a cabin in the same vicinity. The

On ascending another rock we perceived something like a village before us; we pressed forward, but we thought our progress must be either very slow, or else the path we were pursuing only wound round and round the gigantic mountain. We were exceedingly thirsty, continually crying out for water! water! and what annoyed us the more was, the sight of a clear stream of mountain water coursing rapidly down the rugged rocks and cliffs, but inaccessible to us.

So steep was this mountain that wagons, loaded with provisions for the miners about Washington, had large trees fastened to their wheels, and with a push they were started forward and allowed to bring up wherever they could. Oftentimes they upset, scattering flour, bacon and rum in beautiful confusion over the ground

Luther Melanchthon Schaeffer, 1851

The Ophir Quartz Mill in Grass Valley in the late 1860s. Grass Valley area quartz mines produced over $45,000,000 in gold after the accidental discovery of the ledge on Gold Hill in 1850.

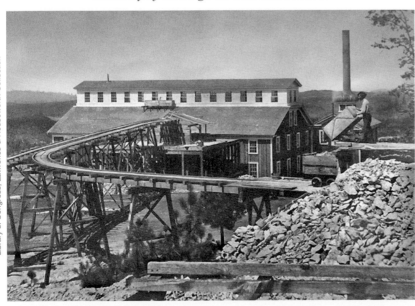

Library of Congress, Lawrence & Houseworth Collection

Grass Valley from the west around 1866.

Theaters were built in Grass Valley, Nevada City and Rough and Ready, as soon as the size of those towns warranted an enterprise of that kind. Since that time many a celebrated actor, singer and lecturer has entertained the people of those places. Among the many that have been here may be mentioned The Robinson Family, The Chapman Family, Lester Wallack, Edwin Booth, Julia Dean Hayne, Mr. and Mrs. James Stark, Kate Hayes, The Alleghenians, Estelle Porter, Bayard Taylor, Horace Greeley, McKean Buchanan, Fanny Davenport, Schuyler Colfax, Mark Twain, James Marshall, the discoverer of gold at Coloma, and many other people of note.

Rhode Island Co. built the Providence Store on the summit of Main street. All these, with a few others, some twenty in all, spent the winter here, and formed the nucleus about which afterwards gathered this bustling, thriving city.

Rev. H. Cummings was president of this company, which arrived on the twenty-third of September, 1849. They built four cabins on the south side of the ravine, which they named after their company, and spent the winter there; the cabins remained many years. On Saturday, September 28, the first Christian burial in Nevada county took place in Boston Ravine, Rev. H. Cummings officiating. An emigrant who had toiled across the plains, only to die on the threshold of his destination, was buried on the south side of the ravine. A number of others settled in Boston Ravine that fall, and in December Jules Rossiere opened a store, and laid the foundation of the flourishing trade the city has since enjoyed.

A few scattered settlers of Grass Valley changed the name of the embryo city to Centreville. Letters were often received addressed "Grass Valley, near Rough and Ready." In November, 1850, a postal route was established between Nevada City and Marysville, J. G. Fordyce carrying the mail on a mule. It was then that the citizens held a meeting and adopted the name Centreville. Letters were then frequently addressed "Centreville, near Boston Ravine." It was not long, however, before it was found that the original name was not only better but had a more pleasing sound, and the people returned to their first love, Grass Valley.

In May, 1850, Rossiere sold his trading post in Boston Ravine to B. L. Lamarque, and in the following June, Fowler Brothers established a second one, but in the fall sold it to William Pattingall and Thomas Fielding, who still lives here and is familiarly known as Uncle Fielding.

Early in November, 1849, Samuel and George Holt, James Walsh and Zenas Wheeler selected a place about four miles below Grass Valley, and commenced the erection of two saw mills. In March, 1850, as detailed elsewhere, Samuel Holt was killed by Indians and the mill burned. James Walsh and Zenas Wheeler, with G. P. Clark, built a saw mill in Grass Valley near the site of Taylor's Foundry, in June, 1850. This was the first business enterprise in the new town.

In August or September, 1850, a man named Morey opened the first store in Grass Valley proper. The first family to settle in-the town was that of Mr. Scott in the summer of 1850, and Mrs. Scott was the first woman to shed the light of her presence upon Grass Valley. Several more families came in

Rocky Bar Quartz Mill in Grass Valley in the late 1860s. The depth of the tunnel in this mine was 475 feet and its production averaged $32 a ton, most extracted through its own ten stamp mill.

An election for town officers was ordered to be held...the new Board of Trustees met and passed sixteen ordinances regulating municipal affairs, and the Marshal made four arrests the first day, one for fighting, one for fast riding and two women for parading the streets in male attire.

A long existing feud between Frank V. Moore and Alexander McClanahan, of Grass Valley, lead to a tragedy which finally resulted in the death of both. Saturday night, February 21, 1857, McClanahan was sitting in Haywood's store, in Grass Valley, engaged in conversation, when Moore entered and asked him if he was armed. He replied that he was not, and was told to arm himself, as he, Moore, intended to shoot him. McClanahan retired and upon his return both he and Moore raised their revolvers and fired simultaneously, McClanahan being shot through the heart and expiring instantly. The light in the room was extinguished by the concussion, and while darkness prevailed some one, stabbed Moore in the back, inflicting a painful but not fatal wound. Moore was arrested, indicted and tried; during the trial an attempt was made by the defence to prove a conspiracy to kill Moore, and the wound inflicted in the dark was cited as evidence of it. The jury brought in a verdict of guilty of murder in the first degree, and Moore was sentenced to be executed.

Every precaution was taken by Sheriff Boring to keep his prisoner safe. A large crowd had collected in the city the day before the morning of the execution, the next morning they as well as the hundreds of others that came pouring into town were much disappointed to hear that Moore had taken strychnine early in the morning and died in a few minutes. The poison had been supplied him by his wife the day before. The succeeding Monday the wife also attempted to destroy herself with the same fatal powder: her life was saved notwithstanding her violent resistance to the physician.

Lola Montez, the gifted, the beautiful and the wayward, came to Grass Valley and made this the scene of her eccentricities for two years.

that fall, so that at a ball given at the Grass Valley House, January 1, 1851, six ladies graced the occasion with their presence. These ladies were the entering wedge of refinement, that has caused such a change in the society of Grass Valley.

The first hotel was built in September, 1850, by J. B. Underwood, who arrived with his large family September 10, and began cutting trees for the construction of a double log cabin the following day. When completed, he called it the Mountain Home, and kept hotel and boarding house in it for some time; it stood on Mill street on the site of the express office. The Beatty House was built soon after, on the southwest corner of Main and Mill streets; this was a frame building, erected by Thomas Beatty.

The great event of the year, and, in fact, the era from which Grass Valley may date her prosperity and prominence, was the discovery of gold bearing quartz, on Gold Hill, then called Gold Mountain, by a man named McKnight, in the month of October. At this time there were but fifteen or twenty cabins in the town, but so great was the excitement and so widespread did the fame of Grass Valley become, that by March, 1851, the town contained about one hundred and fifty buildings, several stores, hotels, saloons and shops.

Grass Valley came near being the scene of a bloody and disgraceful riot in 1852, growing out of the antagonism between the foreign and American miners in regard to the division of claims. The Americans gave notice of an election to be held for Recorder of the district, and the foreign miners held an election prior to that date, choosing a man by the name of Elder. On Sunday, May 23, 1852, the Americans met at the Beatty House, and nominated Captain John Day for the position. The foreigners attempted to take part in the proceedings, and a fight ensued, during which a man was severely wounded and James Nolan killed by being struck upon the head with a rock. Further hostilities were avoided by prudent counsel, the parties referring their differences to the arbitration of the ballot box.

Steadily and firmly Grass Valley climbed the ladder of prosperity. In 1855 the population had increased to 3,500 souls, and at the election that fall 870 votes were cast. At the next election, in the fall of 1856, the number of ballots cast was increased to 1,298. She now leads all the towns in the county, casting, in 1879, 1,105 votes, being 82 more than were cast by Nevada City.

In 1854, Lola Montez, the gifted, the beautiful and the wayward, came to Grass Valley, and made this the scene of her eccentricities for two years. She built a neat cottage on Church street, which is still pointed out by the old residents. Many were her escapades while in the city, but the most prominent one was the attempt to cowhide Henry Shipley, editor of the Grass Valley Telegraph. Between these two there was considerable ill feel-

N. Offenbach Merchant Tailor in Grass Valley, Nov 6, 1891

Searls Historical Library

We reached Grass Valley at four o'clock. It is said to be one of the most beautiful places among the mountains, and is surrounded by some of the richest mining spots. On one side are the famous "Gold Hill" mines, and near are the quartz crushing mills. The population of Grass Valley is estimated at about two thousand, though this must include the floating mining population. We stopped at the hotel (a third-rate country tavern), but on inquiring for rooms, I found that Madame Anna Thillon was "starring" here at the little theatre, and, with her troupe, had taken all the best apartments. The host at last showed us two miserable rooms, which were all he had for us. I then inquired for the ladies' parlor, and was informed that Madame Thillon had engaged it for her dining-room. "Where then"--asked I--"is the lady to sit?" He opened the door of the desolate looking, uncarpeted dining-room, with a close stove at the end, and intimated that this was the only place he had. For the first time since I have been in California, I saw Mrs. Kip's countenance fall, but I did not wonder at it, for the prospect was dismal enough.

William Ingrahm Kip, 1854

There had been a place started there for butchering beeves and packing the meat to the miners. Where these men butchered their beeves we soon found out that the bears would come there in the night to eat the entrails. Sitting around the camp fire one. night there were six of us concluded to try to kill a bear. We made our plans. Five of us, each with a rifle, were to get behind that log. We got all arranged ... finally we heard them coming down the mountain. There were three of them. Finally one bear sat up and I gave the word to fire.

The report was loud. Almost instantly all of us ran to this log cabin and climbed on top of it. One man said, "What did you run for?" Others said, "We ran because you did." The feeling was, I suppose, that we felt safer in the event that we had not killed the bear. The dog heard the shot and smelled the bear. He broke loose from his man and ran. The man climbed a tree and was perched there, looking on. I remarked, "Boys, I hear that dog after the bear; we have crippled one. Let us run quickly and try and rescue the dog." We found the bear and dog rolling over and fighting together. We were afraid to shoot for fear of killing the dog. Thomas slipped up with his axe and gave the bear a blow on the head, which stunned him. Another powerful blow on the skull killed him. I immediately examined the dog, and to my delight found that he was uninjured.

We cut the bear in quarters. We sold it for 75 cents per pound, and as the bear weighed 450 pounds dressed we came out pretty well.

Edward Washington McIlhany,
1849

The Maryland Mine adjoined the Idaho Mine on the east and was part of the same ridge of which the Maryland Mine owned 2,000 feet. Its tunnel reached a depth 675 feet.

ing, and when Mr. Shipley published an article bearing severely upon one of Lola's friends, she armed herself with a whip and hunted for the object of her wrath. She found him sitting in a saloon and at once proceeded to give him a severe castigation, but was disarmed before she had succeeded in striking more than one blow. Both Lola and Shipley published their versions of the affair, each one reflecting severely upon the character of the other. With the subsequent history of the unfortunate Lola Montez all are familiar. Shipley rests in a suicide's grave.

In September, 1862, the gas works were completed and Grass Valley was lighted with gas. At that time the city was seeing "hard times," the silver excitement of the Comstock had carried away hundreds of her miners and thousands of dollars of capital; but 1864, 5 and 6 saw a revival of mining interests here; business became lively, every house in the city was occupied, and Grass Valley once more became the busy, bustling mining town she was before.

Under an Act of the Legislature providing for the incorporation of towns by the County Court, a petition was presented to the court, signed by A. B. Dibble and verified by himself and S. W. Boring, upon which an order was entered. March 5, 1855, incorporating the Town of Grass Valley, with the following boundaries:—"Comprising an area of one mile square, and having for its metes and bounds a perimeter of half a mile due north, due south, due east and due west from Adams & Co."

In the matter of destructive fires and measures adopted for protection from them, Grass Valley has had an eventful history. The first fire organization was a hook and ladder company formed in 1853, before the city had yet suffered from ravages of the flames. This company was allowed to die out in about a year, although they made a parade in uniform October 25, 1854. The first Board of Trustees passed an ordinance, July 3, 1855, requiring the occupant of every house to keep a vessel, holding at least fifty gallons of water, and four fire buckets, for each story of his house. This ordinance was never enforced, and a few months after its passage Grass Valley was almost swept from existence by the most destructive and calamitous conflagration that it has been her misfortune to suffer.

About eleven o'clock on Wednesday night, September 13, 1855, a fire broke out in the United States Hotel, kept by Madam Bonhore, on lower Main street, and rapidly spread to the adjoining buildings. The hoarse cry of "fire!" roused the sleeping citizens from their beds, and they rushed upon the street to meet and combat the enemy. But to no avail, for the frame buildings, dried in the long summer sun, burned too fiercely for the flames to be subdued. The churches and Temperance Hall were saved, being just beyond the limits of the fire. Adams & Co.'s brick building and two other stores supposed to be fire proof were included in the general ruin. Every hotel and boarding house in the town was destroyed. Several merchants saved portions of their stocks in fire proof cellars. The vault

May first: Here I am in Deer Creek. The road first followed the Sacramento and then from Marysville on the Yuba River. A bridge has been laid across the latter river and every person has to pay twenty-five cents for the privilege of crossing it. I will not waste time by washing any more gold, for my sons just met a man who told them that he had earned five dollars yesterday and that this was a rare occurrence. There are seven saloons here and about thirty miners. I did not even unload my wagon, but drove right on.

Herman Scharmann, 1849

*Protection Hose
Fire Company*

On the first day of March, 1851, a man with a small band of mules crossed the South Yuba bridge at Bridgeport and proceeded towards the Middle Yuba river. Not long after his departure a rumor became current in the town that the man was a thief and the mules stolen property. Three or four men, led by a determined character named Spur, immediately started in pursuit, and overtook him at the Grizzly Cañon House on Grizzly Cañon. He was brought back to Bridgeport, and preparations were made for his trial. A miners' court was organized and the man placed upon trial, which proceedings lasted four days. He was adjudged guilty by the mob jury, and was sentenced to be hanged on the fourth day after the decision.

So great was the interest in the case that people gathered here in great numbers, some coming from Yuba and Butte counties, and great preparations were made to enforce the execution of the sentence. To prevent a rescue at least a thousand men guarded every avenue of approach to the town during the four days that were allowed the prisoner. When the fatal hour arrived the man was placed in a wagon with a rope about his neck and driven upon the bridge. The rope was fastened to a cross beam of the bridge, the wagon hauled away, and the man was left dangling in the air before the immense crowd of spectators that had assembled. After hanging half-an-hour, the body was taken down, placed in a rough box and buried on the east side of the South Yuba river.

The Ione Quartz Mill about two miles from Grass Valley, in the late 1860s.

of Wells, Fargo & Co. withstood the hottest of the fire, and preserved its valuable contents. The loss was especially great because the merchants had just laid in large stocks of goods for the fall trade.

Great as was the disaster the people of Grass Valley were not discouraged, but with brave hearts and energetic hands at once commenced the work of rebuilding the burned city and re-cuperating their wasted fortunes. The most notable example of this energy of action was that of A. Delano (Old Block), agent for Wells, Fargo & Co. About an hour after the astonished sun had gazed upon the scene of desolation, a frame shanty was seen moving down the hill from the west end of the town. Slowly but surely it advanced, and was backed up against Wells, Fargo & Co.'s brick vault, which was still standing among the ruins. In a few moments "Old Block" appeared with a ten foot scantling, on which was rudely painted, "Wells, Fargo & Co.'s Express Office."

Notwithstanding the lesson contained in this disastrous visitation of flame, there seems not to have been a regular fire company organized under the law until June 7, 1858. This was known as the Grass Valley Fire, Hook and Ladder.

Another destructive fire occurred here August 9, 1860, which entailed a loss of $40,000 upon the unfortunate property owners.

The fire company was reorganized, June 19, 1861, into Protection Hose Co., No. 1, and the hook and ladder apparatus was turned over to Union Hook and Ladder Co., No. 1, a new company then formed, with N. C. Hammersmith, Foreman; John Blake, Assistant Foreman. When the company reached a good working condition, Hammersmith decamped with two hundred dollars belonging to the company treasury, and the company, unable to survive this financial depression, was dissolved into its component elements.

In speaking of fires it is fitting that the burning of the Washington Hotel, Boston Ravine, should be mentioned. One night, in the month of September, 1852, this building was completely destroyed by fire, and with it were burned a woman named Mary Mahoney and her daughter. The fire was supposed to have been an incendiary one, and Patrick Mooney, the suspected person, was arrested and tried for arson, but was acquitted.

The Grass Valley of to-day, with its brick business blocks, its long rows of stores, its hotels, its handsome residences and

A mixed passenger & freight train of the Nevada City Narrow Guage Railroad on Bear River in 1895. In August 1896 this bridge caught fire and the 200 foot long center span dropped into the river.

Searls Historical Library

Gambling saloons were the first to don fine raiment. Even when in shake buildings with canvas walls, an attempt was made at ornamentation, to render them attractive to the eye and inviting by contrast with the general crudeness of their surroundings. These places had each its band of music, and from twelve to fifteen tables where games of chance were played, monte, faro, chuck-a-luck, twenty-one roulette and many other games. Of all these, monte was the favorite method of losing money. Many a miner has lost his earnings for the week in a few moments on Saturday night, and many another, having accumulated enough to induce him to return home. Bowling alleys were also a great institution, and found many patrons at one dollar per game.

Moore's Flat was the scene of a cold blooded murder, July 11, 1862. Two men named respectively Birckbeck and Echels had a quarrel six weeks previous, and Birckbeck was worsted in a fist contest. The defeated man openly boasted that he would kill Echels. On the night in question Birckbeck went to Echels' cabin and supposing him to be alone, stabbed him to the heart, remarking, "I wouldn't take $500 for that job." He was observed by a Mr. Gibson who was in the cabin, and who was the chief witness against the murderer. Birckbeck was a man sixty years of age and showed a heart of the most depraved character. He afterwards confessed he had brooded over his wrongs, and had plotted the death of his victim, and had it not been for the restraining influence of his wife, would have sated his thirst for revenge long before. He was convicted of murder and sentenced to be executed on Friday, November 28, 1862. November 4 he poisoned himself in his cell and died, thus robbing the gallows of its victim.

Main Street Grass Valley in the 1860s as viewed from the Wisconsin Hotel at the corner of Main and North Auburn Streets.

neat cottages, its large and imposing school houses and church edifices, bears but slight resemblance to the crude and hastily constructed city of board shanties that was burned in the fire of 1855. On every hand are the signs of wealth and prosperity; hundreds of miners and artisans are employed in the mines, and in supporting these many stores, hotels and boarding houses are sustained.

An idea of the size and business importance of Grass Valley can be had from the following list of its component parts. Including Boston Ravine the city contains six hotels, eight dry goods stores, ten grocery stores, five clothing stores, three boot and shoe stores, three book and stationery stores, three drug stores, two furniture stores, one general merchandise store, three variety stores, two millinery stores, one tobacco store, one hay and grain store, one picture frame, paints and oils store, one hair store, two jewelry stores, two hardware stores, one fruit and confectionery store, one hide and tallow store, one candy factory, four bakeries, three merchant tailors, two soap factories, seven markets, three livery stables, four boot and shoe shops, five blacksmith shops, eighteen saloons, four breweries, two lumber yards, one planing mill, two foundries, one stove and tinware establishment, one harness shop, one broom factory, one soda factory, one gas company, one water company, one amusement hall, one bank and broking house, six attorneys, eight physicians, one dentist, two newspapers, two photographers, gunsmiths, carpenters, masons and other mechanics and tradesmen, seven churches, one orphan asylum, nine school houses and a population of over seven thousand. The general office and the repair shops of the N. C. N. G. R. R. Co. are situated here.

The bridges across Wolf creek at Grass valley have been maintained by the city and county at a nominal expense. The bridges across Wolf creek on Auburn and Bennett streets were built in 1872, at a cost of $2,069, of which $500 were paid by the city and the balance by the county. The Broad and Main street bridges at Nevada have met with frequent accidents. The first bridge was built on Main street, in 1852, the one on Broad street during the next year. In 1855, a bridge was built on Broad street, that cost $1,400, raised chiefly by subscriptions. The Main street bridge was also rebuilt in 1856, for $1,000. Both of these bridges were carried away by the breaking of Laird's dam, February 15, 1857, and were rebuilt at an expense of $1,795, of which the county paid $700. The Main street bridge fell under a drove of cattle, May 21, 1863, and had to be reconstructed, and the Broad street bridge was rebuilt in 1867. They have both had a thorough overhauling since.

THE BALTIMORE HOUNDS. Among the early population of Grass Valley were a number of men from Baltimore, who associated together and formed a mutual alliance of offense and defense. They called themselves the "Baltimore Boys," but were

There is a peculiar code among the miners, and they are strong enough to enforce their own laws. One principle is that no mineral lands can be held by proprietors. A village lot can be, but not a field for agricultural purposes.

William Ingrahm Kip, 1854

Nevada City's fire companies parade on a planked street. 1860s or 70s.

Searls Historical Library

I was riding along the side of the mountain and the trail made a sudden turn and at that turn about 100 Indians came suddenly into view. They surrounded me immediately. My mule was very much frightened. I was alarmed somewhat, but did not want to let them know it.

They extended their hands and said "How," but I motioned to them to keep back, for my mule was so badly frightened. They were all painted, had their war materials. They made signs that they wanted tobacco. I had then commenced chewing tobacco and had a big fresh plug that I had not used. I cut it up into small pieces and threw it out among them to pick up. While I was doing this there was a tall, large Indian with long hair that was gray. He pointed his bow and arrow right at my breast. In an instant I opened the bosom of my flannel shirt. He drew the string tight and then let it go, holding to the arrow and said: "Ugh. Much brave Americano."

Edward Washington McIlhany, 1849

Searls Historical Library

When this Grass Valley street was graveled it didn't take long for area residents to discover gold amidst the granite road rock. These men are actually mining the street.

known to outsiders as the "Baltimore Hounds." They were good citizens as a rule, but were apt to avenge an offense against any of them in a summary manner.

It was late in November or early in December, 1852, that one of these men, Burns by name, had a difficulty with Richard Doyle, in which the latter was roughly handled. Not content with this a number of the "Baltimore Boys" went into the New York Bakery, on Main street, and wore about to whip Doyle, when he drew his revolver and shot Burns in the abdomen. Doyle was immediately seized by the crowd and hurried up Main street, towards the slaughter-house on the hill, where it was proposed to hang him at once, even without the usual formality of a miners' jury.

Among the crowd of thirty or forty that went surging up the street were a number of Doyle's friends, who went along with the crowd to render him any assistance possible. As they passed up the street they were met by E. W. Roberts, the County Judge, on his way from Rough and Ready to Nevada City, who rode up in front of the Golden Gate Hotel and inquired the purpose of the crowd, and was informed that they were about to hang a man. Judge Roberts called for half a dozen volunteers to go with him and stop the proceedings, and the call was promptly responded to, and away rushed the men to the rescue. When they arrived on the scene, N. H. Davis was discovered haranguing the crowd, who had a rope around Doyle's neck and over the hooks upon which meat was ordinarily hung. The friends of Doyle had thus far brought the efforts of the lynchers to naught by throwing the noose from his neck every time it was adjusted, but that maneuver had failed to be further useful and the noose was finally secured about the victim's neck, when the party of men came rushing breathlessly up.

Judge Roberts commenced speaking to the crowd, and said the man should not be hung if it could be prevented, and certainly should not unless a majority of those present were in favor of it. He immediately put the question to the crowd who voted that the man should not be hung. Judge Roberts then said: "I am the County Judge, and I order Constable Banks to arrest that man." Bill Banks, the Constable, was also a Balti-

Main Street North San Juan in the mid 1860s shows the voracious use of lumber for all the frame buildings and the enormous flume overhead.

Library of Congress, Lawrence & Houseworth Collection

The last execution was that of George Butts for the murder of William Roberts at Forest Springs, September 6. 1877. The two men had a dispute in regard to an interest in the Norambagua mine, and Butts threatened to shoot Roberts. Roberts then proceeded to the house of Mr. Harrigan, where they were followed by Butts. Here a scuffle ensued, during which the gun was taken from Butts, but he then drew a knife and inflicted a fatal wound upon the body of his adversary. Butts was instantly arrested, was convicted of murder and sentenced to be hanged. On the morning of the execution, October 1, 1878, a large crowd gathered in the city, but their desire to see the doomed man suffer was not realized, as Sheriff Montgomery would not admit them into the jail yard, where the execution took place. Butts was a man of small stature and of inferior mental development and considerable feeling was exhibited by the community at the time of his death, many maintaining that, on account of his intense ignorance and the paucity of his mental faculties, he was not responsible for the terrible crime he had committed.

North San Juan townsfolk, 1860.

The fatal day was the twentieth of June, 1860, and the gladitorial arena was Grizzly Flat, in Yuba county, just across the Middle Yuba river. The ground was paced off by the dignified seconds, sixty good and true paces. As the combatants took their stations with anger in their eyes and rifles in their hands, the moon was smeared with blood. Both fired at the word, and upon discovering that they were still sound in body if not in mind, both champions demanded another shot. A sarcastic individual suggested that they put telescopes on the rifles, but he was quickly squelched, and the work of death went on. Once more did tongues of flame leap from the angry rifles, and once more did the smoke lift from the field of carnage and reveal the virgin sod free from the contamination of blood. A "big talk" was then held, which resulted in an amicable understanding, and both heroes were spared for future deeds of valor.

more man, but he rushed in with the party and threw the noose from Doyle's neck, untied his hands, and moved out of the crowd, warning them that the prisoner was in the custody of the law. Before the "Baltimore Boys " had fully recovered from their astonishment, the party had gathered around Doyle, and all had started down Main street on a keen run. Exasperated at being thus robbed of their prey, the "Hounds" rushed after the retreating men, and struck madly and wildly over the shoulders of the guards in their efforts to reach Doyle with their knives; but all in vain, for he was safely housed in N. H. Davis' office. While the excited crowd were raving on the outside .messengers were sent out, who secured all the saddle horses at the stables and conveyed them to the flat. The party in the office then conducted Doyle out the back way, reached the horses and rode towards Nevada City at a break-neck pace About ten minutes after Doyle was safely lodged in the county jail, some fifteen or twenty of the enraged "Hounds" came tearing into Nevada City, upon team horses that they had secured, and were loud in their execrations when they found that the prisoner was beyond their reach. Bums recovered from his wound in a few weeks, and Doyle was indicted for assault with intent to kill. The following February he was tried and acquitted.

NORTH SAN JUAN. The business, mining and intellectual center of Bridgeport township is North San Juan, a thriving mining town, lying at the foot of the south side of San Juan Hill. The first settler in the immediate neighborhood was Christian Kientz, who prospected on the west end of San Juan Hill, and in the spring of 1853, in connection with Jeremiah Tucker, developed the rich Gold Cut mine. To this enterprising pioneer is ascribed the honor of naming the hill from which the town afterwards derived its appellation. The reasons given for his applying the name San Juan, so unusual in the northern mines, are various, and indicate a remarkable fertility of imagination that does great credit to their authors. Three of these stories are here given with the caution not to give judgment upon such insufficient returns, as there are several stories yet to be heard from.

One of these traditions says that Kientz had been with General Scott's army in Mexico; that one day on approaching San Juan Hill he was impressed with the resemblance it bore to the hill of the castle of San Juan d'Ulloa, and named it accordingly. Another legend, hoary with age and bristling with improbability, is to the effect that the beauty of the scenery so wrought upon his poetic soul, that, being a devout Catholic, he ejaculated "San Juan;" but why a German, even if he was a devout Catholic, should in his rapturous ebulitions use a foreign tongue to express his feelings, and shriek "San Juan" instead of the time honored Mein Gott in Himmel is a riddle too deep for the penetration of the most astute. Another account says that, being a fervent Mason he named it St. John, which, being translated into the pure Castillian of California, becomes San Juan.

A house was built by Kientz where the Halfway House now stands, below the east end of the hill, in the spring of 1853 and kept by him as a hotel. John S. Stidger and George W. Hoard

I can affirm without any exaggeration that thousands of gold diggers are literally starving; they would gladly return home, but have no money to pay their travelling expenses. Of course, there are a few in every hundred who make their fortunes or at least become tolerably wealthy.

Herman Scharmann, 1849

Dutch Flat, Gold Run, Little York and You Bet mining districts. For a more readable view of this map, visit 19thCentury.us/Gold.

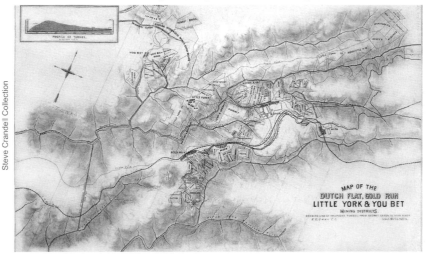

Steve Crandell Collection

I was engaged at the "intellectual" occupation of frying sweet cakes, when I happened to look up, and perceived a woman, fatigued and care-worn, propounding questions to me about Nevada and the best place to pitch her tent; she told me her husband, driving a "wagon and two," was on his way, and she desired to select a location prior to his arrival. I had been listening so attentively to the lady that, upon looking at my cakes, I found not only them, but the leaves around, were burning up, and thus my "extra dish" was lost! However, I selected a delightfully shaded spot for the stranger to locate, and in a short time the husband drove along, and thus another tent was added to the hill. We had lived so many months without the refining influence of respectable women, that each of us felt glad to see our town improving, and women being added to the large crowd of men who needed something to restrain them in their frolics and boisterous conduct.

Luther Melanchthon Schaeffer,
1851

These Birchville miners were likely returning home after a long days work. Birchville was in its heyday around 1865. This Birchville mine relied on hydraulic mining techniques as did many in the area in the mid 1860s.

built a store on the hill at the north end of Flume street and John A. J. Ray opened a canvas built store on the corner of Main and Flume streets. Thus there were three locations, each striving to be the center of the future town. Rich discoveries had been made, and miners were arriving rapidly; the competition became brisk, the stores combined being too strong an opposition for Kientz's location, and the establishment of Ray, leading Stidger & Hoard in the race. Hoard soon sold to Israel Crawford, and Stidger & Crawford continued together for many years.

In the winter of 1853, John Hill, who still resides here, built the first frame house on the present site of the town, near Gaynor & Dickson's saloon, on the south side of Main street. For three years he kept a hotel called the Union House in this building, and it continued under the charge of various proprietors until April, 1872, when it was destroyed by fire. In July, 1853, Crofton Williamson, who had been keeping a boarding house at Hess' Crossing, now Freeman's Crossing came to San Juan Hill, and opened a boarding house. He soon sold to Williams & Son, who discontinued the business two years later. The present National Hotel was built in 1855 by Sears & Green; in 1858 it was bought by Mr. Gordon, who named it the Sierra Nevada House. Henry Pierson afterwards bought it and named it the National Hotel.

Quite a number of people came from San Francisco and settled at San Juan, the street upon which they lived receiving the name San Francisco street. The first brick building in the town was erected in 1856, by Kindt & Grant, and was occupied as a grocery and provision store; it is now used for a store house by A. Harris & Co.

By 1857, the settlement had grown sufficiently to need a post office, and application was made for one. The name San Juan had been long before appropriated, and it became necessary to select another by which the town and post office could be designated and the town christened North San Juan.

But few fires of a destructive character have occurred, owing, chiefly, to the excellent facilities for extinguishing flames. On Saturday, September 5, 1863, a fire originated in an unoc-

Hydraulic mining at French Corral in the late 1860s. This method of mining, while productive for separating gold from gravel, was an ecological disater leaving productive farm land in ruin and killing off huge populations of fish and aquatic wildlife.

Library of Congress, Lawrence & Houseworth Collection

We commenced our march in fine humor and excellent condition--like most travelers afoot, we were talking and laughing as merrily as school boys, until we began to ascend the first mountain on our way, and then didn't we toil and pant? Not a word was now spoken; slowly we pressed on, and when we reached the summit of the rugged mountain we were bathed in perspiration. We had our bedding strapped to our backs, the rays of the sun were beating down upon us, and I began to think, that I at least was paying "dear for the whistle." When about midway to our journey's end, my friend fainted, and fell by the roadside. I was in a pretty predicament, not a drop of water by me, and none in sight; so I sat by him till he revived. He determined to continue on; I insisted upon carrying his pack, and we traveled along pretty well for a mile or more, when over he tumbled again; this time I sought around in various directions for water, but none could I perceive, and when I returned to him he was sitting up, ready to proceed--so on we marched.

At length I espied a path diverging from the main road, and following it we found a cool spring, where we quenched our thirst, washed our faces, and felt much refreshed.

Luther Melanchthon Schaeffer, 1849

French Corral mining camp, 1865.

There is no record of the countless deaths which are taking place from exposure in the mines. Laboring under the hot sun and in the water, sleeping on the bare ground with only canvas overhead, and with unwholesome provisions, the miner, reared, perhaps in ease, sinks into sickness "which is unto death."

William Ingrahm Kip, 1854

cupied building, and destroyed three houses with their contents, all valued at $2,700. October 6, 1864, and September 19, 1865, fires originated in Chinatown, and destroyed a considerable number of the frame buildings in that locality. Still another fire swept Chinatown away, July 4, 1870. The exertions of the firemen saved the balance of the town, arresting the flames in the rear of the National Hotel. The loss to the Chinese was $5,000. One Chinese merchant shut himself up in his vault and was suffocated. The citizens were very much excited, and desired to prevent the rebuilding of the Chinese quarter, as it was a constant menace to the town.

The town at present [1880] contains two hotels, one drug store, two dry goods stores, two clothing stores, two grocery stores, two boot and shoe stores, one book store, one hardware store, one furniture store, three blacksmith shops, four carpenter shops, two wagon shops, one livery stable, one lumber yard, one brush manufactory, one hose manufactory, one jeweler, one tin and sheet iron shop, one millinery and dressmaking establishment, three millinery establishments, three saloons, one bakery and confectionery store, one barber shop, one newspaper, one bank, two lawyers, four physicians, one dentist, two undertakers, and one brewery. The population is about nine hundred, exclusive of some one hundred Chinese; there have been in former times as many as four hundred Chinese here.

The Ridge Telephone Co. was organized here in 1878, and has its principal office at North San Juan. The line is owned by the Milton Water and Mining Co., the North Bloomfield Gravel Mining Co., and the Eureka Lake and Yuba Canal Co. The line cost $6,000, is sixty miles long, running from French Corral to Milton, in Sierra county, with a branch to Foucharie; in all there are twenty-two stations on the line, and the chief use it is put to is the management of the ditches and mining claims.

BIRCHVILLE. The little village of Birchville lies on the gravel channel, three and one-half miles southwest of North San Juan, and has long been the center of extensive mining operations.

The first prospecting was done here by David Johnson, in 1851, and the place was known for some time as Johnson's Diggings. The same year the Miners' and Mechanics' Steam Saw Mill was built by Jenkins, Webster, L. D. Brown, Harvey, Beckwith, Capt. Allers and others, and continued in operation

To look at pictures of hydraulic mining you might think how pretty the powerful jets of water looked. But, they left a big environmental mess that would take years from which to recover. In their quest for gold, miners would do about anything. Sometimes whole settlements would be torn down to mine the ground underneath.

Library of Congress, Lawrence & Houseworth Collection

Ever dear and much loved Wife,

One day last spring while living in Nevada; I was passing through the City with a load of lumber, when two little girls came to me, and asked for a ride. I stopped and placed them on the load. They rode about a quarter of a mile and then left me. A few weeks after that I was at the Sabath School for the first time. I immediately recognized these same little girls among the scholars. At the close of the school I called the little girls to me and ascertained that they were sisters. I asked the eldest if she recollected me. She said she did not. I then told her about her riding on the lumber. She replied "I recollect the circumstance very well, but I cannot recognize your countenance". These were her own words.

Horace Root,
April 5, 1852

During the first winter of its existence as a town. Little York was infested by a gang of ruffians that went by the name of the Decker family. These men were the terror of the town. Fisher was a large, powerful brute, and several times beat inoffensive men in a cruel manner. If they desired a new pair of boots, they simply entered a store, fitted themselves and walked away. One day in the spring of 1853, several of them entered a clothing store kept by a Jew, and proceeded to array themselves in new garments. Upon the Jew making objection to the transaction they became offended and proceeded to pitch him and all his goods into the street. Quite a crowd collected to witness the affair, but no one dared to interfere. Among the spectators was Tyce Ault, who remarked that he should think some one would shoot them some time. This remark was reported to Fisher who threatened to whip Ault. Fisher was arrested for this offense and had become incensed at the jury, one of whom was Ault. He sought out the object of his wrath and confronted him, with a pistol in his hand. Ault endeavored to avoid him and entered E. H. Gaylord's store, but was followed by the ruffian. Ault then drew his revolver and shot Fisher, who quickly retreated to the street, followed by Ault, who continued shooting until his antagonist lay dying in the street. The defeat and death of Fisher completely destroyed the power of the Decker family, and they hastily left the town. This was the first and last homicide in Little York.

Cherokee, 1870s.

until 1853, when it was destroyed by fire. The first building located on the top of the hill was built by Stevens, Everett & Co., in 1852, and opened as a store and boarding house. The firm was changed to Evens & Ross, who pulled down the building in 1855 and erected another across the street; in 1856, they sold to John Thompson who closed out the store and kept the boarding house until 1869.

In 1853 quite a large number of miners had settled here, and by common consent the town was named Birchville, in honor of L. Burch Adsit, a prominent citizen.

Birchville reached the hight of its prosperity in 1865 and 6, but the leading claims have been since worked out, and the village now contains a population of only half a hundred souls.

CHEROKEE. This once flourishing and now by no means dead mining town is situated on the ridge, about four miles east of North San Juan.

The locality was known as Cherokee before the town sprang up, the name being derived from some Cherokee Indians, who moved here in 1850. Crego & Utter built a house here in 1851, and the following year the Grizzly Ditch was brought to the place. This gave an impulse to the settlement, and in 1852 the population reached four hundred. Of these there were but two families, that of John Ryan, and the family of Eugene Turney, who kept the Grizzly Hotel, and a store in the same building.

From 1856 to 1865 the village saw the era of its greatest prosperity. During these years a drug store and a resident physician were among the adjuncts of the town. Owing to the decline in mining operations in the vicinity the village has lost ground since that time, and now contains a population of about two hundred. There are two hotels, one store, one blacksmith shop, one butcher shop, one shoemaker shop and two saloons.

FRENCH CORRAL. This is the last of the series of mining towns that lie on the ridge between the Middle and South Yuba rivers. Its altitude is but 2,000 feet above the level of the sea, and the climate is pleasant and agreeable.

A corral was built at this point in 1840, by a Frenchman from Frenchman's Bar, on the Main Yuba, to be used as an enclosure for mules. From this fact the locality and afterwards the town received the name of French Corral. Mining was carried on in the ravines about this place in 1849, and a man named Galloway opened a store in a tent. He afterwards moved to the vicinity of Downieville.

Surface diggings were discovered here in 1851, and in the spring of 1852, a ditch was brought in from Shady creek, and miners began to settle here rapidly, so much so that the town soon had a population of four hundred. The hill diggings were discovered in 1853, another ditch was brought in, and the town was progressing finely, when fifty of the seventy houses that composed the village were destroyed by fire. The next summer

Logs being dragged along a horse chute to a landing. A chain is spiked to the last log so the whole bunch can be dragged together.

Searls Historical Library

The night ride on the stage over a rough road, especially in the late summer when the dust is thick, is very uncomfortable and wearisome; yet it has a certain strange interest. The large head and side lights to the stage, alias "mud-wagon," cast weird reflections on the deep cuts in the rocky hillsides, and on the ranks of gray-trunked oaks or dusty thickets of underbrush. At the stations, placed at intervals of twelve miles, sleepy hostlers come out with fresh relays of horses, and their half unwilling talk with the drivers reveals queer glimpses of lonely wayside life, with its paucity of incident and topic.

Benjamin Parke Avery, 1850

In the fall of 1850 Studley & Withers kept a store in Rough and Ready. Withers was a married man and had his family living with him at the store. A friend found a nugget of gold on Kentucky Flat, valued at $312, and brought it to Withers to keep. It was shown to a great many interested people and was kept in a drawer behind the store counter. One morning the nugget was missing, and Withers charged his partner with the theft. A civil suit was brought against Studley before Justice W. G. Ross, which ended in judgment being given for the amount of the loss. Studley's interest in the store was sold out to satisfy the judgment, and then a lot of the "hounds," headed by one Howard, and encouraged by Withers, who was the real thief, seized Studley, tied him to a tree and proceeded to give him fifty lashes. While they were still laying the lashes on their victim's back, which was quivering and bleeding from thirty cruel blows, Judge E. W. Roberts and several other gentlemen rushed into the crowd, threw the men right and left and made their way to the tree. They told the "hounds" that they should not whip an innocent man, and that the guilty thief was Withers, who stood trembling by. They were able to unbind Studley and conduct him to a place of safety without opposition.

McKilligan & Mobley Store, North Bloomfield

another fire destroyed the balance of the town, but by the energy of the citizens the town was quickly rebuilt, and continued to thrive and prosper. The era of prosperity lasted for a number of years, and even now the town is in good condition and the center of large mining operations. There are in the town two hotels, one store, one saloon, one bakery, four blacksmiths, two carpenters, one physician and a number of dwelling houses; the population is about three hundred.

The employment of Chinese in the mines so incensed the people that they organized, and December 1, 1867, drove away the Celestials and destroyed their cabins. Twenty-seven of the rioters were arrested, arraigned before a Justice of the Peace in Nevada City, and granted separate trials. Upon trial of David Norrie the evidence showed that there were from eighty to one hundred men engaged in the movement, miners, merchants, tradesmen, and men of wealth. Considerable difficulty was experienced in securing a jury, and when the case was submitted to them and they returned with a verdict of "guilty," upon being polled one of them said it was not his verdict. They were sent out again and soon returned with the same verdict. Norrie was fined one hundred dollars. The charges against the others were dismissed.

SWEETLAND. This little mining locality is situated midway between North San Juan and French Corral. It has been and still is the scene of large mining enterprises. H. P. Sweetland, from whom the town derived its name, settled here in 1850, and from that fact the locality became known as Sweetland's. The place was early noted on the ridge as a trading post, and gradually became settled. The town did not assume the proportions of its neighbors at first, but afterwards overtook some of them, and has maintained its standing. There are now in the town two hotels, four stores, one saloon, one tailor shop, one shoemaker shop, two carpenters, three masons, three blacksmiths and a population of about four hundred.

NORTH BLOOMFIELD. The town of North Bloomfield, the center of one of the leading gravel mining districts of the county, is pleasantly situated on the ridge between the Middle and South Yuba rivers, at an altitude of 3,300 feet above the level of the sea. Originally the town rejoiced in the suggestive name of Humbug, which it acquired in a legitimate manner from Humbug creek, on which it is situated. Upon the origin of the name there hangs a tale. In the winter of 1851-2 a party, composed of the incongruous elements of two Irishmen and a German, prospected along the creek, near which they discovered a rich deposit of gravel, yielding them a goodly quantity of dust. When their supplies became exhausted, one of the sons of Erin was dispatched to Nevada City for provisions, being strictly enjoined to preserve due silence in regard to their good fortune. Money and a secret are too much to confide to an Irishman when whiskey is plenty, and the consequence was, that, after purchasing the supplies and a mule to carry them, he invested liberally in "corn juice," his purse strings and his tongue both

For the purpose of conveying the pure water of the Yuba to Nevada City a narrow flume covered with planks has been built through this gorge. Over this pathway one can walk into the rocky chasm for two miles. The construction of the flume was a work of difficulty and danger. The face of the rock had to be blasted to make way for it, and the blasting could be effected in places only by letting men down from the top of the cliff with ropes, and they drilled and charged the powder holes, hung in mid-air. One poor fellow, who put off a blast prematurely, was blown from his airy perch across the river and dashed in pieces.

Benjamin Parke Avery, 1850s

Miner Harry Stryker in front of his cabin.

The village of Newtown on the fourth of March, 1852, witnessed the most cruel and heartless exhibition of mob violence. A robbery had been committed and a Negro named Brown was arrested upon suspicion of being the guilty party. A jury of twenty-four declared the man to be guilty and left the degree of punishment to be fixed by the crowd. The turbulent mob clamoured for his death, and it was so decreed. A rope was placed about his neck, Brown was mounted in a wagon, and the end of the rope was fastened to a limb of the tree. The rope was a little too long, and when the man was pushed off from the wagon, the limb bent sufficiently to allow his toes to touch the ground. As he hung there slowly strangling, his breast heaved as he gasped for breath and his body writhed in agonized contortions. One of the mob, more compassionate than the rest, perhaps, climbed the tree and leaped upon his shoulders, in order to break his neck. The gymnastic hangman fell sprawling in the mud.

The rope was then untied and when the poor, tortured wretch regained consciousness he entreated his tormentors to hang him decently. A sailor fastened the rope to a higher and stouter limb, the noose was again adjusted about the victims neck and he was pushed from the wagon. He was left to hang struggling in the air for some time, when he was cut down. A physician gave it as his opinion that if left above ground five minutes the man would revive, and he was therefore hastily dumped into a grave that had been dug and was half full of water, and quickly covered from sight.

Searls Historical Library

Flumes were everywhere. These people posed on top of one for this photograph taken in the 1880s.

becoming loosened at the same time, Erin go bragh, familiarly translated "Erin go brag," was here exemplified, and he boasted of his rich "strike," declining, however, to give the location. When he took his departure the next morning, a crowd of ravenous gold seekers tracked him to the camp. Up and down the creek they wandered, panning a little here and a little there but in no place finding the rich diggings they anticipated, and the disgusted crowd returned to the city, calling the creek a humbug, which name has always clung to it, and which it later bequeathed to the town.

J. B. Clark commenced mining near the site of the present town in 1852, and Owen Marlow, Roger McCullough, G. W. Carter, Dickerson, A. Jacobs, John Newman, Francis Blair and others came in 1853 and 1854. By 1855 the camp began to assume the appearance of a town, twenty or more houses forming the bustling hamlet of Humbug City. In that year Madame August, a French lady, built the Hotel de France, which was roofed with canvas. In 1850 Antone Mayhew and Pettijean built a store, and Franz & Esher a saloon, which latter building is now occupied by P. Lund as a hotel. In this year the city took a sudden impulse forward, the population increasing to four hundred and the number of frame houses to seventy.

Having made application for the establishment of a post-office here, it became necessary to change the name of the town, California being too full of Humbugs to suit the Postal

Department. In April, 1857, a public meeting was held, at which a resolution was passed, changing the name of the town to Bloomfield, the word North being added because there was another office in the State by the same name. The same year a public school-house was erected, the United States Hotel was built, and Bloomfield had connection with San Juan by daily stage, and thus to other points. In 1859, Samuel M. Irwin built the Irwin House in the lower part of the town; it is now being used as a dwelling house. Mr. Irwin also erected a large stable for the use of the California Stage Co.

The town began to decline in 1863, and became nearly depopulated; but when the North Bloomfield Co. began operations in 1867, things assumed a different aspect, and population and business increased more rapidly than they had declined. At present [1880], including the Malakoff settlement, which is practically a part of Bloomfield, the population is about twelve hundred.

When the town began to decline the public school was discontinued, but in 1866 it was revived, with an attendance of twelve. In 1873 a new school-house was erected, at an expense of $3,700 which is well furnished and has an excellent library. Religious services are held in the school-house by Catholics, Episcopalians and Methodists, at different times. In the summer of 1878, a large hall was erected by Edward Cummings. which is used for dancing parties and miscellaneous entertainments.

Empire Mine mill clean up.

Searls Historical Library

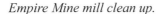

The gallows was erected upon the side of Lost Hill, about one-half mile from the court house. The prisoner and attendants were escorted to the scene of the execution by the Nevada Rifles, who formed about the gallows and maintained order. The hill was covered with a crowd of spectators, at least five thousand people from Nevada and Sierra county being present to witness the legal taking off of a fellow man.

Nevada City in the 1860s was a center of commerce for the region. Note the heavily laden freight wagons in the background.

It is never safe in California to judge of a person by his dress. You are thrown into contact with rough-looking people in a stage coach, and before you have travelled five miles, find they are college-bred,--perhaps professional men at the East. You speak to a miner in a red flannel shirt, about the geological formation of the mine in which he is working, and the first sentence of his answer--the very wording of it--shows him to be scientifically educated, and, by his training, an accomplished man. The proprietor of a book store in one of the mining towns told me, that the roughest looking men came in to ask for classical works on these and on every other scientific subject. Astronomy seemed to be a particular favorite with them.

William Ingrahm Kip, 1854

Saturday, October 28, 1876, the French Hotel at Malakoff was destroyed by fire. A man named Harmon was burned to death, and it was supposed that he was the cause of the fire, as he was in the habit of smoking a pipe while lying in bed.

North Bloomfield is on the line of the Ridge Telephone Company, the principal office of which is at San Juan.

LAKE CITY. Pleasantly situated on the ridge down which runs the pliocene river channel, on the road from Columbia Hill to North Bloomfield, and about two and one-half miles from the latter, the little town of Lake City has passed on almost uneventful existence of twenty-three years.

A little cabin was built here in 1853 by a man named Joiner, and in 1855, John H. Helwig, John Schroder, Henry Bowman, Fred Thane and two others, commenced mining operations, being known as the Dutch Hill Company. In 1855 and 6 Lake City became connected with North Bloomfield and Columbia Hill, although there were then but a few cabins, and no effort had been made to build a town. A hotel was built in 1855 by Saul and William Bell, and the locality was known as Bell's Ranch. When the Eureka ditch was completed in

1857 the settlement received quite a forward impulse. A town was then laid out and named Lake City. The same year the Bremont House was built by M. Bremont, and remained until a few years ago, when it was destroyed by fire.

COLUMBIA HILL. Situated on the ridge at the junction of the North Bloomfield gravel channel with the one from the Blue Tent. W. L. Tisdale and brother settled here in October, 1853, erected a log cabin and commenced mining operations. In 1855, a man named Fleming opened a store, and the settlement began to assume the aspect of a village. The name of the place changed to North Columbia, although it is generally spoken of as Columbia Hill. About a year ago the old town site was abandoned, and a new town built about one-fourth of a mile distant. The old village was built on the gravel channel, and here as in other places the town had to move when the site was wanted for mining ground.

RELIEF HILL. This place is situated on the South Yuba river, about three miles east of North Bloomfield. Captain Monroe, J. K. Reed, Burnham, Tuttle and some others located here as early as 1853, and engaged in mining. By 1856 the settlement had attained a population of seventy-five people, and rejoiced in one store, two saloons, one butcher shop, two boarding houses, one blacksmith shop and several dwellings. The town steadily increased in size and importance until 1858, at which time it contained one hundred voters. It then began to decline very speedily; but in 1862 it was revived, and remained a thriving camp for a number of years.

One of Louis Voss' sawmills, the earliest of which was built in the 1850s. Most of his mills were near You Bet, Red Dog, and Chalk Bluff Ridge.

Searls Historical Library

In the fall of 1849, a tall, handsome young fellow, dressed in a suit of fine broadcloth, and mounted upon a splendid horse, stole a purse of gold-dust from an honest miner, and fled from the camp. The thief took the plain wagon-road that led around a tall mountain, while his pursuers took a shorter route across, reached a mining camp where there was an alcalde in advance of the thief, and quietly awaited his arrival. In due time the thief appeared, mounted upon his splendid steed, and was at once arrested, and promptly tried before the alcalde. After hearing all the testimony, the alcalde said to the prisoner: "The Court thinks it right that you should return that purse of gold to its owner." To this the culprit readily assented, and handed over the purse. The alcalde then informed him that the Court also thought he ought to pay the costs of the proceedings. To this the culprit made not the slightest objection (thinking he was very fortunate to escape so easily). "Now," said the alcalde, "there is another part of the sentence ... that you receive thirty-nine lashes on your bare back, well laid on." The punishment was promptly inflicted, and, of course, the transgressor thought his way hard. He could only boast that he was "whipped and cleared."

Peter H. Burnett, 1849

If I would buy the goods and pack the goods into their bar for them, they would give me a fourth interest in the claim, which was very rich. I accepted their proposition, loaded the four mules and started. The traveling was tedious and the boys sometimes had difficulty in following the trail, as there was more or less melting snow on the ground. Finally we wound our way down the mountain and came to the bar. We went to the camp, unloaded the mules and all of us being very tired. After awhile a man came to the camp--a stranger to my friends. He had a pint cup in his hand and had it about half full of coarse gold. They asked him if he knew where the man was that they had left in their camp. He said that he did not know and he had bought him out and he had been gone several days. The matter was talked over that night in camp. This man had bought the claim honestly and paid for it, and he would not think of giving it up. He had possession of the claim, that being nine points in law. They finally made a compromise in some way, that these two men still held an interest, but I was cut out. I did not feel disposed to have trouble in any way, as I was making money and had plenty provisions with me. I let the boys have enough of the provisions to give them a pretty good stake to start on and sold the balance for a big price.

Edward Washington McIlhany,
1849

An 1853 view of Rough & Ready.

YOU BET. This mining camp was first settled and named by Lazarus Beard, son of the man whose name was given to Beardstown, Kentucky. He built a small saloon about 12x12 feet on the hill opposite Walloupa, and three hundred yards east of the site of the present town. The ground on which the saloon stood has been washed away. This was as early as 1857. People came here from Walloupa to have a good time, and Beard located his place as a town lot. Having done so he cast about him for a name, and called to his assistance Wm. King and James Toddkill from Walloupa, who frequently repaired to the saloon and drank free whisky while employing their brains in this service. They were always careful to suggest and urge some name that they were sure he would object to, so as to protract the deliberations and the accompanying whisky as long as possible. If Beard used one slang expression more than another, it was "you bet," which was a great favorite with him, and in a joking way the two privy counselors suggested that as a name for the town. To their surprise it met with favor and was adopted, and their free whisky was stopped.

On Saturday, April 24, 1869, You Bet was completely destroyed by fire. The fire originated in a Chinese wash house and in a few minutes consumed the whole of the town proper, some thirty buildings, including Mrs. Stitch's Hotel, Kennebeck Hotel, Beard's Hotel, Good Templar's Hall, four stores, five saloons, two variety stores, butcher shop, shoemaker shop, two blacksmith shops, tin shop and post office.

The town was partially rebuilt, and many houses were moved over from Red Dog.

In 1863 a school house was built midway between You Bet and Red Dog. There are two old cement mills standing here, that have not been in operation since 1872.

HUNT'S HILL OR GOUGE EYE. This place was first located by a French company about 1855. The claim was "jumped" by another company and a fight ensued, during which one of the Frenchmen lost an eye. It was this circumstance that led Thomas Concord to name the place Gouge Eye when a little mining camp sprang up. In Hunt's Hill the blue lead was discovered in 1857, and a great many claims were staked off. The little town that grew up was known both as Hunt's Hill and Gouge Eye. At one time an effort was made to change the name to Camden, but it was unsuccessful. There are now one small store and saloon combined and a few houses here.

ROUGH AND READY. The history of the town of Rough and Ready is like that of many a mining town in California. A discovery of rich diggings, an influx of miners and merchants, a sudden growth of population and business, prosperity and importance as long as the mines continued to yield, gradual deterioration with the decline of the mines, and, finally, resolved into a small village, with but little more than the memory of other days to live upon.

The first settlement was made in the fall of 1849 by the Rough and Ready Company, from which the town derived its name. The leader of this company was Captain A. A. Townsend. Captain Townsend had served under Gen. Taylor in

Seventy-five miles from Sacramento City, not far from the Yuba River, there is a gold mine called the Rough   and Ready. There are no less than thirty thousand people working there.

Herman Scharmann, 1849

Blacksmith, W.H. Fippin, 1905.

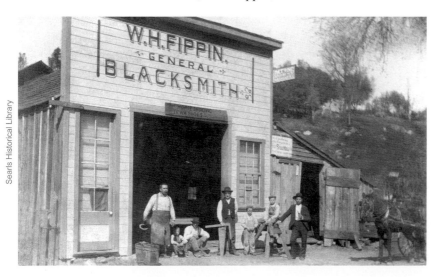

A most amusing duel occurred in Nevada City, July 12, 1861, between Messrs. Tompkins and Curley. One of these gentlemen having become offended, became thoroughly convinced that nothing but blood would cleanse the stain upon his honor, challenged the other to deadly combat upon the bloody sands. The challenged party was as thoroughly convinced that water as a cleansing agent was far superior to blood, and besides that he had more of it to spare, so he accepted the challenge to fight, instead of the bloody sands the scene was to be the muddy pavement, and instead of the death dealing pistol, which might miss both of them, the weapon was to be a section of hose, from whose unerring aim there was no escape. The terms were agreed upon; seconds were chosen; everything was conducted after the manner prescribed by the code. Each was armed with a twenty-five foot hose with a quarter inch nozzle, the hose attached to hydrants in which there was a pressure of one hundred and fifty feet. When the word was given the water was turned on and for sometime the air was rent with the hilarious shrieks and yells of the spectators as the drenched but valiant combatants dodged the rushing streams of water. Neither would submit or call for a truce, and the aqueous strife was only terminated when the hose of one of the parties suddenly "busted." It was here demonstrated that in removing stains of honor one drop of blood is equal to a thousand gallons of water.

Searls Historical Library

Working animals had to be cared for if they were to provide the power for the many hard tasks of the day. Horses didn't pull heavy loads well so oxen and mules were most often used to pull freight wagons, plows, etc. This ox is getting a new pair of shoes.

the Winnebago war, and for this reason the company was styled Rough and Ready. The company crossed the mountains by the Truckee route, and arrived on Deer creek, near the mouth of Slate creek, September 9, 1849. Here they mined in the bed of the creek for several weeks with good success. Grizzlies and deer were plentiful, and while one of the company was out on a foraging expedition after game, he came to the ravine below Randolph Flat. Being thirsty he stooped to slake his thirst in the clear stream at his feet, and in doing so discovered a piece of gold lying exposed upon the bed rock. The company prospected here, and finding rich ground, removed their camp from Slate creek to this place. Two of the men were dispatched with a wagon to Sacramento to procure provisions, the route chosen by them being the same afterwards known as the Telegraph road.

But a short time after the settlement here of the Rough and Ready Company, another, the Randolph Company, appeared and located on Randolph Flat. The Rough and Ready Co. had endeavored to keep their success a secret, they had located the whole ravine, and had even taken up claims that were known to be of no value, in order to keep others away. They maintained their monopoly whenever any miners began prospecting in the neighborhood, by going to the place they were at work and claiming the ground. This was the state of affairs when the Randolph Co. appeared and located on some ground claimed by the others. This proceeding threatened to result in a difficulty between the two companies, but a compromise was effected, and the two parties divided the ravine between them.

These companies were very successful in their mining operations, and Captain Townsend returned East in the spring to procure some more men. He made up a company of forty men, whom he had under contract to work for him one year for the wages that then prevailed in the States. All are familiar with the magical growth of mining localities in the summer of 1850, and when Townsend arrived with his new party in September, he was both surprised and disappointed to find four or five hundred people in a town composed of a motley collection of tents and shanties, where but a few months before stood only the cabins of the two companies. He was obliged to hire his men out to the owners of claims, and to buy an interest in a claim for himself.

The first family at Rough and Ready was that of a Scotch-man, named Riddle, who came here with his wife from South America. In April, 1850, James S. Dunleavy came with his wife and built the first frame house, paying $200 per thousand feet for the lumber at the mill near Grass Valley. Mr. Dunleavy had come to this coast as a minister, and had for several years previously resided in San Francisco, where he was elected by the inhabitants of that place in 1847 to represent them in the Council called by Fremont, the acting Governor. The reverend

I made a little money, and went to Sacramento City and bought two wagon loads of goods, went back to Grass Valley and started a hotel, ran it a few weeks, and the first thing I knew I was "busted."

Lell Hawley Woolley, 1849

Hydraulic mining at Jim Cameron's Mine in Relief Hill, 1895.

Searls Historical Library

Searls Historical Library

Altoona Mining Company boarding house on Alta Hill in the Randolph & Bunker Hill area of Grass Valley, 1898.

Saturday, December 28th. ''Hitched up'' our fast team about 4 P.M., and started forward. The road was very rough, and the slow motion of our team suited very well now. Reached the ''Zinc House,'' delightfully situated near never-failing streams; and while we washed our faces and enjoyed a rest in the welcome shade, our breakfast was prepared, and when the word was given, we lost no time in doing ample justice to the excellent repast mine host had spread before us. Bidding the landlord the ''top of the morning,'' we followed after our patient and sure-footed oxen, and reached ''Rough and Ready'' during the afternoon; took a bird's eye view of the rough, but not ready looking place, and proceeded on until night overtook us, when we halted at the ''Madison House,'' a rough, ill-shaped log hut, the meanest public house on the road.

Luther Melanchthon Schaeffer, 1849

gentleman got drunk on the night of the election, and seems to have retrograded rapidly, for upon his appearance in Rough and Ready he opened the first saloon in the new town, and a few months later dedicated the first ten-pin alley in the county.

The settlement began to grow. The roads which the severe weather of the preceding winter had rendered impassable for wagons, began to free themselves from mud, and there was a great rush of miners from below to Deer creek, the fame of whose marvelously rich diggings had gone abroad. Claims were taken up on all available ground, tents were pitched on the flat and along the ravines, everywhere; a few shake and board shanties were built. Merchants came in with there stocks of goods and whiskey. The first store was opened by H. Q. Roberts, in a tent, consisting of the mainsail of a vessel, that some sailors had originally taken to the Anthony House, supported by pine poles stuck in the ground. This was in March, 1850.

It was during the uncertainty of 1850, when everything was new, and government of a legal kind was yet a stranger to the town, that E. F. Brundage conceived the idea of a separate and independent government. He issued a high sounding manifesto, and called a mass meeting to organize the State of Rough and Ready. About one hundred men adhered to him for a while, but the whole affair was so severely ridiculed that the State of Rough and Ready vanished like mist.

The population increased so rapidly in 1850, that at the election in October there were nearly 1,000 votes cast. A number of cases of cholera, that fearful scourge from which the State suffered so severely in 1850, appeared in Rough and Ready.

The size of claims, at first limited to fifteen feet square, was extended to thirty feet square, and all the long, dry season the miners threw up heaps of dirt, awaiting the time when the rains of winter should provide the water for washing their treasure. They waited in vain, for the wet season of 1850-1 was a dry one, as it were, and the consequent lack of water led to the construction of ditches to supply the deficiency. In November a party commenced a ditch from Squirrel creek to run to Rich Flat, which they completed before the end of the year. Another company surveyed a line from Deer creek, but found a party of Nevada City men bent on the same purpose. They united and constructed the Rough and Ready Deer Creek Ditch, which was completed in the fall of 1851. The scarcity of water, while waiting for the completion of the ditch, paralyzed the mining industries and business of the town. Miners departed for more favored localities, business was at a complete pause, merchants failed in large numbers, buildings were torn down and removed, and the town presented a most dilapidated appearance. The appearance of water had a reviving influence, and the town regained, to a degree, its former prestige.

The now prosperous town was visited by a devastating conflagration, on the night of Tuesday, June 28, 1853. A careless person left a lighted candle too near a canvas partition when he retired to sleep, and the result was that in a few moments

Washington's Town Band, 1866

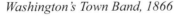

Searls Historical Library

...since the rainy season set in, and the community were confined to quarters, the system of dividing the day was no longer practicable, and the yawning miner, devoid of any mental resources, embraced the indulgences of degrading appetites and propensities as a cure for ennui, stimulating the dullness of unenlightened rumination with intoxicating drink, and ministering to the cravings of the lust for acquisition and excitement by gaming in its most odious guise, giving rise to unintermitting scenes of disgusting debauchery, that partook in their grossness of the reckless character of the class who flocked to snatch up fortunes, where there were no curbs or restraints to check the natural bent of their dispositions. The seed once sown in so congenial a soil, shot up with luxuriant rapidity, the prolonged period of idleness affording ample time for the full maturation of its odious and contaminating fruit.

Matters thus daily deepened in repulsiveness, until even my own mess became imbued with the vicious contagion, when I fairly lost all heart, and yearned piningly for the pleasures of rational companionship.

William Redmond Kelly, 1849

Searls Historical Library

Four miners at their cabin in Nevada County.

During the year 1851 pretended assayers convinced gullible stockholders in quartz veins that their rock yielded from ten to fifty cents per pound, when the real value was perhaps nothing, receiving of course good pay from their grateful customers. Under the spur of such welcome information, hundreds made themselves poor by misapplied capital. The "Bunker Hill Co." is an illustrious instance. They erected a costly mill upon Deer Creek, to use a certain roasting process by which they smelted the quartz in an immense furnace, expecting the gold to drop in a receiving chamber below. It is perhaps needless to say that they poked in vain in the ashes below for the oro.

Believing the experiment had failed through intrinsic defects in its philosophy, and not that their ledge was destitute of Gold, (for had it not been assayed with brilliant results?) the Company next erected stamps. Unluckily, the tailings were very pure quartz and the affair was a failure. The loss by the Company is computed at $85,000.

the whole business portion of the town, including forty hotels, stores and houses, was burned to the ground.

In December, 1856, the people of Rough and Ready met in public convention, and resolved that a proper observance of the Christian Sabbath required the suspension of business on that day, and agreed to close their stores on Sunday for one year, commencing January 1, 1857. The meeting was held and these good resolutions passed in a no less place than the Union Saloon.

Nearly the entire town was destroyed by fire on Friday, July 8, 1859. Subscriptions were taken in Grass Valley, Nevada City and other localities for the relief of those so suddenly deprived of their homes.

From this blow the town never recovered. The rich surface diggings that had drawn the people here had become nearly exhausted, there was nothing to induce the people to remain and build up another town. A few who still had paying claims remained, and there was population enough to maintain a store, saloon, post office and express office. Such has been the condition of Rough and Ready ever since the fire that blotted it out, and such is its condition to-day [1880]. Where once stood some three hundred houses, stores, saloons and shops, Masonic Hall, Odd Fellows' Hall, and a town throbbing with busy life, are now some two dozen houses scattered about a single store.

SPENCVILLE. The copper discoveries led to great excitement in 1865-6, and thousands rushed to the copper belt to take up claims. Towns were laid out, and there was an immense "boom." Spenceville, Hacketville, Wilsonville, Queen City, and several others made great pretentions, but the subsidence of the fever left them without any population, and now even their sites are hard to find. Spenceville, however, still remains, and is quite a little village, where the San Francisco Copper mine works are situated. A school and post office are situated at this point. Three general merchandise stores and a hotel, are well supported by the miners and the surrounding farming community.

WASHINGTON. The little town of Washington, from which the township in which it is situated derived its name, lies on the South Yuba river, twenty miles from Nevada City. It was one of the first settled of the mining camps in the county, dating back to 1849.

In the fall of 1849 a company from Indiana arrived at this point, and decided to remain through the winter. The place of their location was called Indiana Camp. The winter was a severe one, and the snow lay on the ground to such a depth that but little work or prospecting could be done, and they, therefore, amused themselves and supplied their larder with bear steak and venison by hunting the bears and deer that the severity of the winter had driven down the mountains from the higher altitudes. When returning spring removed the embargo of snow,

Empire Mine Crew 1905

The miners would give us buckskin purses containing from $500 to as high as $3,000 to keep for them. There were no safes then. They had their names marked on the purse. We threw the mony in the shoe box for safety and never was a cent lost and men coming in and going out constantly.

Edward Washington McIlhany, 1849

Searls Historical Library

Monday, June 9th. The trees which flourished best in our neighborhood were the oak and pine; and at that time wood cost nothing; so every miner kept up a blazing fire. I came near losing my palatial habitation on one occasion. I greatly feared that I should be overrun by the million of ants that were holding a mass convention near me, and I saw they had agreed ''by acclamation'' to take possession of my provisions ''sans ceremonie.'' So I threw hot ashes over the first battalion, and passed on to the city, hoping, upon my return, I would find that my enemy had ''retreated.'' As I was returning, not dreaming of anything amiss, some friend sang out to me, ''look ahead, your cabin is on fire.'' I hastened my steps, and soon discovered that the hot ashes had ignited the dried leaves lying around, and the flames were fast extending towards my cabin. I took things very calmly; reached for my long shovel, and pitched the burning leaves as far off as possible. Fortunately, they lodged upon a bank of clay, and thus I saved my hut, drove off the ants, and sitting down, partook of a frugal repast, grateful that I still possessed a shelter, humble though it was.

Luther Melanchthon Schaeffer, 1851

Saloon in Washington. If you look closely at the man in the back left corner, it looks at though he's thumbing his nose at the photographer.

deer hunting was abandoned and gold hunting resumed. The river was found to be quite rich and many others were attracted to the spot. Another party had made its way to this vicinity in the fall of 1849. This was a company from Oregon, led by a man named Greenwood. They prospected up the South Yuba river as far as the Indiana Camp, their success drawing after them quite a number of others from farther down the stream. They located that fall at Greenwood's Camp, afterwards called Jefferson, a mile and a half below Indiana Camp. In the spring a majority of those who had spent the winter in Greenwood's Camp came on to the river in the vicinity of Indiana Camp, and these were soon followed by crowds of men from below, so that quite a town began to make its appearance. The new town was named Washington by its patriotic inhabitants.

By the month of August, 1850, there were about one thousand men at work on the river, constructing dams, canals, etc., for the purpose of working the bed of the stream. In the vicinity of Washington in 1850-51 there were probably three thousand men. The town of Washington, which was the headquarters of this busy hive of workers, had become a thriving, bustling, animated mining camp, with hotels, saloons, restaurants, bowling alleys, stores and all the accessories of a successful mining town. When the work of laying bare the river channel was completed, it was found that the golden visions of the laborers were not realized in their fullness, and a great many deserted Washington to seek more favored localities. This gave Washington a bad name, and it is well known that it has as fatal an effect on a mining camp as it has on a dog to give it a bad name, and progress was necessarily slow. Those who remained made an ounce or two per day, and many of them returned East with considerable wealth. The region gradually became developed, and the population somewhat increased. Rich gravel banks were discovered in the neighborhood, hydraulic mining was introduced, and Washington became and has always remained the most considerable town in the township. In the vicinity and tributary to it were the rich diggings on Poorman's creek, Gaston Ridge and Fall creek. In 1858 the town of Washington had five provision stores, two clothing stores, two hotels, one billiard saloon and the usual complement of liquor saloons and gambling rooms. The population was in the neighborhood of two hundred. In 1860 Washington was about the same size as in 1858, containing two hotels, several stores and saloons, a butcher shop, a shoe shop and a population, including a considerable number of Mongolians, of about three hundred and fifty.

Washington still remains the principal locality in the township, and unlike most mining towns, has never had the misfortune to be destroyed by fire. A store was burned in October, 1867, and the proprietor in kicking about in the ashes discovered $1100 in gold coin, which he had laid away so carefully that he had forgotten the fact, and had charged parties with its theft. The town now contains two hotels, two stores,

When we left our tents we always felt sure our valuables would be safe, because the miner's law was the law, and their justice was meted out quick and sure--no quibbling and tedious wrangling. I have seen, at a distance, men flogged for committing crimes, and then drummed out of camp. Was a miner robbed, was a miner murdered, the report flew around the camp with lightning speed. The culprit, if caught, was summarily dealt with; and if persons think this harsh and cruel, they must only place themselves in a country without laws, without proper courts of justice, and then ''circumstances alter cases.''

Luther Melanchthon Schaeffer,
1849

Unknown Grass Valley Mine

Courtesy of the Bancroft Library, University of California, Berkely

Hydraulic Mining in Nevada County, c. 1870.

Gold hunting is, without doubt, the most exciting life a man can lead. No matter how unsuccessful, no matter if the result of a hard day's labor yielded barely sufficient to pay necessary expenses, the hope, the pleasurable hope of finding the ''big lump'' next day, fills the miner's breast with joy and delightful anticipation, and keeps up the spirits of men who otherwise would despond.

Luther Melanchthon Schaeffer, 1849

two saloons, shoe shop, market, post office, school house and a population of about two hundred and fifty, exclusive of Chinese.

GOLD HILL. Another of the early mining camps where hill diggings were found was Gold Hill, two miles west of Washington and a little way south of the river. Gold Hill was almost entirely destroyed by fire October 2, 1856. The fire originated about four o'clock in the morning in the store of J. Job, and the flames made such rapid headway that all attempts of the excited people to oppose them were unavailing, and nearly the entire town was laid in ashes. The origin of the fire is uncertain, but some men had been up nearly all night playing cards, and had retired less than an hour before the flames broke out. The town never recovered from this blow, and the mines soon after becoming exhausted, the place was abandoned.

This is William Shaughnessy's eight horse team in Sierra City heading toward Downieville. They're hauling hay from the Sierra Valley, the northernmost part of Highway 49. It was one of many freighters that would haul animal feed as well as food supplies for the early pioneers as well as later residents. The Sierra Valley was, and still is, the bread basket for Northern California & Nevada mining communities.

Chapter 4: Sierra County — Downieville, Goodyear's Bar, Sierra City and vicinity

Sierra County lies in the north-eastern part of the state of California, its entire area being included within the great range of the Sierra Nevadas. The topography of the county, with the exception of Sierra valley, presents a continuous succession of lofty hills and deep cañons, many of the former rising to dizzy heights, and hundreds of the latter sinking into bewildering depths, with precipitous walls of rock and earth. Most of the hills are covered with magnificent coniferous forests of red spruce, balsam fir, cedar, sugar and yellow pine; while the valleys or cañons furnish a rich growth of oak and all the varieties of trees found in the foot-hills of California. Most of the mining towns in Sierra county are situated far above the snow-line, at elevations ranging from three to six thousand feet.

The steep and lofty mountain directly fronting the little village of tents, was so rugged and sudden in its declivity, that wagons could not descend; hence, mules packed with about 200 lbs. of provisions were started ahead, and sometimes, cautious in his step as this animal is known to be, he would miss his foothold, tumble over and over, until he reached the base, and not unfrequently plunge into the river, where the poor beast found rest in death.

S. M. Schaeffer, 1851

We sped merrily onward until nine o'clock, making the old woods echo with song and story and laughter. It seemed to me so funny that we two people should be riding on mules... and, funniest of all, that we were going to live in the Mines! In spite of my gayety, however, I now began to wonder why we did not arrive at our intended lodgings. At every step we were getting higher and higher into the mountains, and even F. was at last compelled to acknowledge that we were lost!

Totally unprepared for such a catastrophe, we had nothing but the blankets of our mules, and a thin quilt in which I had rolled some articles necessary for the journey... I sobbed and cried like and repeatedly declared that I should never live to get to the rancho. F. said afterwards that he began to think I intended to keep my word, for I certainly looked like a dying person.

Every one congratulated us upon not having encountered any Indians, and it is said they would have killed us for our mules and clothes. A few weeks ago a Frenchman and his wife were murdered by them. They generally take women captive, however; and who knows how narrowly I escaped becoming an Indian chieftainess, and feeding for the rest of my life upon roasted ;hoppers, acorns, and)werseeds?

Dame Shirley,
Rich Bar,
September 13, 1851.

Grizzly bears were prolific in Northern California when the early miners and settlers arrived. They were greatly feared and aggressively hunted. Consequently, grizzly bears were killed off entirely in this part of the country. The bear in this photo, however, is not likely a grizzly. His size indicates that he might be of a smaller and less dangerous variety, but that didn't save him from this unfortunate fate.

The water obtained from the numerous mountain streams is of the purest possible quality, being fed by the vast masses of snow melting from the summits. The crystal torrents on every side, dashing and foaming over the rocks, pursuing their serpentine ways through the wild yet always beautiful cañons of the Sierras, rushing with mighty swiftness along their narrow channels and singing the ever-sweet song of rushing waters, are laden with countless numbers of beautiful mountain trout, choice prizes for the eager angler.

The isolated peaks of Sierra county are Table Rock, Saddle Back, Mount Fillmore, Fir Cap, Mount Lola, and the Sierra Buttes. Fir Cap attains an altitude of 6,500 feet, Sierra Buttes 8,950 feet, and Mount Lola, the highest point in the county, about 9,200 feet. The Sierra Buttes mountain is one of the landmarks of the state rendered prominently conspicuous by the sharply-defined, cone-shaped, serrated, basaltic lava in its formation.

The primal cause of the settlement of Sierra county was the desire for gold, almost fabulous amounts of which have been found in many parts. The proportion of agricultural to mineral land is exceedingly small, not one acre in fifty being suitable for the plow.

EARLY HISTORY. The first explorers of this region are not all known. Along the cañon of the North Yuba men were mining as early as the summer of 1849. Philo A. Haven came up the North Yuba early in September, 1849, and at that time found notices of seven different claims posted on Big Rich bar, signed by Hedgepath & Co. He located on Little Rich bar, and was joined by Francis Anderson, who, on the fourteenth of September, found the first gold discovered in the neighborhood of Sierra's capital town. Several other settlements were made within the present confines of the county, either prior to the discoveries on the North Yuba, or simultaneously with them. By November several of them were quite populous camps. A few days prior to Mr. Anderson's discovery at the Forks, he was in Indian valley with John C. Fulton and —— Elliott. There they abandoned their mules, and packed their culinary and mining utensils over to where Mr. Haven was on Little Rich bar with his party. Mr. Anderson went up to the Forks, and discovered gold at a point immediately above where the Jersey bridge at Downieville now stands. The value of the find was not large but it encouraged him to proceed farther up in hopes to discover larger pay. The traces of Indians were apparent everywhere. A tree on Jersey flat was still burning, while a white log lay across the river-on which were a number of deer skulls. Other indica-

In 1854 the bars on the river at Goodyear's were alive with men, and sanguinary quarrels were of almost daily occurrence. The gambling-saloons were generally the pest-houses from, which emanated the bloody crimes, and in one of these a man named Hawkins was killed one day by a Spainard. No sooner had the deed been committed than the murderer was fiercely attacked by the spectators, who cut and hacked him without mercy, causing his death almost instantly. On his body were ten deep knife-wounds.

Hitchcock & Reis Mills, below the Sierra Buttes

Courtesy of the Kentucky Mine Museum

These gentlemen stopped their drinking long enough to get their photo taken. This is a pretty calm scene in this Sierra City saloon.

The fatal quarrel of the two Taylor brothers occasioned some excitement when it occurred. In 1852 they lived in their cabin on the point, seemingly on amicable terms. About noon one day several Indians were seen near the door of the cabin, making violent gesticulations and yelling. The miners working a distance off thought the Indians had been up to some deviltry, and started for the place, ready to take dire vengeance on them, providing anything of a sanguinary character had been perpetrated. In a moment the younger brother emerged, tore open his shirt, and exclaimed, "See what my brother has done," expiring as he fell to the ground. The boys, while sitting at their dinner-table, had quarreled over some trivial matter, when the younger rose to strike the elder, who was a less powerful man. Seizing a long bread-knife from the table, the elder Taylor plunged it into the body of his brother. He was afterwards tried, convicted, and sent to the penitentiary.

tions were seen of a fishing party having been there. Anderson was standing in the water taking out from ten to twenty dollars to a pan, when he heard a loud noise on the hillside, and saw a party of men dressed in various bright colors descending towards him. They were whooping and yelling as they clambered down the steep descent, and Andersen's first impression was that they were Indians thirsting for his gore. Grasping his knife firmly, he determined to sell his life dearly, but was soon pleased to find no necessity for the exercise of his native valor, as they proved to be the Jim Kane party. Rushing down to the river bank, they paid no attention to Anderson but began at once to wash gravel with their rocker. They were very fortunate in their selection of a point to work, for they cleaned up all the rest of that day three hundred dollars to a pan. Anderson went down to Little Rich bar in the evening, full of enthusiasm, and guaranteed to Mr. Haven, if he could wash a hundred pans of dirt in a day with a rocker, $30,000 for his trouble. Of course the result fell far short of his extravagant expectations, the Kane party having at first struck a natural sluice, where the gold had accumulated, but which was worked out in a few hours. Notwithstanding, the yield on the following day, and for several days thereafter, was by no means insignificant. The morning's work for the Kane party on the fifteenth netted $2,800.

Philo A. Haven's account of the finding of gold on Little Rich bar is quite amusing. About the last of August, 1849, while working at Cut Eye Foster's bar, just below and near Indian valley, in Yuba county, he, with his three companions, saw an Indian who had a larger nugget than any they had found. On being asked to tell where he found it the native became exceedingly reticent on the subject; but after much parley, he agreed to point his finger in the direction of the place he had taken it from, in consideration of what he and his son, a half-grown youth, could eat then and there. The bargain being made, enough bread was brought out to supply two meals for the four white men, and as a sort of trimming to the repast, Mr. Haven began frying pancakes. The company soon saw visions of a famine. Even the great American pie-eater would have hung his head in shame had he beheld the delicate mouthfuls and the quantity of food devoured on this occasion. But even an Indian's capacity is limited, and the feast was finally finished, greatly to the relief of the gold-hunters. Then the company awaited with ill-suppressed impatience the performance of the Indian's part of the contract. With great dignity poor Lo arose, and calling the attention of his son to the way he was about to indicate, faced to the bluff, and holding his finger straight out before him, turned completely around, the index digit taking in every point of the compass; after which he sat down with a loud laugh at having so easily sold them. Mr. Haven joined heartily in the laugh, and said it was a good joke, telling the jocose aborigine that he was "heap smart—much too smart for white man"; by which compliments he secured his assent to a bargain to allow his son to show the place; the conditions being that if nuggets the size of small walnuts were found, the Indian was

Miners in a stamp mill, perhaps the Sierra Buttes Mine.

Courtesy of the Kentucky Mine Museum

John Kelley, commonly known as "Kelley the Fiddler," earned his living by scraping a violin. William S. Spear was one of the first members of the Sierra county bar. Both were rollicking, good-hearted men, but unfortunately they became enamored of the same woman; and to decide as to which should enjoy her exclusive favor, and which should furnish a job for the undertaker, a meeting was arranged for. The place selected for the bloody work was on Smith's flat a mile above Downieville. The woman who was at the bottom of the trouble took a position across the river. She wept violently at the prospect of losing one or both of her lovers. The matter was no secret to the public, and a large crowd assembled to witness the spilling of blood. At the appointed signal both fired, neither receiving a scratch. The conditions were that they should continue shooting until one was disabled or called for a cessation of hostilities. Spear immediately recocked his weapon, and took a deliberate aim at his adversary. But Kelley was in hot water; the hammer of his pistol refused to be raised. He tugged and pulled without success, all the time Spear getting his aim down to an exact certainty, and being in no hurry to shoot until he had a bead on his victim. Kelley threw his pistol at Spear. The suspense was over for Spear had dropped his weapon and fled. The spectators caught the frightened duelist and made the parties clasp hands across the bloodless chasm. It is said that the seconds, fearing an accident might occur, had prudently withdrawn the bullets.

Mining is certainly what brought most settlers to this area originally. Their presence required lots of services. Hotels sprang up everywhere like this one in Sierra City. This building also housed the express service, which would transport letters, gold, and people throughout the area. The building still stands but the third floor is gone. For many years it was known as the Busch & Herringlake Building.

...what a lovely sight greeted our enchanted eyes as we stopped on the summit of the hill leading into Rich Bar! ...It was worth the whole wearisome journey--danger from Indians, grizzly bears, sleeping under the stars, and all--to behold this beautiful vision. While I stood breath-less with admiration, a singular sound, and an exclamation of "A rattlesnake!" from F., startled me into common sense again. I gave one look at the reptile, horribly beautiful, like a chain of living opals, as it corkscrewed itself into that peculiar spiral which it is compelled to assume in order to make an attack, and then, fear overcoming curiosity, although I had never seen one of them before, I galloped out of its vicinity as fast as my little mule could carry me.

Dame Shirley,
Rich Bar,
September 13, 1851.

to have one gray blanket; and if only the size of corn or beans, a new blue shirt. The next morning they started up the river. About two o'clock of the second day they arrived opposite what was afterward known as Big Rich bar. Here the Indian pointed to gold lying around, and asked for his recompense. Perceiving Hedgepath & Co.'s notices posted in various places, claiming seven claims of thirty feet each, they said it would not do, and that not a single piece should be touched. He then led the way to the place where he had found the nugget, which was near the edge of the river opposite the place now known as Coyoteville, and pointing to a crevice, said: "Dig, you ketchum here." Mr. Haven soon raked out a piece weighing an ounce and a half. On the same day he located Little Rich bar a little way up the river. The next day he went upon the ridge and saw the Forks, now the site of Downieville. A week after the Hedgepath claims were jumped by several parties. On the Sunday following their location at Little Rich bar, Philo Haven and Carlos Haven, his nephew, strolled up the river and picked up $700 in pieces between their claim and the mouth of the middle fork of the North Branch. While returning to camp, they fell in with a miner who had some jerked venison, and rather than continue on their way that night, they offered the man its weight in gold for a piece of meat weighing eight or nine ounces, which rather liberal offer was summarily refused.

In April, 1858, Major Downie published in the *Sierra Democrat* a series of personal reminiscences of 1849, containing his recollections of his first entry into what is now Sierra county, and his settlement on the present site of Downieville. He and his party arrived at San Francisco June 27, 1849, in the ship *Architect*. He was soon en route for Nye's ranch (Marysville), to which place he and his companions navigated a barge from Benicia. The North Fork being reputed rich in gold-dust they started in search of it, but had great difficulty in finding the stream. At Bullard's bar, on the Yuba, he tarried for some time agitating a rocker, all the time hearing fabulous stories from prospectors of rich finds elsewhere, none of whom would indicate the precise place where wealth could be so easily secured. He finally resolved to go farther up the stream; but those whom he asked to accompany him had not the courage to brave the hardships of the unknown country above. After many disappointments he met with some colored sailors, ten in number, who were willing to go, and also induced an Irish lad, Michael Deverney, to make one of the company. On the 5th of October, 1849, they started. At Slate range a Kanaka, Jim Crow, joined them. The succeeding Sunday was spent with "Cut Eye Foster," who was reputed to be a professional horse-thief, and employed Indians to carry on his nefarious business. His corral was the highest up in the mountains, and many a stray mule found its way into it. However, old Foster is represented by Major Downie as being a very philanthropic, if a dishonest, man.

Courtesy of the Downieville History Museum

Two miners drilling a face in the No. 9 Tunnel of the Sierra Buttes Mine. The Sierra Buttes Mine, best known of all the area mines, operated in Sierra City from the early 1850s until 1937 with a forty-stamp and twenty-stamp mill, producing in excess of $17 million in gold. The date of this photo is unknown, but looks like the early 1900s.

The hill leading into Rich Bar is five miles long, and as steep as you can imagine. Fancy yourself riding for this distance along the edge of a frightful precipice, where, should your mule make a misstep, you would be dashed hundreds of feet into the awful ravine below. Every one ... said that it would be impossible for me to ride down it. I, however, insisted upon going on. About halfway down we came to a level spot, a few feet in extent, covered with sharp slate-stones. Here the girth of my saddle, gave way, and I fell over the right side. I was not in the least hurt, and had the accident happened at any other part of the hill, I must have been dashed into the dim valleys beneath.

F. soon mended the saddle-girth. I mounted my darling little mule, and rode triumphantly into Rich Bar at five o'clock in the evening. The Rich Barians are astonished at my courage. Many of the miners have told me that they dismounted several times while descending it. I, of course, feel very vain of my exploit, and glorify myself accordingly, being particularly careful not to inform my admirers that my courage was the result of the know-nothing, fear-nothing principle; for I was certainly ignorant of the dangers of the passage.

Dame Shirley,
Rich Bar,
September 13, 1851.

"I left Forest City for Downieville. I heard a shot fired. I rode on to where the sound came from, and could see no one. Two men jumped out from the side of the road, with shot-guns, and demanded my money. I went for my revolver, but they shouted 'Don't you draw that; if you do, you are a dead man!' ...they ordered me to dismount, ...two ordered me to follow the mule; when I did not go fast enough they punched me in the back with the muzzle of their guns. They tied the mule, and tied me, too, to a tree. I expected to be killed, for I saw one of them was a Spaniard, and he had a knife at least a foot long, which he flourished around my body. The leader of the gang said he ought to kill me, for he said I was eyeing him until I would know him if I saw him in hell. They took what gold-dust I had, amounting to nearly $5,000.

Two of these robbers were afterwards arrested. George Walker, the captain of the gang, was captured at Sacramento and brought to Downieville. He obtained his freedom by inducing the jailor, Bob Drake, to open his cell door, when he slid out and locked the obliging officer inside. He was afterwards killed near Stockton.

Express Rider

A Forest City gathering in memory of Ulysses S. Grant who died on July 23, 1885. The speaker in the center is Tirey L. Ford, who was the 18th Attorney General of California. Tirey was charged with taking a bribe and later aquitted after a long trial. Later he published a well-received novel, Dawn and the Dons: The Romance of Monterey.

At the Mountain house site the Downie party found the trees blazed to indicate the road to Goodyear's bar; but they kept up the divide, expecting to find the big pieces of gold on higher ground. They camped that night on the north fork of Oregon creek. At Secret cañon they found the first gold since leaving Bullard's bar. They began to think they were nearing nature's treasury, and crossed the river and camped on O'Donnell flat. Here they prospected a day or two, but failed to discover the rich deposits there, afterwards brought to light. Four of them crossed the hill from the flat and saw the deep East Fork cañon below them. Following the ridge, they went towards the Forks. He says:

"When we got to the first island above the Forks the boys insisted on going back. I had my attention turned to the low ridge that divides the North fork from the South. There had already been so much speculation that one did not like to urge his surmises very strongly; so I said but little, yet felt assured that there was a fork of the river just beyond that ridge. I agreed that if the boys would go with me around that point, I would then go back to camp with them. They consented to do so. Turning the point, we saw the forks of North Yuba, which have since become so famous. The spot where the town stands was then the handsomest I have ever seen in the mountains. Long willows waved on the banks of the north fork, small pine and spruce trees stood in beautiful groups where the saloons now stand; the hillsides were covered with pretty oaks, stretching out their strong branches and thick foliage, sheltering the Indian wigwam; and here and there a tall pine towered above everything. But the miner and the trader spared none of these; the willows were uprooted, the pine and spruce were cast out upon the Tuba's current, the branches were lopped from the oaks, and their trunks made heat for sordid slapjacks; the tall pine was laid low, and all was changed."

When they came to the junction of the two streams, they noticed that the water of the north fork was not so clear as the other. An exploration of the upper regions revealed a party at work on a small bar just below the Blue banks. They were very reticent about the diggings; and in answer to a question if they intended to stay long in the mountains, they replied that they "mout stop a spell longer, and then again they moutn't." They seemed to entertain the idea that when their crevice was worked out, gold digging in California would be over with. The remain-

As the miners worked they required more lumber. Some built cabins, but far beyond that need, they built miles of flumes, used timbers in mine tunnels and on ore rail lines, not to mention the commercial buildings that, in many communities, were rebuilt many times over due to fires. This need provided paying work for many a would-be miner who realized that "making their pile" from mining was anything but assured.

Courtesy of the Kentucky Mine Museum

A gentleman came to me and wanted a lot of Christmas goods packed to Downeyville, on the Uba river, about seventy-five miles.

He said choice wines, liquors, cigars, tobacco, and canned goods, and some bar fixtures. I told him I would charge him a dollar a pound, which he agreed to give.

A small mule that was loaded with the bacon lost his footing and fell and commenced rolling over, and before any one could get to him he was rolling so that the boys could not catch him. He rolled on until he went out onto a very large rock that was level on the top and it was ten feet from the edge of the rock to the ground. Just as he had got to the edge of the rock he had almost stopped. There was force enough to carry him over, and he commenced rolling faster and faster till he finally struck the bottom. The pack saddle was so built that it protected the body of a mule. In rolling his head never struck a tree or a rock. We finally reached the bottom without any further accident. I went with one of the boys to the mule. I gave him a lick on the head and spoke to him. He struggled immediately to get up. We assisted him and the little fellow was soon on his feet and we found that there were no limbs broken. We soon got to the store and delivered the goods, nothing being broken. There was a very large crowd of miners around to see that train and all the fine goods come in. They anticipated having a fine time at Christmas. I think that my freight amounted to about $3,000 in gold dust that trip.

Edward Washington McIlhany, 1849

Monday, June 10th. After breakfast at the ''French Restaurant,'' I purchased two pounds of ham for $2 25.--This, with my flour, cooking utensils, mining implements, clothing and bedding, were strapped to my back--a load more fit for a mule than a human being to carry....on we went, and soon found another stupendous mountain in our road, and I began to think if we ascended many more such mountains we would reach the clouds. The change in the temperature was very perceptible; when we arrived at the summit snow was seen ahead of us. Our feelings were not so gay as when we started, but still we endeavored to cheer each other, hoping that ''Gold Lake'' would be reached before long....we began to fear that we had lost our reckoning of the probable latitude of Gold Lake.

We sat down upon the hard frozen snow, and endeavored to study out whether we were going to, or from the coveted lake. Far away over the mountains we could see the lurid smoke arising from the wigwam of the hostile Indian. The only tracks we could perceive were

continued in far right column

Drinking and gambling was a favorite pasttime of miners, loggers and the other early adventurers. It was common that a miner who was doing well in his mining operation would lose his entire "pile" the minute he hit town.

der of the party came up the next day, and they unpacked on Jersey flat. While encamped on Jersey flat Jim Crow one day killed with a small crowbar a salmon-trout which weighed fourteen pounds. It was boiled in the camp kettle, and the major says that afterwards gold was found in the bottom of the kettle. As crevicing was better up the fork, they broke up camp on Jersey flat, and moved up to Zumwalt flat, where each man could make about five ounces a day. A day's work was then three hours and a half. Fourteen ounces a day was no uncommon crevicing. They found gold all along the banks of the north fork, seldom using a shovel, the implements being a butcher-knife, a tin pan, and a crowbar. The party intended to winter on a rough-looking bar up the south fork half a mile.

Eight of the boys started below for provisions, taking all the mules with them, and promising to be back in a few days. Jim Crow went with the party. None of them came back with the necessary commissary stores. The only one who returned was Jim Crow, and he came back in the spring with a number of Kanakas and about five hundred white men, whom he was leading to the rich diggings at the Forks, supposing that the Downie party was frozen or starved to death. The winter was spent at the Forks by the party, who experienced great hardships and privations, both from the weather and the scarcity of food.

Many of those who prospected through the eastern part of Sierra county in 1849 returned to the lower camps in the winter, and told glowing tales of the fortunes to be made there. The substantial sacks of dust and nuggets they displayed convinced the doubting miner that his paltry fifty dollars a day or less could be many times increased by seeking the upper country. When the sunshine and rains of spring had melted the deep snows from the ridges, they poured into Sierra's territory by the hundreds. In 1850 many flourishing and populous camps were formed, some of which still exist as substantial, well-built towns. Among them were Downieville, Goodyear's bar, Forest City, Allegheny, Howland Flat, and Gibsonville. The famous Gold Lake excitement, though disappointing many in their Aladdin expectations, yet served to open up and settle many localities through the vigorous exertions made to discover that supposed valuable sheet of water.

DOWNIEVILLE. John Potter cut the first tree used for building a cabin, which was erected about the last of December, 1849, with the assistance of Kelley and others, at the mouth of the ravine on the north side of town, and came to be known as the Kelley cabin. Another log cabin was immediately built on Jersey flat, by a man named Lord. In January, 1850, Anderson brought B. F. Parks, now of Marysville, and six others, to the Forks, the Kelley and Lord cabins being the only ones there at the time. The population of the Forks upon their arrival consisted of Mr. Marey, with his party of eight men, and Major Downie, with his three companions, a detachment of eight hav-

Sierra County Courthouse, Downieville, built in 1853 and destroyed by fire in 1947. It originally had a porch with columns.

Courtesy of the Kentucky Mine Museum

continued from far left column

the footprints of deer and bears; and each man, but myself, (as I carried no weapon) examined his gun and prepared for the worst.

At length we decided to proceed in a northerly direction, and began the ascent of another mountain; after awhile, on looking up, we thought we saw on the summit the ruins of some old castle or monastery, but when we reached the top of the mountain, we found that what we supposed to be some ancient ruin, was nothing but huge boulders projecting from the highest point of the mountain. We found the valley on the other side, filled to the tops of tall pine trees with snow, and we were puzzled how to proceed, until we finally hit upon the laughable expedient of each man placing his wash pan on the snow, then getting into it, and with a gentle shove, down we went pell mell, over and over, rolling and tumbling, until we reached the base.

Luther Melanchthon Schaeffer,
1851

...about dark we camped on the mountain side half a mile from Downieville.

One of our company came into camp saying, "I reckon somebody has struck it rich down there, and covered up their prospect hole so as to hide it."

With picks, shovels, and pans, three of us accompanied him to the bottom of a deep, wild glen; not that we intended to "jump" any one's claim, but as a possible clue to diggings above and below on this side of the river.

Spading away the soft earth to the depth of about three feet, we found--not a gold mine, but that which made us start back with horror--a blue shirt sleeve on the arm of a corpse. Gently the body was uncovered and raised to the surface; water was brought and, washing away the mire, disclosed the features of a young man, of probably twenty years.

His pockets were empty and there was nothing about him to reveal his name. Traces on each side of his head indicating where a bullet had passed through, were the only marks of violence upon his person. Evidently he had been murdered but a few days since and his body concealed in this wild glen. To use a phrase common among mountaineers, he had been "rubbed out."

Rev John Steele,
Jan. 29 & 30, 1851

Durgan Bridge, Downieville -- the first Durgan bridge was a double A-frame construction. This bridge was destroyed during the flood that occurred December 14-15, 1861. Rebuilt, the new bridge was once again swept out by a flood in February 1881. The next bridge was constructed by the California Bridge Company, in the short space of two weeks, on a contract calling for $3,200. The current bridge replaced one destroyed by the flood in 1937.

ing been sent below in December for provisions. Albert Callis was then with Major Downie, and was suffering from a severe illness which nearly cost him his life. The snow was very deep during January and February, most of the members awaiting idly for its clearance before going to work. Those who employed their time in searching the crevices beneath the snow were generally repaid by making from one to two hundred dollars a day. From the last of February to the middle of March the snow fell in such quantities as to put a stop to the work on all such diggings, the party having no bank claims opened. Not knowing the length of time they would be obliged to wait for a fresh supply of provisions, the men were put on rations. Downie went below and succeeded in obtaining two head of cattle, together with a little rice and a few dried apples. Before the food was entirely consumed, they were relieved by the arrival of a large number of miners fully supplied. The news of the rich diggings spread rapidly, and with the return of spring came great numbers to mine. In February a town was laid out by James Vinyard, and a meeting to christen it was held, sufficient locators being there to require a permanent title. Considerable rivalry existed in regard to the selection of a name. Some favored Marey-ville, while others wished to perpetuate their own names or those of their friends in the camp. It was finally left to Mr. Parks to propose a name, and he suggested Downieville, which obtained unanimous approval. On the same evening the south side was christened Washingtonville, and the flat above, on the south side, Murraysville. In the fall of 1850 James Durgan built the first sawmill in Sierra county, on the south side, and soon that part of the town was called Durgan Flat instead of Washingtonville. The name of Murraysville did not prove popular, and the Jersey company, owning the river claim at that point, invested it during the year with the title of Jersey Flat.

In the early spring Parton opened a store on Jersey Flat, while James Hawkins brought a stock of goods, and sold them in Downieville. The prices were enormous, whisky being sixteen dollars a bottle, and other necessaries bringing worse than "war prices." In April, 1850, the first eating-house was opened by Mrs. Judge Galloway in a large log cabin, and the pioneer meat market owed its origin to Ned Barker soon after. The town grew as if by magic. Hundreds came in every day, without cessation, for weeks. It is estimated that in April not less than five thousand people were at Downieville, coming and going all the time. Numerous stores and saloons were opened in tent houses, the proprietors having no time to indulge in more substantial architecture. Woods soon put up his large hotel, which became the must popular caravansary in that neighborhood.

As early as March a miner's meeting was held, at which thirteen resolutions were passed, forming the laws governing the people in their relations to each other as miners. Claims were fixed at thirty feet to a man. Downieville soon became crowded,

We invested in a four-ounce donkey, that is, we paid four ounces of gold for him, just an ounce apiece for four of us--W. L. Manley, Robert McCloud, Lyman Ross and John Briggs. We piled our blankets in a pack upon the gentle, four-ounce donkey, and added a little tea and coffee, dried beef and bread, then started for the Yuba River, ourselves on foot. We crossed the river at Park's Bar, then went up the ridge by way of Nigger Tent, came down to the river again at Goodyear Bar, then up the stream to Downieville. This town was named after John Downie, a worthless drunkard. I remember that he once reformed, but again back-slid and died a drunkard's death.

William Lewis Manly, 1851

This family's livelihood may have relied on placer mining for many years. They proudly display their "pile." Because of the women and children in this photo it was probably taken in the 1860s or 1870s.

Courtesy of the Kentucky Mine Museum

The roads were in a miserable condition, and occasionally we halted to scrape off the putty like mud which impeded our progress....On we pressed, scaling mountains, crossing valleys and creeks, then ascending high hills, almost exhausted, until at last we came in sight of the ''Mountain House,'' at which place we proposed to spend the night. The ''Mountain House'' was simply a large tent; and the bull dog-visaged landlord, notified the many travelers who had met there, that supper would be ready soon, and all who partook and paid for it, were entitled to spread their blankets under the tent--of course. We all agreed, and about 8 o'clock, supper was announced, which consisted of half baked bread, salt beef, salt fish, and something called coffee--for which each paid two dollars. We spread our blankets on the ground, and expected to have a comfortable night's rest; but the rain descended fast and heavy, and we had to shift about to protect ourselves from the storm.

Luther Melanchthon Schaeffer, 1851

Courtesy of the Kentucky Mine Museum

As necessary as building materials were for mine timbers, houses, flumes and other essentials of the day, logging took a tremendous toll on the area's resources as this massive operation shows the deforested hillsides. Donkey engines supplemented the manpower to get the job done.

and it was with difficulty that the multitudes could secure their board. Of course all the lazy, worthless fellows, who by a little labor could have made fifty dollars a day, protested that all the paying claims were taken, and that the dimensions were too large. Too indolent to perform the labors that others had done, and discover new mines, these malcontents demanded a division of the claims already found and located. But it was not long before hundreds left diggings that paid fifty dollars a day, to search for the famous Gold Lake, and the pressure was removed. They were also drawn away by the discoveries of digging sat Eureka, Howland flat, St. Louis, and other places.

Downieville presented a different aspect then from what it did a year or two later. The great pines that grew down to the water's edge were scarcely touched by the miners, except when they wished to get them out of the way. Myriads of tents covered the flats, in which the rude arts of the pioneer cuisine were practiced in all their primitiveness. S. W. Langton started, in the spring, his express to Marysville, and the arrival of the expressman with letters that cost the homesick miner a dollar apiece was far more anxiously looked for than is the mail-bag in these days of rapid communication, when the score is settled with Uncle Sam at the beginning of the journey.

The building of Mr. Durgan's saw-mill soon altered the appearance of Downieville. The trees began to fall on every side; saw and hammer awakened the echoes; building commenced in real earnest from lumber that cost eighty dollars a thousand at the mill, and carpenters were in demand at sixteen and twenty dollars a day. Gambling and drinking became the prevailing vices, as in all new camps, with their accompaniments of bois-terous music, big, yellow nuggets, and oceans of coin strik-ing the eye and ear at once. Whisky was retailed at four bits a

When you look at the timbers used in the mines themselves as well as their mills (visit the Kentucky Mine in Sierra City for a look), you have to wonder how these ingenious men conquered the forest and milled the monstrous trees they found. It was no small task that these hearty men accomplished.

...one of the party gave out, and we agreed to remain with him. We gathered fire-wood, kindled a fire, and after resting a while, began to feel a disposition for supper; we had no alternative but to roast the acorns we found on the ground, and drink for our tea, water that had, fortunately for us, lodged in a mud hole!

Luther Melanchthon Schaeffer, 1851

Courtesy of the Kentucky Mine Museum

Pack mules in front of St. Charles Hotel, Downieville

"There was an absence of women in 1850, and well on to 1851. There were not half a dozen women in town, white or Spanish. In the fall of 1851 I was mining on Durgan flat, and was in the shaft drifting, when suddenly I heard the most exciting yells and hurras on the surface. My partner at last hallooed down, 'Come up—come up; they are coming.' 'Well, who is it?' 'Why, the women!' All hands knocked off, and soon the flat was alive with men. The trail then was nearly straight down Galloway's hill, and they were in view from town for about an hour. They were four or five of the demi-monde, under the care of the afterwards notorious Rose Cooper; as they neared town it grew dark, and the miners crowded in from up and down the river, cheering and yelling up the crowded main street, till they landed in the Gem saloon. "

George Barton for
the *Messenger*

drink, and was mostly made in the back rooms of the saloons. This explains why there was never a scarcity of whisky in the mountains, even when flour and beans were worth nearly their weight in gold.

The general idea in 1849 was that all the gold must be in the rivers; but in 1850 the rich flats, the deep bars, and the high benches began to be worked with surprising results. Some fluming of the river-bed was done during the year, and in 1851 this kind of mining had become almost a mania. Between Downieville and Goodyear's, a distance of four miles, the river was carried nearly the whole way in flumes, costing an immense amount of money. Though a great deal of gold was taken out, these enterprises, on the whole, failed to supply very large dividends, in consequence of the tremendous losses occasioned by incipient floods. The fluming companies generally were deceived by the holes in the river-bed, which, when pumped out, were often entirely barren. The richest company working on the bars was the Steamboat, on Steamboat bar, which for some weeks in 1851 averaged $5,000 a day. The Virginia company, of which S. B. Davidson was secretary and general manager, had a claim below the mouth of Slug cañon, running down to Steamboat bar were nine in the company. In 1851 their highest day's work produced $2,617, and on the five succeeding days they secured $2,200, $1,659, $1,120, $2,138, and $2,135, consecutively. It was the custom among all the companies to divide the gold every night, thus avoiding complications with defaulting cashiers. The Jersey company, in 1850, had a claim above the present site of the Jersey bridge, embracing the spot, where Frank Anderson had made the first discovery of gold. Twenty persons formed the company in the fall, who worked twenty rockers. Their yield was very gratifying, even in those days, the gold being weighed nightly on the steelyards in the butcher-shop, and divided with even-handed justice. Their harvest ran from twenty to sixty pounds of gold-dust every day. On Durgan flat, Frank Anderson, Charles Lewis, James Irwin, and J. W. Hamilton had a claim sixty feet square. On this they worked eleven days, and took out $12,900, one day's yield amounting to $4,300. Then they sold the precious piece of land to other parties, Anderson's partners going back to the states. The new company did somewhat better, averaging $1,500 per day to each man, working also eleven days. The Bennett boys then took their chances on what remained, and averaged $1,200 per day per man, until they disposed of the property to others. During the six months from the time of opening this claim it passed into several other hands, yielding, in the aggregate, over $80,000. Around Downieville every foot of ground paid rich returns. The Tincup diggings, proved a mint to those who worked them, for a long time. It is said that in 1850 three men always

The duel fought near Brandy City, in September, 1855, between Judge Lippincott and young Tevis, was not so bloodless an affair. Lippincott was interested to some extent in a temperance paper at Downieville, called the Old Oaken Bucket. Tevis belonged to the know-nothing party, of which he was a leader, and was a candidate for district attorney. The dispute that led directly to the meeting was caused by an article from the pen of Lippincott casting reflections on the character of a Mrs. Pellett who was lecturing in the town on temperance. Tevis replied with a sharp letter that greatly exasperated Lippincott. He sent the young man a challenge to fight a duel. The weapons were big, double-barreled shot-guns, loaded with ball. The parties left Downieville for the scene of conflict, and arrived there at daylight. Benjamin Green gave the signal, and at the first fire Tevis fell to the ground a corpse. A piece was shot out of the shoulder of Lippincott's coat. No proceedings were ever entered against him. The body of Tevis was brought to Downieville, where ceremonies [were] conducted by the Good Templars.

Courtesy of the Kentucky Mine Museum

Miners at Sierra Buttes Mines

There has been quite an excitement here for the last week, on account of a successful amputation having been performed As I happen to know all the circumstances of the case, I will relate them to you as illustrative of the frightful accidents to which the gold-seekers are constantly liable, and I can assure you that similar ones happen very often. A stone, unexpectedly rolling from the top of Smith's Hill crushed his leg in the most shocking manner. His physician made every effort to save his shattered limb, but, truly, the Fates seemed against him...

F. was called in to see him. He decided immediately that nothing but an amputation would save him. A universal outcry against it was raised by nearly all the other physicians on the Bar.

They agreed, en masse, that he could live but a few weeks unless the leg--now a mere lump of disease--was taken off.

It was a great responsibility for a young physician to take. Should the patient die during the operation, F.'s professional reputation would, of course, die with him; but he felt it his duty to waive all selfish considerations, and give W. that one chance, feeble as it seemed, for his life. Thank God, the result was most triumphant.

Dame Shirley, September 22, 1851.

There wasn't much entertainment available in the 19th century. "Stag" dances were popular with the miners early on before women were in the area. All they needed was a fiddler. Later, many communities got together bands or small orchestras like the Sierra City Brass Band pictured.

made it a point to fill a tin cup with gold, before quitting work at night, and they didn't wear themselves out at labor either. On a low bar just below, George Barton and party were working. One day they sunk a hole five feet deep, and panned out $2,500 in two hours, consisting of coarse gold that ranged in size from two bits to eleven ounces. In the fall of 1850 the largest piece known to be found on the river was excavated at Gold bluff, two miles above town, on the Sailor claim. It was pure gold, almost round, and weighed twenty-five pounds. Other pieces from the same claim weighed from one to five pounds.

Eight hundred miners were working on Durgan flat in 1851. Durgan erected a little footbridge across the stream to Downieville, and the inhabitants of that section were taxed each four dollars a month for the privilege of walking across it. On the night of February 19, 1852, Downieville was entirely destroyed by fire. There were so many cloth tents and plain board shanties that the fire fiend made quick work of it, and the morning sun shone on a flat waste of ashes. The loss was about $150,000. Houses of a more substantial character soon replaced the old ones. On the following day a great meeting of the inhabitants was held. Robert Keifer, George A. Booth, and another man were appointed to lay off the streets, which they did on the twenty-first. The citizens could not agree at first about the width to make the thoroughfares, but at length, after holding three meetings, in which the matter was fully discussed, it was decided to make the streets forty feet wide. McNulty opened the St. Charles hotel two days after the fire. It was an immense, light frame, covered with cotton, with benches and tables running lengthwise of the structure. On the anniversary of Washington's birthday McNulty took in, for meals alone, $2,600. Craycroft & Co. in a short time put up their immense saloon, which had a counter in it seventy-five feet long, that on many an occasion lightened the purse of the rash individual who called the whole house up to drink, and to whom the long perspective of expectant men waiting to be served at his expense must have been a cheering sight. A brief glance at a few of the business men stationed here in the summer of 1852 may not be inopportune. In the line of dry goods, E. W. Haskell & Brother led the trade; Knapp & Paull kept a variety store; Sam Rosinsquy dealt in boots and shoes; Ferdinand Reis supplied the miners with implements and tools; while William B. Hamblin & Son sold them pots, kettles, and tinware; Hawley, Simmons, & Co. and Thomas Tobin & Co. wholesaled and retailed groceries and liquors; S. Walton & Co. traded general merchandise for gold-dust; A. A. Cochran owned the Sierra drug-store; Green & Shepard worked in precious-stones and metals ; George A. Reynolds bought gold-dust; Dr. B. N. Freeman, Dr. George Chase, Dr. Wilson Carr, and Dr. C. D. Aiken attended to the physical ailments of the camp. The National theater, with J. J. McClosky as manager, supplied Thespian amusements to the pleasure-seekers; while Reverend R. R. Dunlup preached Methodism to the religiously inclined. Among the numerous hotels were the Arcade, kept by A. Wheeler, and the Bridge house,

The whipping of the innocent young man in 1854, at Downieville, for the alleged robbery of sluice-boxes, is related. At Cox's bar, in 1852, a different kind of punishment was given a man for sluice-robbing. He was tied to a tree, with a large board hung around his neck, on which was traced in bold characters the word "thief." All who passed along the road from Downieville to Goodyear's on that day stopped to jeer at the unlucky sign-board. When the shades of night had fallen he was released and given the customary warning.

Pack mules in Downieville

Courtesy of the Bancroft Library, University of California, Berkeley

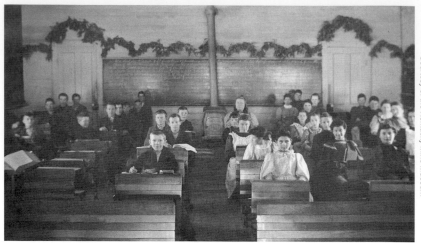

Scholars at the Sierra City schoolhouse, late 1800s.

Company K, sixth regiment California volunteers, had a short time before been recruited in Sierra county, with headquarters at Downieville. By the premature discharge of a cannon fired in honor of the capture of Vicksburg, from the bluffs below town, Lieutenant M. M. Knox and Second Lieutenant William A. Donaldson were horribly mangled and killed. Knox was blown down the declivity two hundred feet, while Donaldson had his eyes blown out, his wrists torn off, and was otherwise mutilated. Military rites were performed over the grave by the National Guard, the Sierra Guards, and the fire companies.

by Mrs. E. Lowry & Co., together with McNulty's and Wood's caravansaries. In 1851 Craycroft & Cheever had built a sawmill above town, which was in operation; and in 1852 Philo A. Haven erected another farther up the East Fork. Haven's flume headed two miles above Downieville, carrying water and lumber right into town. It was a successful enterprise, and is still in existence, the property of Benjamin Pauley, who has owned it a great many years. Mr. Haven sold to John Cummings and John Angle, in 1854. Craycroft & Co. held their mammoth raffle December 31, 1853, for $3,000 in cash, and other property, amounting in all to $55,000.

In 1856 W. H. Ladd & Co. were running a bank in Downieville. The Reis house had passed into the hands of Grippen & Day, and many other changes in business had occurred, among others the establishment of the United States hotel by Nicholson & Pearce. It was at this time that Lola Montez, countess of Landsfelt de Heald, the wonderful spider dancer, made her appearance on the boards of the National theater, creating a profound sensation in the susceptible breasts of the population. She was greeted with crowded house, and so strong was the impression left behind by this Teutonic beauty that her name was immortalized in the christening of a lofty peak, Mount Lola.

Downieville was a second time baptised with fire, on the first day of January, 1858. The flames got beyond the control of the citizens, and swept with remorseless fury over the fated town, destroying everything within their reach. But a vestige remained on the Downieville side of the once sightly and crowded business streets; ghastly ruins stared at the spectator from every side. Many lost all they had in the flames, and some distress was felt; but the neighboring towns came promptly to their relief. The donations received were as follows: Nevada City, $402; Forest City, $318.50; Monte Christo, $315; Alleghany and Smith's flat, $278; Marysville, $221.50; sundry persons, $69.25; whole amount received, $1,604.25. Forest City, in addition to her money contribution, gave twenty-six pairs of blankets.

Downieville rapidly recovered from this blow. The inherent germs of progress were too deeply planted for even such a catastrophe to prove disastrous, and with the resuscitating faculties within her, commonly ascribed to the fabled Phœnix, she could do no less than rise from her own ashes better than before.

In a few years the question of incorporating the city was raised and agitated. It became apparent that the interests of the two flats were closely identified with those of the town itself, from which narrow streams of water should not separate them. These ideas found fruition in an act of the legislature approved March 18, 1863.

In a few years the expense of a city government became irksome to the people; interest in the election of officers began to flag, and finally these elections were discontinued altogether.

An act was passed in March, 1863, establishing a fire department in Downieville, to consist of chief engineer, first and second assistants, president, secretary, treasurer, and a board of

In the vicinity of Forest City, Alleghany, and Chip's flat petty robberies by Chinamen were very frequent during the year. 1865. P. Curry owned a store-house at Chip's, which was broken into several times, and goods stolen. To put a stop to them he employed a man by the name of Newhouse to watch nights and discover who the rascals were. The first morning after assuming the duties of night-watchman, Newhouse was missing. Search was made for him, but without success for a time. In looking through a Chinaman's cabin one day, blood was discovered, which was sufficient to fasten suspicion on the proprietor. He was induced by threats and rough treatment to confess having killed Newhouse, and agreed to tell where the body was. He conducted them to the trail in a ravine, where the remains of poor Newhouse were found to be buried. To facilitate the carrying of the corpse to this place, John had cut it in two, putting a half on each end of his pole. Short work was made of the murderer. A lynch court was immediately organized, a short trial given the prisoner, and he was hung without more ado. Before death had relieved his sufferings, the men began throwing rocks at him, one of which crushed in his skull; and he was otherwise mutilated. After this hanging, the thefts in that vicinity ceased entirely.

Schoolhouse Downieville, 1890.

The following peculiar court opinion is ascribed to a Downieville justice, though to whom the credit belongs of the brilliant decision no one is able to decide. When the county seat had reached its zenith of prosperity, a man began building a house on Jersey flat. Before the work had progressed very far, he was notified by another party not to build, as the ground was his mining claim, and he intended to work it before long. No attention was paid to his warning, and the building was completed. Mining was soon begun near the structure, and day by day the earth was torn away and washed for the precious metal. Steadily the foundations of the house were undermined, until it scarcely could preserve its equilibrium, and the owner ran considerable risk every time he entered it. Matters were now in a suitable shape for a lawsuit; attorneys looking for a job easily induced the house owner to rush into court, and W. S. Spear was retained by the plaintiff. During his argument before the court, he was asked by the judge if he admitted that his client had been notified not to build his house there. "Yes sir," he replied, but unabashed, continued to argue his case. Again the judge interrupted him with,"Mr. Spear, what is the use of all this talk? You have admitted that your client has no redress in law." Still the persistent attorney kept on, and would not be silenced. At last the judge jumped up and blurted out:

"It is the opinion of this court that a mining claim reaches up to heaven and down to hell. Now, Mr. Spear, if you can't get above or below that, please sit down."

Courtesy of the Kentucky Mine Museum

Panorama of Downieville in the 1860s. Photo continued on next page.

delegates of three from each hose company.

Downieville was made a post-office in 1852. A man named Kempton started the first private school in Downieville, in the spring of 1853.

In the flood of February, 1881, the Durgan bridge was swept out. The present bridge was constructed by the California bridge company, in the short space of two weeks, on a contract calling for $3,200.

Downieville is supplied with water by numerous ditches and pipes, owned by five different water companies. S. D. Hill & Son furnish water to Durgan flat by pipes running from the Oro tunnel. Jersey flat is partially supplied by M. H. Mead, who carries the water in pipes from the South fork. S. M. York & Brother's ditch taps the East fork two miles above; while the old Haven flume, owned by J. M. Hall & Co., with John Hughes as agent, commences on the East fork, at Pauley's saw-mill, and supplies Busch's brewery, Chinatown, and a number of residences with what they require. H. Spaulding's flume, which is the main water supply of town, heads at the Good Hope mine, runs a mile in length, and conducts through pipes laid along the streets the quantity necessary for the usages to which it is put. This ditch has been in operation many years. A reservoir on the hill west of town furnishes water to protect the village from fire. On Main street there are six fire-plugs, with a fall sufficient to throw a stream far above the highest buildings. Jersey flat has three plugs, supplied from the ditch of S. M. York & Brother,

Panorama of Downieville in the 1860s.

and Durgan flat owes its protection to the water supply of S. D. Hill & Son. McGuire & Wilbern have a private ditch a mile and a half in length, heading in Hungry Mouth ravine.

Downieville is connected by daily stages with Marysville and with Sierra City. The former route is owned by Dan T. Cole, Warren Green, and John Sharp. The distance is sixty-five miles, and twenty-four horses are in use constantly. Weir & Mead own the route to Sierra City, the distance being twelve miles. The Alta California Telegraph company built a line of telegraph from Nevada City to Downieville in 1855. W. W. Smith, the first operator, was succeeded by A. C. Chapman the same year. A district telegraph system has been in operation for a number of years, connecting several business houses and residences with the court-house. Wells, Fargo, & Co.'s express succeeded that of Langton & Co., in 1866.

The Downieville foundry and machine shop is an important institution, being the only one in the county. Solomon Purdy erected the first foundry, in 1855. Prior to 1860 it was owned and run for several years by Oland & Noble.

The dam across the North fork was built in 1867, at a cost of $3,000, furnishing a splendid water power to propel the machinery. Thirteen thousand dollars were paid at the last sale for the property. Pennsylvania Lehigh coal is used in the furnace, costing forty-four dollars a ton laid down at the foundry. The works were burned in 1869, and again in 1872.

Tom Bell and a companion named Bill Gristy met a traveler going from Downieville to Marysville, and demanded his money. The traveler fired upon them and fled, but was brought down by a bullet in the thigh from Gristy's pistol. After relieving him of his cash, Dr. Hodges dressed the wound, and placed the man in a wagon that happened to come along, telling the teamster to "Drive slow and pick your road," not, however, until he had prospected the driver's pockets and "found color," a clear case of "pocket mining."

There's little left of the vibrant Forest City shown in this 1880 photo. The flags fly proudly for what was likely the Independence Day celebration. The town was originally known as Bald Mountain, hence the name for the Bald Mountain Hotel in the foreground.

The Empire is the only two-story building in town, and absolutely has a live "upstairs." Here you will find two or three glass windows, an unknown luxury in all the other dwellings. It is built of planks of the roughest possible description. The roof, of course, is covered with canvas, which also forms the entire front of the house, on which is painted, in immense capitals, the following imposing letters: "THE EMPIRE!"

Dame Shirley, September 15, 1851

Quartz-mill building and repairing have for a long period been the loading features of the work performed. The two breweries of Downieville make an excellent quality of beer. The amber fluid was first brewed here in 1854, by Borge, who two years after sold his brewery to Scammon & Schultz, and they to John Hupp and another party. Ferdinand Busch bought the property in 1858, and still owns it. The Monte Christo brewery was built in 1861. L. Nessler and Joseph Wackman became the proprietors the same year. The brewery was burned in 1864, involving a loss of $10,000, and a second time was consumed in 1870.

H. Scammon's banking house has been conducted by him since 1866. The principal business houses of Downieville may be enumerated as follows: St. Charles hotel, McDonald hotel, dry goods, B. Latreille, Brilliant & Co., Cohn Brothers; groceries, Spaulding & Mowry, A. Garibaldi, J. M. B. Meroux; hardware, drugs, C. C. Smith, watches and jewelry, furniture, livery stable, butcher-shops, L. Byington, John Coster; blacksmith shops, George Ift, "W". D. Nolan. The town supports a large number of saloons, several of them being elegantly fitted up.

FOREST CITY AND ALLEGHANY. The thriving town of Forest City is very pleasantly situated at the junction of the forks of Oregon creek, seven miles from Downieville, and four from the Mountain House. Diggings were first struck at this place in the summer of 1852, by a company of sailors. The site of the town was then covered with a growth of oaks so dense that the rays of the noonday sun scarcely could find a spot of earth on which to shine. The pedestrian, upon descending the side of the hill, suddenly entered a region of almost perpetual twilight, a cool and shady retreat most welcome during the hot summer months. The settlement rapidly grew to respectable proportions. Among the arrivals of that year was that of Peter Vermoish, who is still a resident of the vicinity. The camp took the name of Brownsville, from one of its locators, by which it was known until the following spring, when, there being at least a thousand residents of the place, it began to be called Elizaville, from the wife of W. S. Davis, now of San Francisco, who had accompanied her husband thither. Mrs. Moody, who came in 1853, originated the name of Forest City.

Charles Heintzen removed from Downieville to this place September 1, 1853. At the time there were several-stores and two hotels. The diggings on the flat paid at the time about an ounce a day clear to the man. There were a good many companies engaged in drift mining, several of which took out great quantities of gold; the best paying among the claims being that of the Live Yankee company. Near it were the Dutch company, the Empire, and the Hawkeye. On the north fork of the creek were the Little Rock company, the Rough and Ready, Can't Get Away, Don Jose, Manhattan, American, and Washington. Among the numbers on the flat were the Great Western, Free

The Mechan home at Forest City in September 1880.

Courtesy of the Kentucky Mine Museum

Coming out of the Bay, a fishing vessel sent a paper on board, which contained the death of Mr. Clay, the well-known American statesman. It also informed us of some duels, in which "General" Denner kills Mr. Gilbert, editor of the "Alta California," a newspaper; Mr. John Morrison kills Mr. Legget of Rich Bar; and W. S. Spear, "Esq.," encounters John Kelly at Marysville, fire three harmless rounds, then withdraw, and bury animosity in friendly "drinks."

"Fatal Duel.--We learn through Wells, Fargo and Co.'s Express, that a duel took place on Tuesday last at Rich Bar, on the North Fork of Feather river, between a Mr. Wm. Legget and Mr. John Morrison. The parties fought with Colt's pistols, at a distance of ten paces.

On the third interchange of shots, Mr. Legget fell mortally wounded, and immediately expired. The cause of the difficulty is not known. None of Mr. Legget's shots took effect."

"Another Duel.--We understand that W. S. Spear, Esq., and John Kelly, two Downievilleans, met the other morning to settle their difficulties before breakfast. Three rounds--nobody hurt. Result--a shake of hands, and toddies for all."

Sir Henry Vere Huntly, 1852

Mr. B., the landlord of the Empire, was a Western farmer who with his wife crossed the plains about two years ago. He settled at a mining station until he removed to Rich Bar. Mrs. B. is a gentle and amiable looking woman, about twenty-five years of age. I will give you a key to her character, which will exhibit it better than weeks of description. She took a nursing babe, eight months old, from her bosom, and left it with two other children, almost infants, to cross the plains in search of gold! When I arrived she was cooking supper for some half a dozen people, while her really pretty boy, who lay kicking furiously in his champagne-basket cradle, and screaming with a six-months-old-baby power, had, that day, completed just two weeks of his earthly pilgrimage. The inconvenience which she suffered during what George Sand calls "the sublime martyrdom of maternity" would appal the wife of the humblest pauper of a New England village.

Dame Shirley,
Rich Bar,
September 15, 1851

The stage line between Downieville and Sierra City, taken in 1908 at Sierra City. Although stage travel was starting to be replaced by autos, it still played an important role in transporating people and goods well into the 20th century. You can see the fire bell standing at the right of the photo.

and Easy, and Girard companies. Like all the early mining camps, Forest City was at first built principally of cloth tents, notwithstanding the profusion of timber.

Forest City rapidly developed and prospered until 1856, when it decayed with the same rapidity, owing to the failure of mining around it, and the formidable rivalry of Alleghany, which drew the population away to the other side of the hill.

The Sierra Democrat was started at Forest City in 1856, by John Platt and W. J. Forbes, but a year after was removed to Downieville.

Prior to 1860 all the transportation of goods and commodities into this region was done with pack-mules. Colonel Platt of the Sierra Turnpike company succeeded in getting a road built from the Mountain House in 1860, aided by contributions from the citizens. This road is invariably passable at all seasons of the year. A line of tri-weekly stages is run by James M. Scott to the Mountain House. The Henness pass road also runs through Forest City to San Juan. In 1872 the town began to revive, in consequence of the heavy mining enterprise in progress under Bald Mountain, and has steadily grown to be the most important mining center in the county. The place is supplied with water from springs to the south-east, owned by

Thomas Ellis, who brings it into town with pipes laid along the principal streets.

At Alleghany the Union quartz-mine was opened in 1862, and the first pay struck in the summer of 1863, when four men in six days took out $11,600. A mill was built in December, after which the first twelve days yielded $37,400, and the week following $9,000. This mine has changed hands several times; in April, 1881, it was sold to a New York company called the Golden Gate Milling and Mining company. The Kentou quartz-mine, now the Harlem, was also located in 1862. At Chip's, the American mine was located in 1857. A mill was put up, but legal complications broke the company. Then J. O. Groves, one of the company, asked leave to invest five hundred dollars more, which was spent in prospecting, and the result was the discovery of the bonanza which has since yielded $250,000 in ore, under the management of Mr. Groves.

GOODYEAR'S BAR. This celebrated old mining camp, one of the first located within the present confines of Sierra county, is picturesquely situated on the North Yuba, four miles below Downieville. Beautiful pine-clad hills surround the place, conspicuous among which is the noble crest of Grizzly peak. In the distance may be seen Saddle Back, Fir Cap, Monte Christo, and many other points of interest alike to the practical miner and the lover of nature. The first inhabitants of Goodyear's bar

Forset City in 1880. Look at the barren hillside and then all the wooden structures. These buildings and homes represent only one of the many voracius needs for lumber in the 19th century.

Courtesy of the Kentucky Mine Museum

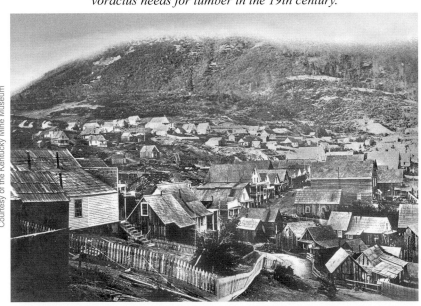

...there are three other women on the Bar. One is called "the Indiana girl," from the name of her pa's hotel, though it must be confessed that the sweet name of girl seems sadly incongruous when applied to such a gigantic piece of humanity. I have a great desire to see her, which will probably not be gratified... But I can say that I have heard her. The far-off roll of her mighty voice, booming through two closed doors and a long entry, added greatly to the severe attack of nervous head-ache under which I was suffering when she called. This gentle crea-ture wears the thickest kind of miner's boots, and has the dainty habit of wiping the dishes on her apron! Last spring she walked to this place, and packed fifty pounds of flour on her back down that awful hill, the snow being five feet deep at the time.

*Dame Shirley,
Rich Bar,
September 15, 1851*

A poor, destitute man was caught in the act of stealing a small article from a store. He was immediately secured, and a crowd quickly gathered around. The first cries were to "hang him," but a suggestion from somebody that he be whipped averted the fatal stroke, and he was taken by his captors to a tree close to town, to which he was tied, with his back bared to the waist. A burly sailor produced an ugly-looking raw-hide, which was applied to the writhing flesh of the victim with an energy that the occasion hardly demanded. The terrible lash rose and fell with even stroke until the regulation number of thirty-nine stripes had been administered, when the master of ceremonies raised his hand and said, "Enough." The ropes were untied that bound the wretched man, and he was ordered to put on his clothes. He was asked:

"Have you any money?"

"No."

"Any more clothes?"

"No."

An ounce of gold-dust was weighed out and given to him, accompanied by the instruction that if he were seen in town that night at ten o'clock he would be hanged. Without reply the man arranged his clothes, took his ounce of gold, and a few minutes after disappeared over the hill.

Courtesy of the Kentucky Mine Museum

Only 30 residents are left in the once thriving Goodyears Bar mining community. It its heyday 3-5,000 men (and a handful of women) mined the river, only 4 miles from Downieville. This building was built in 1864 after a fire distroyed the first structure on the site. The building served as a hotel, stage stop and dance hall. Stages would pass through on the way to Mountain House. As the story goes, Mountain House stages would ring a bell high atop its cliffside perch as stages would leave. The road was so narrow and dangerous that two stages could not pass each other. Stages headed up the mountain had to wait for the coach from Mountain House to go by. This building is still there and currently operating as a bed and breakfast. Photo 1890.

were Miles Goodyear, Andrew Goodyear, Dr. Vaughan, and a Mr. Morrison, who settled here in the late summer of 1849. At that time the hand of man had not molested the beautiful groves of oak and other valley growths that fringed the turgid waters of the Yuba, Rock creek, and Goodyear creek, then dashing their silvery torrents over primeval rocks, or explored the rippling depths where lay the yellow sands so highly prized for ages. The scene was soon changed. Discoveries of rich gold deposits caused others to settle in the neighborhood, who had left the lower diggings and followed up the stream in search of a more rapid road to wealth. Philo Haven, Frank Anderson, and the Downie party passed here during the fall at different times, seeking the North fork.

Great hardships were experienced at Goodyear's bar during the succeeding winter. Food was terribly scarce, and the prospect of famine drove nearly all the pioneers to the lower country to obtain the necessities of existence. Flour was the most needed and the most difficult to procure. Even the nutritious bean, the pioneer's loadstar in all new countries, was not to be had. Famishing parties from other places came to Goodyear's to sate their vigorous appetites, but most had to go away hungry for what their abundance of gold would not buy. What was sold brought the uniform price of four dollars a pound, were it food, tools, or blankets. Before supplies arrived the inhabitants of the bar were compelled to test the unsavoriness of beef bones from a dead animal lying on the bar, and the last bone had been deprived of all animal matter ere relief came. With the return of spring came a great horde of eager miners, and long ere the snows had vanished from the ridges thousands were delving every foot of ground that showed promise of returns. Andrew Goodyear was located on a point, with several Indians who were working for him, and had very rich pay ground. At a meeting of the miners the size of the claims was fixed at thirty feet square. Daniel Cowley, who arrived that spring, was forced to content himself with half a claim, not another spot being vacant. James Golden, now a well-preserved old gentleman of 82 years, arrived at the camp on the thirty-first of March. The buildings were nearly all of canvas. Many of them were called hotels, where a fare rude and plain enough for an anchorite was charged for at the fancy prices which prevailed. A man named Woodruff opened the first regular store, in a log building; other stores were soon run by James Golden and a Mr. Vinyard.

Several rich bars were settled on, above, and below Goodyear's. Two miles below was St. Joe bar, above it was the Nigger Slide, and farther up was Woodville bar, first named Cut-Throat bar, because of a sick German who had cut his own

Stages were the main mode of travel for many years. They were often filled to capacity with people and express shipments and traveled over roads that today, we wouldn't attempt without a 4-wheel drive vehicle. Travel the Mountain House Road (4-wheel drive not necessary) if you'd like a little adventure and tiny taste of stage travel of yesteryear.

Courtesy of the Kentucky Mine Museum

In 1858 a Chinaman was kicked by a mule at Goodyear's bar, in consequence of which injury he dissolved partnership with earth, and was gathered to his antipodal fathers. The great sanhedrim of celestials was immediately convened, and the Chinaman to whom the guilty mule belonged was summoned to appear before that tribunal with his vicious property. The animal was trotted up without saddle or bridle, and after a protracted "chiug-chuug-how-ee-lum," the jury of seventeen Chinamen proceeded to ballot on the question of shooting the long-eared prisoner at the bar, without giving him a chance of speaking in his-own defense. Sanguinary counsels prevailed, and six pistol balls entered the mule's hide; after which his brains were clubbed out. Then it was resolved that the offending member must be cut off; but as mules kick promiscuously with both hind legs, it became a difficult problem as to which hoof should be loppod off. Numerous citations were made from Confucius and other Mongolian authorities, when it was decided that both legs should be amputated, and thereby get a dead sure thing on the mule; which order of the court was faithfully carried out.

Goodyear's bar was the scene of a whipping affair in 1853. A tall, pock-marked Chinaman had been detected in the act of robbing the money-drawer of a butcher-shop of a small amount of stray silver. John D. Seellen, the constable, made the arrest in due form, and Justice Stanwood proceeded to try the case. The Chinaman was easily found guilty, and the punishment devised was fifteen lashes, to be laid on by the constable. Mr. Seellen, who was a gentleman, would much rather have been freed from such an unpleasant duty. Though the tender-hearted officer tried to evade its performance, he was finally forced to comply. The man was tied to a post in front of the St. Charles hotel, and got his whipping, but Seellen laid on the blows as lightly as possible, giving the Chinaman about as severe a lashing as the stage Uncle Tom gets from his master in the theatrical performance of "Uncle Tom's Cabin."

Four miners in Sierra Buttes Mine.

throat there. Ranty Doddler bar and Hoodoo bar were close to town. The origin of the latter name is ascribed to the peculiar enunciation by an Indian of the salutation, "How-dye-do?" rendering it "Hoodoo." Two hundred yards above Goodyear's, a wing-dam was built in the summer by Dr. William Todd, John Scellen, and others. Cox's bar was located two miles above the town. Sickness prevailed at Goodyear's during the fall of 1850, erysipelas becoming an alarming epidemic, from which a large number died. In the winter of that year a log cabin was put up for hospital purposes, and supported by donations from the large-hearted miners. Daniel Cowley was deputed to the office of making the collections for the sick, and many times his leathern purse was packed to the top with freely given gold-dust. Dr. Barkdul, an Ohio man, officiated in the capacity of physician at the hospital.

In 1850 the old ditch that supplies water to the town was built by Colonel T. M. Ramsdell, James Harpman, and John Lake. The water supply was from Rock creek, and the ditch supplied many of the miners with water to work the long toms. The North Yuba tunnel was constructed in 1852, the company being a consolidation of several others. The tunnel was three hundred feet in length, twelve feet wide, and ten feet in height. It cut off a point around which the river flowed, and into it the waters were turned, leaving the bed of the stream dry for some distance. The enterprise was not prolific in returns, paying slender dividends on the investment. Under-the beautiful ranch now owned by H.H. Kennedy numerous tunnels were run, the bed-rock being below the present bed of the river. Several years ago some miners were exploring one of them, when they came across a place that was caved in. Digging through this obstruction they came upon a pool of water from which they obtained a basketful of trout that were adapted by nature for their subterranean abode, having no eyes at all. This curious circumstance shows that in a comparatively short space of time species of the finny tribe can undergo important changes in their physical structure.

In 1852 a dozen well-patronized whisky-shops were in operation at Goodyear's, sufficient indication of a wild and rollicking camp. It was at Goodyear's that Peter Yore made his first lucky find. Having several men working at the north end of Kennedy's ranch, he saw one of them standing over a long torn, holding up his hands and exclaiming, "My God! my God!" He proceeded to the spot, and found that from one wheelbarrow of dirt had been cleaned up two thousand dollars of gold-dust. The news was kept secret from the other miners, and the harvest of dust for some time continued large. In 1852 extensive fluming operations were carried on between Goodyear's and Downieville. Flumes were erected all along the water-course, and with but short breaks here and there, the river was conducted from the latter town, four miles to Goodyear's, on the flumes. Hundreds of miners were working the bed of the river. In Novem-

Hauling timber for the Sierra Buttes Mine in Sierra City. This may have been one of Wm. Shaughnessy's teams.

Courtesy of the Kentucky Mine Museum

Hermitage Rancho,
January 1 st

Downieville is one of the richest mining towns in the State. Upwards of $2,000,000 has been dug there this season by some three or four thousand men. The last 50 miles of the way to Downieville is only a mule trail, no wagons are seen in the streets, everything is packed and yet in this 'hole in the ground' as it is called, you will find two hundred buildings, two saw mills, a theatre and all the necessaries of life and cheap, too, for this country. Downieville is only 20 miles from the summit of the Sierra Nevada which is covered with snow the year round.

Franklin Agustus
Buck, 1852

Harris Freeman's Stage traveled from Sierra City to Blairsdon. High water often brought disaster to a stage, its passengers and cargo. This 1914 photo, taken at Gold Lake, reminds us that stage coaches served us well into the era of the automobile.

The old fiddler who always presided at these strange orgies knew but half a dozen notes of one sickly tune, which he repeated over and over during the long nights of revelry. But when a real "live woman" appeared on the floor, the joy of the miners knew no bounds. Upon the arrival of one in camp, she would be greeted with rousing cheers, throwing up of hats, and a general jubilee.

ber, 1852, heavy rains came on, which raised the stream to a volume greater than the flumes could carry, and they were all swept out. Vast quantities of timber went down the swollen torrent, the puerile strength of man being powerless to overcome the irresistible forces of nature. The losses by these floods were enormous. In 1852 Mr. J. C. Stewart arrived at Goodyear's. At that time the whole flat was covered with houses.

In 1851 George Young came to Goodyear's bar, where he remained a number of years. Stores were then owned by Robinson & Wood, James Golden, Hugh Lynch, and Sam Davis. A hotel was being run by Edward Echstein; the Mansion house was under the supervision of Mr. Wellman, while the Eldorado, about the first of the permanent caravansaries, was managed by James Harpman and John Lake. The saw-mill, as it now [1880] stands, was erected in the summer of 1852. The flume which brings water from Woodruff creek to the mill was first built in 1858, and has been rebuilt once, at a subsequent period.

A post-office was established at Goodyear's in 1852. Langton's express started through this place in 1850. Wells, Fargo, & Co. established an office here in 1858, with John D. Scellen as their first agent. Some years ago the office was discontinued. A private school was first taught at Goodyear's, in 1856, by Mrs. Massey.

The customs of the early days are so often described by able writers that perhaps not more than a casual mention of a few peculiarities is necessary here. The scarcity of the softer sex in the mining camps is a fact so often rehearsed as to be proverbial of the times. In the pioneer dances, impersonations of females for partners were made with the utmost care. Men would don muslin head-gear and tread through the mazy waltz with as much composure and propriety as though they had always played maiden parts on the theater of life; and their rude admirers would cavort and salute with as much suppleness of limb and excessive politeness as they had ever exercised in the more brilliant circles of eastern society where they had formerly moved. In 1852 a celebrated singer came to Goodyear's, accompanied by her husband, who was a gambler. Though dressed in male attire, she did not escape the congratulations invariably vouchsafed to her sex.

Life at Goodyear's bar was not always one of pleasure. Adam's sentence, imposed for disobedience, has been inherited by all his descendants; but to no one was given a larger legacy than to the miner of this region who earned his daily bread by a liberal flow of cranial perspiration. Hard work was the programme of the hour to a large majority of the miners, but the rewards were generally proportionate to the intensity of the labor, and every body made money, and was willing to spend it.

In 1852 people who walked on the road to Downieville noticed, two miles above, at the McGintie place, a horrible stench arising from decaying matter on the bank of the river. Henry Foster saw a piece of canvas close to the river, and descended the bank to obtain it. Lifting it up, he saw a leg protruding; then two human bodies in an advanced state of decomposition were revealed to his astonished gaze. They were well-known Germans, who had been murdered and buried there weeks before. Bullet holes were numerous on their persons, and the head of one was crushed and beaten. Lying around were several Indian arrows, placed there to throw suspicion on a few miserable savages who lived in the neighborhood. The mystery enveloping the death of these men was never cleared; nobody was suspected, and the world heard no more of the affair.

This Sierra City photo was taken in 1906 in front of the Busch & Herringlake Building. The man on the veranda with the white beard is A.C.Busch, the proprietor who also served as sheriff of Sierra County.

Courtesy of the Kentucky Mine Museum

S. W. Langton started his express from Marysville to Downieville in 1850. He delivered letters to [the miners] at the rate of a dollar apiece. In 1853 Mr. J. N. McMillan was on the route from Minnesota to Nevada City, which was considered a very dangerous one, as four men had been killed on the ridge. One day he had about two hundred ounces of gold-dust in the express bags, and after leaving Chip's flat, going down to Kanaka creek, the bags slipped off. He retraced his steps searching for the treasure. He soon saw a man in the act of taking the bags. McMillan dismounted [and] found that the straps of one side were unbuckled, and the contents gone. He told the man that one purse was missing; but the latter claimed to know nothing about it. Being sure that the man had the gold, McMillan proposed that they should go to Chip's together, and let the agents know what had happened. The stranger, who carried a pig in a sack, agreed to this, and they went back. They went on and told their stories. McMillan was put under arrest by the justice, while McGury, the pig man, was allowed to go. A subsequent search revealed the purse hidden which led to the arrest of McGury.

Loggers working their way through the lush forest to satisfy the voracious needs of the rapidly expanding settlements.

Courtesy of the Kentucky Mine Museum

Scenes betokening a not very high civilization were frequently enacted at the bar.

The road was completed that connects Downieville with Goodyear's, Mountain House, and Camptonville, July 4, 1859. The stage came up from Camptonville, decorated profusely with flags and banners, and the horses were decked out in proper colors. This was a great day of rejoicing in the mountains, for it meant the abandonment of the time-honored pack-mule, who had painfully threaded the narrow trails for so many years.

On the fifth of September, 1864, a fire broke out in P. Cody's saloon, which spread rapidly and consumed the business portion of town.

SIERRA CITY. Twelve miles above Downieville, on the south fork of the North Yuba, at the base of the Sierra Buttes mountain, Sierra City is very prettily located. The town owes its origin and present existence, in a large measure, to the proximity of the Great Sierra Buttes quartz-mine, where a large number of men are employed. In the spring of 1850 P. A. Haven and Joseph Zumwalt came over the divide where the great mine is situated, and were about the first white men in this locality. Signs of Indians were plenty along the river, but there were no indications that any crevicing or prospecting for gold had been done prior to this time. Later in the year a settlement was made where the town now stands, and the Sierra Buttes quartz-ledge had been located upon by a man named Murphy and another party whose name is unknown. In 1851 John Lavezzolo settled on Charcoal flat, but removed to his present place in the fall of 1852, his ranch below having been jumped during the year. Locations were made on the Independence lode in 1851, and considerable quartz was soon worked by arrastras. In 1852 twenty arrastras, run by mules, were pulverizing rock in the neighborhood, which, with the numerous tunnels piercing the hill in every direction, caused the employment of a large working force. Sierra City then consisted of two large buildings (one on the site of the Catholic church), a baker shop, and several gambing-houses and saloons. During the succeeding winter the town was entirely demolished by the heavy snows, so much of this element accumulating on the roofs of the frail buildings as to crush them to the ground. Food being exceedingly scarce, everybody went away, and not a soul was left in the embryo village. At this time a snow-slide on an adjacent hill covered up and killed two men who were trying to get away. A third miner named Dillon escaped the fate of his companions, and lives a half mile below the town. For some years matters did not look very promising for a revival of the settlement. Each of the mines had its own little settlement, with its store-house and saloon; and it was not until 1858 that a permanent town got a foothold on the soil now covered by so many pleasant homes and sightly business houses. The discovery of rich diggings on the flat caused a large number to rush to the spot; shanties were erected, and the real inauguration of the village commenced.

Stage from Sierra City to Sierraville, early 1900s

Courtesy of the Kentucky Mine Museum

Just above our camp stood several large dead pines, probably fire killed, but overgrown, from bottom to top, with long, yellow moss. After dark we set this on fire and the flames soon streamed far above the woods, making immense torches, and illuminating our camp; and, as the wood was filled with pitch, they continued to burn most of the night.

After all my companions had lain down to sleep, while writing up my journal, I noticed that one of the burning trees was about to fall, and, fearing it might come down upon the camp, I watched it until there was evidence that it would fall across the rocky slope above us. Therefore, without waking my companions, I spread down my blanket, and was about to join them on our bough-built bunk, when the tree fell; it broke into several pieces on the rocks and one great fiery mass, rolling directly over our bed, stopped against the logs which composed our campfire.

The crash awakened the sleepers, and while they all escaped, there was no time to remove the bedding. However, shaking the coals from the blankets, and changing the boughs to another place, most of them were soon again sleeping soundly.

Rev. John Steele, Jan. 30, 1851

Miners from the Keystone Mine

One enterprising man who was anxious to make money easily, took a notion to try his luck in trade, so, as rats and mice were troublesome in shops and stores, he went down to the valley and brought up a cargo of cats which he disposed of at prices varying from fifty to one hundred dollars each, according to the buyer's fancy.

William Lewis Manly, 1851

In 1855 Doyle & Co. put up a saw-mill at Sierra City, which remained in operation until 1878, when it was washed away by a flood. At the time of its erection there was one solitary log cabin standing back of Peter Goff's present residence. Harry Warner first visited the place at that time, but did not settle here until three years later, when the Buttes, Independence, and Keystone mines were in full blast. Stephen L. Clark came to the Independence mine in 1858; oaks were then growing on the site of Sierra City; Lavezzolo had resumed mining on Charcoal ranch, and also had a potato ranch east of Scott's hotel, where he raised fine tuberous specimens. Lafayette Thompson, uncle of the immortal Philander Doesticks, and the father of that pleasant humorist, built a hotel soon after on ground which is now the Goff place. In 1860 Michael Carrigan and several others built a saw-mill on the flat, which afterwards fell into the hands of John Doyle. One year after Wilcox & Hutchinson put up another hotel on the site of Scott's hotel, which two years after was owned and run by Samuel Williamson. In 1866 Mr. A. C. Busch purchased the property, and for six years it was a popular place of resort under his management. In 1872 Stephen J. Clark and Alexander Black became the possessors. Mr. Black was murdered on the second of November, 1872, a mile above town, by Winchester Doyle, who is serving out a thirty-years term in the state penitentiary for his crime. In 1873 the Yuba Gap hotel, as it was called, was sold to J. A. Scott, who has since run it. The present roomy structure was erected in 1874, the main part of which is three stories in height, and covers an area of 56 feet by 86. With side additions and the back part, Scott's hotel forms one of the largest and best-regulated institutions of the kind in Sierra county.

Miss Hannah Riley, now Mrs. John Scott, started a private school in Sierra City, in the winter of 1863. She had only seven scholars.

A post-office was established at Sierra City in 1865. Wells, Fargo, & Co. established an express office here in 1871. In 1870 the county voted bonds to the amount of $20,000 for the construction of a wagon road from Downieville, through Sierra City, to Sierra valley. Sierra City is connected by a line of daily stages with Downieville, a distance of twelve miles, the route being owned by Weir & Mead; she has communication by tri-weekly stages with Forest City, twenty-five miles distant, under the management of J. F. Mayott; G. H. Abbe runs tri-weekly stages to Sierraville, where connection is made with G. Q. Buxton's line southward, that extends to Truckee, fifty-four miles from Sierra City. A telegraph line from Downieville to Taylorville, via Sierra City, was built in the fall of 1874. To aid in its construction, the people of this town subscribed one thousand dollars, five hundred of which were given by the Sierra Buttes Mining company. Another line runs to Forest City, while telephonic communication is had with the Buttes mine. Mr. Busch is the operator at this point.

Several breweries have at various times been in operation at Sierra City, but the present one, called the Sierra Buttes brewery, was erected in June, 1881, by Casper Joos and William Junkert. In October F. L. Fisher bought out Joos' interest. An

Stage Leaving Sierra City to Sierraville

Courtesy of the Kentucky Mine Museum

The unfortunate killing of Fred Willet happened in Pine Grove, on the first day of January, 1855. A fallen tree having broken in Kavanaugh's house, a large number of Irishmen congregated to assist in setting the place to rights. Opposite to Kavanaugh's was Peter Glenn's hotel, where a man named Mullen lived. Glenn went over, and in the course of the conversation said that his man Mullen could whip Willet, who was among the crowd that had assembled. Willet, being under the influence of liquor, went at once to Glenn's hotel to try his prowess on Mullen, who, being a timid man, refused to fight, and started to go out of the room. Willet intercepted him before he reached the door, when he received a fearful wound in the abdomen from a knife in the hand of Mullen, from which he died on the fourth day afterward. Mullen gave himself up to Squire Hill, at St. Louis, but no one appearing against him, he went away. For his hand in the affair Glenn was arrested soon after, with his wife as an accessory. They were kept in prison at Downieville for nearly a year, when they were liberated by the verdict of a jury exonerating them.

Crossing the summit between Sierra City and Sierraville, winter of 1906.

On a bright Sunday morning in September, 1855, the bodies of five murdered Chinamen were found about a mile from St. Louis, on Slate creek. They were mining in the neighborhood, and lived in a cloth tent. In the night some men had jumped on the side of the tent, and killed three of the poor Chinamen as they lay in their beds, stabbing them through the canvas. Another had been murdered on the outside, while the body of the fifth had been thrown in the mud at the bottom of a prospect hole. The sixth one got away. The Chinamen had a hundred ounces of gold with them, which had been taken. Three Spaniards, who were considered suspicious characters, were arrested and taken before the citizens' court, but there being no evidence tending to show their guilt, they proved an alibi, and got away.

excellent article is manufactured here. The business of Sierra City is considerable, a large section of country drawing its supplies from this place. Dr. J. J. Sawyer, surgeon of the Buttes mine, enjoys a very large practice throughout the county. Two saw-mills are at present in operation: one on the South branch, owned by the South Branch Water Company, is situated a mile and a half above the town; the other is about the same distance and is the property of James Kirby, who erected it in 1872.

MORE FROM THE CRIMINAL ANNALS.

HANGING OF THE SPANISH WOMAN. The Fourth of July, 1851, had been a great day in Downieville. The anniversary of the birth of our republic had been commemorated with grand parades. Those addicted to the use of stimulating beverages—their name was legion—had held high carnival. Later in the night these jolly spirits became mischievous, and some of the rougher sort went around breaking open the doors of houses, among others, attacking the domicile of the ill-fated Juanita, occupied at the time by herself and a man of her own race. In the crowd was Jack Cannon, a Scotchman of magnificent physical strength and herculean proportions. When the hilarious band had broken up, at a very early hour the next morning, Cannon went back to the Mexican house. His purpose in returning thither is of course unknown. Mr. V. C. McMurry, who was probably the only outsider who witnessed the killing of Cannon, states that he saw Cannon go up to the door of the house, inside of which were standing the Mexican and the woman Juanita, and heard him address the latter with the Spanish word for prostitute. She immediately went into a side room, while Cannon, leaning each hand upon a door post, stood directly in the doorway conversing with the man. In a moment she re-entered the hall, with one hand held behind her. Coming rapidly to the front, and passing her companion of the night before, she plunged a long knife with tremendous force into Cannon's breast. Cannon fell dead .

But a moment was required to spread the news far and wide. He was a popular fellow with the crowd. Threats of vengeance came from many a throat, and for safety the woman who had done the deed left her house hastily, and entered Craycroft's saloon, asking for protection. Her movement was noticed. A mob surrounded the place, so as to give her no possible chance of escape. Some one raised the cry, "Hang her!" and the idea met with an instant general approval.

A judge and jury were appointed by those present, together with a lawyer for the "people," and one for the defendant. A young lawyer lately from the states undertook her defense, and right bravely he denounced the act about to be committed. While in the midst of his peroration the barrel on which he stood was kicked from beneath him, hat going one way and spectacles another, while he was flung on the heads of the mob below, and carried a hundred yards before he touched the ground, receiving blows and kicks from all sides. After taking evidence, the jury retired, but returned with a verdict of guilty.

Blacksmiths were perhaps the most critical 'support' service needed in the 19th century. They went far beyond simply shoeing horses and would build and mend wheel rims, tack, and mining equipment.

Courtesy of the Kentucky Mine Museum

Those who worked in these mines during the fall of 1850 were extremely fortunate, but, alas! the monte fiend ruined hundreds. Shall I tell you the fate of the most successful of these gold-hunters? From poor men, they found themselves, at the end of a few weeks, absolutely rich. Elated with their good fortune, seized with a mania for monte, in less than a year these unfortunates, so lately respectable and intelligent, became a pair of drunken gamblers.

*Dame Shirley,
Rich Bar,
September 20, 1851*

In the fall of 1850, when Richard Galloway was alcalde of Downieville, a suit was brought before his court. The parties were a couple of darkies on the one side and several white men on the other. The negroes had located a claim and being industrious, were soon amassing considerable of this world's goods. Their good fortune excited the cupidity of some men, who failed to perceive that a negro had any rights which a white man was bound to respect. So they claimed to have made a prior location of the mining ground. Through the spirit and determination of the darkies they failed in their designs, and the matter was brought into court for adjudication. The court-room was the space included by a spacious canvas tent. A jury was called, and the trial began. The evidence adduced was rather damaging to the cause of the white plaintiffs, who, having been obliged to furnish substantial sacks of dust as security for costs, began to perceive that unless something were done to turn the tide of affairs their wealth would soon swell the plethoric purses of the alcalde and jury. Kind fortune gave them an opportunity. A full hour had passed since the learned judge had partaken of alcoholic stimulants, and he adjourned the court for a drink. So judge, jury, and audience rushed out at the welcome sound, leaving the negroes alone. After reassembling, the plaintiffs brought in a sack of flour, which they proceeded to empty over the heads of their black opponents filling their eyes, nostrils, and wool. Amidst shouts of laughter they left the court-room, and could not be induced to return; in consequence of which, the case was decided against them.

J. G. Rose's Livery Stable in Sierra City.

The woman was taken to her cabin, and given one hour to prepare for death, without a priest. Confronting with an unflinching, steady gaze the angry crowd surrounding her, she sat the whole time; when, her hour being up, she was called forth, and passed fearlessly down the street, chatting and smiling with as much ease as any one there. From the top of the Jersey bridge a rope dangled over the side, while beneath it a timber six inches wide was lashed to the bridge, and swung out above the stream. Three thousand excited spectators were present, many of whom now live to tell the tale. On the plank she stood, quietly surveying the crowd. Perceiving a friend, she took off her Panama hat, and gracefully flung it to him, bidding him good by in Spanish. She took the rope in her own hands, placed it about her neck, and adjusted it beneath her beautiful black hair with her own fingers. A white handkerchief was thrown over her face, her hands tied behind her, and at each end of the plank, ax in hand, stood a man ready to cut the lashings. Another fired a pistol as a signal, and the axes fell. She dropped three or four feet, meeting death with scarcely a struggle.

SHOOTING OF THADDEUS PURDY. In the fall of 1853, a gambler named Muntz and a miner, "Baltimore Jack" quarreled over a game of cards at Foster City. Muntz wounded Jack dangerously with a knife, and hastened to Downieville to give himself up to the sheriff. The present court-house and jail were not finished, and Sheriff William Ford placed him, with a guard, up-stairs in Craycroft's building. Jack had lived in Downieville, and was a gay, frolicking, social kind of fellow, a good singer, and had warm friends among a certain class. On the night of Muntz's arrival, Baltimore Jack had died. His friends were determined to lynch the gambler; and on the following day a great number started for Downieville, bent on this purpose. The first intimation the town had of the coming storm was a dark, moving mass of men on the trail, coming down Galloway's hill; there must have been two or three hundred, armed with great clubs, knives, and revolvers. Twenty gamblers and several officers defended the stairs as the surging, angry crowd surrounded the building. The miners were furious, and frequent shouts of "Let's drive the d——d gamblers out of town," were heard on every side. That portion of the body politic began to tremble as much for their own safety as for the life of their prisoner. Among the objectionable characters at the head of the stairs was one Cheever. Philo A. Haven stood at the bottom, and Thaddeus Purdy, then district attorney, about half-way up. Perceiving the trouble likely to ensue, Mr. Haven said that Cheever had better come down and let a miner take his place. At this juncture some of the miners crowded up the stairs, when a pistol was fired from above, and Purdy dropped, mortally wounded. Somebody raised the cry, "It is an accident," which served to quell the fury of the mob. A vague stillness followed the report; the loud voices fell to a lower tone as they carried Purdy to the center of the saloon, and friends stood by helpless to assist him in his death agony. In a few minutes all was over for him on earth, and tears coursed down many a rough cheek, from even some of the mob that had caused all the disturbance.

In the early years woman were extremely scarce in the area. This photo was taken probably in the late 1890s. These men and women were clearly visitors to the Sierra Buttes Mine. A mule train awaits a trip into the tunnel for more ore.

The big saloon was owned by John Craycroft, formerly a mate on a Mississippi River steamboat, who gained most of his money by marrying a Spanish woman and making her a silent partner.

During the summer Kelley the fiddler came up in the mines to make a raise, and Craycroft made him a pulpit about ten feet above the floor in his saloon, having him to play nights and Sundays at twenty dollars per day. He was a big uneducated Irishman, who could neither read nor write, but he played and sang and talked the rich Irish brogue, all of which brought many customers to the bar. In the saloon could be seen all sorts of people dealing different games, and some were said to be preachers. Kelley staid here as long as he could live on his salary, and left town much in debt, for whiskey and cards got all his money.

William Lewis Manly, 1851

Courtesy of the Kentucky Mine Museum

The Outcasts of Poker Flat [Excerpt]

It [Poker Flat] was experiencing a spasm of virtuous reaction, quite as lawless and ungovernable as any of the acts that had provoked it. A secret committee had determined to rid the town of all improper persons. This was done permanently in regard of two men who were then hanging from the boughs of a sycamore in the gulch, and temporarily in the banishment of certain other objectionable characters. I regret to say that some of these were ladies. It is but due to the sex, however, to state that their impropriety was professional, and it was only in such easily established standards of evil that Poker Flat ventured to sit in judgment.

Mr. Oakhurst was right in supposing that he was included in this category. A few of the committee had urged hanging him as a possible example, and a sure method of reimbursing themselves from his pockets of the sums he had won from them. "It's agin justice," said Jim Wheeler, "to let this yer young man from Roaring Camp--an entire stranger--carry away our money."

A body of armed men accompanied the deported wickedness of Poker Flat to the outskirts of the settlement. Besides Mr. Oakhurst, who was known to be a coolly desperate man, and for whose intimidation the armed escort was intended, the expatriated party consisted of a young woman familiarly known as the "Duchess;" another, who had won the title of "Mother

continued in far right column

Crossing Yuba Summit from Sierra City to Sattley in the winter of 1908.

A POKER FLAT FIASCO. According to the entertaining narrative of Bret Harte, entitled "The Outcasts of Poker Flat," this place was once the scene of a triple hanging; but the charge is indignantly denied by all who have lived in those classic precincts, and we must sadly deposit this story on the shelf in the liar's corner. But Poker flat has not always sustained her present good behavior. From a choice collection we select one little circumstance that happened on the tenth of January, 1859.

John Burk and Jimmy Lyons were eating supper at Kelly's, when the latter, finishing first, took the former's pipe and began to smoke it. Burk became offended at this familiarity, protesting in no very elegant terms at the other's impudence. Burk drew a butcher-knife and stabbed Lyons to the heart. It looked as though Burk would furnish a disagreeable duty for the sheriff to perform, considering the cold-bloodedness of the crime. Edwin Irwin was sheriff and Sawyer Clapp under-sheriff, at the time. A letter was received from relatives of the prisoner, offering Clapp a large sum if he would enable Burk to escape. The trial occurred in August, when Burk was found guilty of murder in the second degree, and sentenced to the state prison for a term of twelve years. In April, 1863, Burk was convicted of murder in Nevada county, and hung.

HANGING OF THE INDIAN PIJO. The first legal hanging in Sierra county occurred on the sixteenth of September, 1853, and an Indian named Pijo has the honor of being the candidate on that occasion. On the thirtieth of May three Chinamen were at work on Cañon creek, in Indian valley, when they were surprised by a band of Indians from the Middle Yuba, consisting of twenty or more, and two of the foreigners were slaughtered, the third making good his escape. Some time after, Chung Chong, the survivor, came to the ranch of S. H. Cook and told him about the occurrence. Cook immediately went to the spot, in company with several Americans and Chinamen, but failed to find the bodies. Chung said he saw an Indian, who had an ugly scar on his lip, kill the two Chinamen on the road, and was certain he could identify him. Charles Stanwood, justice of the peace at Goodyear's bar, issued a warrant for the arrest of the murderer, and three days after a party went in pursuit of him. With the help of a friendly savage, Pijo was caught at Cold Spring ranch, his own chief pointing him out as the man, forty Indians being present. Pijo was dragged to the house, tied to a post, and by threats of hanging was induced to disclose the burial place of his victims. His knife was taken away, and he led his captors to the scene of the murder, where he pointed them out. Upon their return to Cook's house, the Chinamen took Pijo, and would have hung him, "Mel-ikee fashion," to a neighboring oak, had he not been rescued from their hands.

The grand jury found an indictment for murder against him, July 20, 1853. William J. Ford was at that time sheriff of the county. Not being a man of very strong nerves, he dreaded the performance of his official duty, and as the day approached he shrunk from it. However, he found no difficulty in shirking the work, for a man with an itching palm volunteered to hang Pijo for fifty dollars. The Indian paid the penalty of his crimes on the scaffold which had been erected up the South Fork.

Sierra City family poses for a photo.

Courtesy of the Kentucky Mine Museum

Shipton;" and "Uncle Billy," a suspected sluice-robber and confirmed drunkard.

...A horseman slowly ascended the trail. In the fresh, open face of the newcomer Mr. Oakhurst recognized Tom Simson, otherwise known as the "Innocent" of Sandy Bar. He had met him some months before over a "little game," and had, with perfect equanimity, won the entire fortune--amounting to some forty dollars--of that guileless youth. After the game was finished, Mr. Oakhurst drew the youthful speculator behind the door and thus addressed him: "Tommy, you're a good little man, but you can't gamble worth a cent. Don't try it over again." He then handed him his money back, pushed him gently from the room, and so made a devoted slave of Tom Simson. There was a remembrance of this in his boyish and enthusiastic greeting of Mr. Oakhurst. He had started, he said, to go to Poker Flat to seek his fortune.

...He excused himself to the Innocent by saying that he had "often been a week without sleep." "Doing what?" asked Tom. "Poker!" replied Oakhurst, sententiously; "when a man gets a streak of luck,--nigger luck--he don't get tired. The luck gives in first. Luck," continued the gambler, reflectively, "is a mighty queer thing. All you know about it for certain is that it's bound to change. And it's finding out when it's going to change that makes you. We've had a streak of bad luck since we left Poker Flat--you come along, and slap you get into it, too.

continued next page far left column

...with small food and much of Homer and the accordion, a week passed over the heads of the outcasts. The sun again forsook them, and again from leaden skies the snowflakes were sifted over the land. Day by day closer around them drew the snowy circle, until at last they looked from their prison over drifted walls of dazzling white that towered twenty feet above their heads. It became more and more difficult to replenish their fires, even from the fallen trees beside them, now half-hidden in the drifts. And yet no one complained. The lovers turned from the dreary prospect and looked into each other's eyes, and were happy. Mr. Oakhurst settled himself coolly to the losing game before him. The Duchess, more cheerful than she had been, assumed the care of Piney. Only Mother Shipton--once the strongest of the party--seemed to sicken and fade. At midnight on the tenth day she called Oakhurst to her side. "I'm going," she said, in a voice of querulous weakness, "but don't say anything about it. Don't waken the kids. Take the bundle from under my head and open it." Mr. Oakhurst did so. It contained Mother Shipton's rations for the last week, untouched.

"Give 'em to the child," she said, pointing to the sleeping Piney. "You've starved yourself," said the gambler. "That's what they call it," said the woman, querulously, as she lay down again and, turning her face to the wall, passed quietly away.

Bret Harte, 1868

This gallows was built in 1885 and used once for the execution of 20-year-old James O'Neill for murder. It's still standing near the courthouse as California State Historical Marker number 971.

HANGING OF HARLOW. Mordecai E. Harlow, for the murder of a man named Smith, committed October 12, 1854, at Rabbit Creek was hung in Slug cañon about eighteen months after. Harlow was known to be an utterly unscrupulous and a dangerous man, and withal a very cunning thief. In 1858 the good citizens of Goodyear's bar had proved a theft on him, and in addition to the administering of a severe castigation, he was branded with the letter "T" on his cheek. Harlow and the wife of Smith, at Rabbit Creek, had formed an intimacy not altogether consistent with the laws of society, which improper connection is supposed to have led to the murder of Smith, for the purpose of getting him out of the way. On the day alluded to, Harlow and Smith were chopping trees in the woods, when the former split the latter's head open with an axe. The wife was suspected of conniving at the murder of her husband. A sentence of death was pronounced by Judge Searles.

The job was not performed very artistically. At the first drop the rope stretched so much that the victim's feet touched the ground. Immediately several strong hands grasped the rope and hauled the writhing burden to a more elevated position, where he died in a few moments.

Epilogue

The discovery of gold and the consequent rush of people to Coloma deprived J. W. Marshall, the discoverer of gold, of his right to land. It would be no more than right and just that he should receive some reward due him for the discovery of gold.

The first idea of recognizing the obligation of the State to give some aid to Marshall, was brought up in the State Legislature, in session of 1860 to 1861. This bill, however, was killed.

James Marshall (1810-1885). Marshall was born in 1810 in New Jersey and took up his father's trade as a skilled carpenter and wheelwright. At age eighteen he decided to head west, settling as a farmer near Fort Leavenworth, Kansas for a time then joining a wagon train for California in 1844. In July of 1845, Marshall arrived at the Sacramento River settlement run by John Sutter, who employed him as a carpenter. He joined forces with John C. Fremont early in 1846 to stage the Bear Flag Revolt. He served in Fremont's California Battalion, then returned to the Sacramento Valley to find that his cattle had been stolen. Forced by financial necessity to sell his ranch, Marshall formed a partnership with John Sutter to construct a sawmill along the American River, agreeing to operate the mill in return for a portion of the lumber. On January 24, 1848, Marshall looked down through the clear water and saw gold.

Courtesy of the Bancroft Library, University of California, Berkeley

Saml Kyburg errected or established the first Hotel in the fort in the larger building, and made a great deal of Money. A great Many traders deposited a great deal of goods in my Store (an Indian was the Key Keeper and performed very well). Afterwards every little Shanty became a Warehouse and Store; the fort was then a veritable Bazaar. As white people would not be employed at the Time I had a few good Indians attending to the Ferry boat, and every night came up, and delivered the received Money for ferryage to me, after deduction for a few bottles of brandy, for the whole of them. Perhaps some white people at the time would not have acted so honestly.

John Sutter, May 21, 1848

The first party of Mormons, employed by me left for washing and digging Gold and very soon all followed, and left me only the sick and the lame behind. And at this time I could say that every body left me from the Clerk to the Cook. What for great Damages I had to suffer in my tannery which was just doing a profitable and extensive business, and the Vatts was left filled and a quantity of half finished leather was spoiled, likewise a large quantity of raw hides collected by the farmers and of my own killing. The same thing was in every branch of business which I carried on at the time. I began to harvest my wheat, while others was digging and washing Gold, but even the Indians could not be kept longer at Work. They was impatient to run to the mine, and other Indians had informed them of the Gold and its Value; and so I had to leave more as 2/3 of my harvest in the fields.

John Sutter, April 7, 1848

Again, in the Spring of 1870, the following call made the circuit of the press: "J. W. Marshall, the discoverer of gold in California is living at a place called Kelsey, El Dorado county, in this State. He is old and poor, and so feeble that he is compelled to work for his board and clothes, being unable to earn more." But meagerly was this call responded, nothing was done on the side of the State.

The San Francisco Pioneers, in 1873, petitioned the State Legislature for a pension for Captain Sutter, with the result that $250 per month, as a pension, were paid to the latter out of the State Treasury; while Marshall, petitioning at the same time in his own behalf, running out of money became pennyless, and the Pioneer Society of Sacramento forwarded him one hundred dollars.

A bill for the aid of Marshall was introduced in the Senate, in session 1877 to 1878. This bill allowed James W. Marshall the sum of one hundred dollars per month for a period of two years.

These two years have expired a long time, but other steps for his relief have not been made since, as far as we know, and Marshall, when we saw him last, was still walking straight and upright, apparently promising to outlive many a younger man.

John Augustus Sutter (1803-1880). John Sutter saw his immense wealth and power overrun in California's Gold Rush. Sutter was born John Augustus Sutter in Baden, Germany, though his parents had originally come from Switzerland. In 1834 he decided to try his fortunes in America and set sail for New York. There he decided that the West offered him the best opportunity for success. After three years in Missouri

as a trader on the Santa Fe Trail. He then set off along the Oregon Trail, arriving at Fort Vancouver in hopes of finding a ship that would take him to San Francisco Bay. His journey involved detours to the Hawaiian Islands and to a Russian colony at Sitka, Alaska, but Sutter made the most of his wanderings by trading advantageously along the way. When he finally arrived in California in 1839, Sutter established a settlement along the Sacramento River. Sutter was granted nearly fifty thousand acres and authorized "to represent in the Establishment of New Helvetia [Sutter's Swiss-inspired name for his colony] all the laws of the country, to function as political authority and dispenser of justice, in order to prevent the robberies committed by adventurers from the United States, to stop the invasion of savage Indians and the hunting and trapping by companies from the Columbia."

Ironically, as headquarters for his domain, Sutter chose a site on what he named the American River, at its junction with the Sacramento River and near the site of present day Sacramento. Here he built Sutter's Fort. Two years later, in 1841, Sutter expanded his settlement when the Russians abandoned Fort Ross, their outpost north of San Francisco and sold it to him for thirty thousand dollars. Paying with a note he never honored, Sutter practically dismantled the fort and moved its equipment, livestock and buildings to the Sacramento Valley.

Sutter had achieved a success he long dreamed of: acres of grain, orchards, a herd of thirteen thousand cattle, even two acres of Castile roses. His son came to share in his prosperity in 1844 and the rest of his family soon followed. Sutter's Fort became a regular stop for the increasing number of Americans venturing into California.

Then, on the morning of January 24, 1848, James Marshall discovered gold at Sutter's Mill in Coloma. Marshall took his discovery to Sutter and within a few months the gold rush was on.

Suddenly all of Sutter's workmen abandoned him to seek their fortune in the gold fields. Squatters swarmed over his land, destroying crops and butchering his herds. "There is a saying that men will steal everything but a milestone and a millstone," Sutter later recalled; "They stole my millstones." By 1852, New Helvetia had been devastated and Sutter was bankrupt. He spent the rest of his life seeking compensation for his losses from the state and federal governments, and died disappointed on a trip to Washington, D.C. in 1880.

The travelling to the Mines was increasing from day to day, and no more Notice was taken, as the people arrived from South America, Mexico, Sandwich Islands, Oregon, etc. All the Ships Crews, and Soldiers deserted.

John Sutter, May 25, 1848

WILL BE EXHIBITED
FOR ONE DAY ONLY!

AT THE STOCKTON HOUSE!
THIS DAY, AUG. 12, FROM 9 A. M., UNTIL 6, P. M.

THE HEAD
Of the renowned Bandit!

JOAQUIN!
AND THE

HAND OF THREE FINGERED JACK!
THE NOTORIOUS ROBBER AND MURDERER.

"JOAQUIN" and "THREE-FINGERED JACK" were captured by the *State Rangers*, under the command of Capt. Harry Love, at the Arroya Cantina, July 24th. No reasonable doubt can be entertained in regard to the identification of the head now on exhibition, as being that of the notorious robber, *Joaquin Murietta*, as it has been recognised by hundreds of persons who have formerly seen him.

Bibliography

BOOKS & JOURNALS

Sioli, Paolo *Historical Souvenir of El Dorado County California*, 1883

Thompson & West, *History of Nevada County*, 1880

Thompson & West, *History of Placer County*, 1882

Thompson & West, *History of Sierra County*, 1882

INDIVIDUALS.

AVERY, BENJAMIN PARKE (1828-1875) was a New York journalist who emigrated to California. He became part owner of the *Marysville Appeal* in the 1850s and later published a newspaper in San Francisco and served as state printer. Californian pictures in prose and verse (1878) contains his "word-sketches," which are largely confined to California scenery, although some picture Native Americans and miners whom he knew when he prospected on the Trinity River in 1850 as well as the city of San Francisco.

BUCK, FRANKLIN AGUSTUS (1826-1909) A native of Maine, was working in New York City when he heard of the gold strikes and set out for California in January 1849. A Yankee trader in the gold rush (1930) contains Buck's letters to his sister in Maine. They chronicle his first dozen years in the West: a voyage round the Horn to San Francisco; prospecting and storekeeping in various gold camps and the towns of Sacramento, Downieville, North Fork, Marysville, and Weaverville; and a trading voyage to Tahiti and Hawaii. Politics interest Buck, and he pays close attention to the issues in the 1852 election, local secessionist debate, and the impact of the Civil War. In the 1860s, Buck turns to agriculture, raising fruit and cattle at farms in Weaverville, Oakville, and Red Bluffs. Discoveries of silver lead him back to mining at Treasure City, Meadow Valley, and Pioche, Nevada.

BUFFUM, EDWARD GOULD (1820-1867), a New York journalist, came to California as an officer in the 7th Regiment of N.Y. Volunteers during the Mexican War. He stayed on to seek gold and edit a California newspaper before returning east to become Paris correspondent of the New York Herald. Six months in the gold mines (1850) is Buffum's vivid account of his regiment's voyage west in 1846 to help secure California for the United States. He describes his discharge from the army in Monterey and his subsequent adventures as a gold seeker, sailing up the Sacramento to reach the Sierra Nevadas above Sutter's Fort. He describes prospecting along the Bear and Yuba Rivers, Weber Creek, and Middle and South Forks of the American River, Foster's Bar, and Weaver's Creek, 1848-1849. He concludes with the story of his work for Alta California in San Francisco and the growth of San Francisco.

BURNETT, PETER HARDEMAN (1807-1895) spent his early years in Tennessee and Missouri, serving as a district attorney in the latter state. In 1843 he joined an emigrant party bound for Oregon, where he became a prominent and controversial lawyer, judge, and politician in the new territory. In 1848, he went to California in search of gold and soon became a business and political leader of that territory. Recollections and opinions of an old pioneer (1880) contains Burnett's recollections of his early life in Missouri, his career in Oregon, and his decision to join a wagon train to California in the summer of 1848. There he seeks gold for six months before resuming the practice of law and the pursuit of politics. Elected a judge in August and governor in December 1849. Burnette resigned as governor on January 8, 1851 "as a result of certain personal prejudices." Coming from a slave state, Burnett argued that black immigrants should simply be barred from entering the state. Burnett turned to the practice of law in the 1850s and the business of banking in the 1860s. He touches on his various professional pursuits and his home life in Sacramento.

CLAPPE, LOUISE AMELIA KNAPP SMITH wrote the Shirley letters from California mines in 1851-52; being a series of twenty-three letters from Dame Shirley to her sister in Massachusetts.

CLEMENS, SAMUEL LANGHORNE (1835-1910), better known as "Mark Twain," left Missouri in 1861 to work with his brother, the newly appointed Secretary of the Nevada Territory. Once settled in Nevada, Clemens fell victim to gold fever and went to the Humboldt mines. When prospecting lost its attractions, Clemens found work as a reporter in Virginia City. In 1864, Clemens moved to California and worked as a reporter in San Francisco. It was there that he began to establish a nationwide reputation as a humorist. *Roughing It* (1891), first published in 1872, is his account of his adventures in the Far West. He devotes twenty chapters to the overland journey by boat and stagecoach to Carson City, including several chapters on the Mormons. Next come chronicles of mining life and local politics and crime in Virginia City and San Francisco and even a junket to the Hawaiian Islands. The book closes with his return to San Francisco and his introduction to the lecture circuit. Regarding some of the clips from the *Territorial Enterprise*, Twain writes for a monthly magazine, *The Galaxy*: "...I certainly did not desire to deceive anybody. I had not the remotest desire to play upon any one's confidence with a practical joke, for he is a pitiful creature indeed who will degrade the dignity of his humanity to the contriving of the witless inventions that go by that name. I purposely wrote the thing as absurdly and as extravagantly as it could be written, in order to be sure and not mislead..."

DAME SHIRLEY, see Clappe, Louise Amelia Knapp Smith

HARTE, BRET (1836-1902) was born in Albany, New York. By the age of eleven, Bret had published a number of poems. Bret had become a self-supporting young man at age fifteen. In late 1854, Bret and his sister joined the family in California. They traveled by steamship to California, encountering storms at sea, revolutions, and shipwreck. These experiences helped to color Harte's later writings. Harte's first years in California were not easy ones. He thought of himself as a failure but finally went to work as a printer for the Northern Californian. He related well to the many characters who made up the new culture of the West. His colorful stories about the West made California famous. During the Civil War, Harte wrote twenty-two poems and he made an outstanding contribution to the Overland Monthly, founded in 1868 with Harte as its editor. Two of his most memorable pieces were published in this magazine, "The Luck of Roaring Camp" and "The Outcasts of Poker Flat".

HUNTLEY, SIR HENRY VERE (1795-1864) was a British naval officer and colonial administrator. *California: its gold and its inhabitants* (1856) contains his experiences in California in 1852 as the San Francisco-based representative of a British gold quartz-mining company. He describes business and social life in San Francisco as well as visits to Marysville and Sacramento and two months at Placerville supervising large-scale mechanized mining operations. Special attention is given to shipping news, crime and violence and political corruption and disasters such as the Marysville flood and Sacramento fire.

JOHNSON, THEODORE TAYLOR of New Jersey sailed to California in February 1849 and had returned home by the end of June. Sights in the gold region (1849) is the first published book to relate authentic personal experiences in the California gold fields. Johnson describes his voyage to California and Panama crossing and prospecting in the Culomma Valley. He also writes of his return to San Francisco in the hope of finding work at the end of spring and his discouraged decision to take passage home, again crossing the Isthmus again at Chagres. Personal recollections are fleshed out with second hand discussions of the state's history and culture.

KELLY, WILLIAM REDMOND (1791-1855), an Englishman visited California in 1849 and 1850, and his account of that trip was widely read. An excursion to California (1851) is the two-volume account of that journey. The second volume was published separately the next year as "A stroll through the diggings of California." Here Kelly describes gold prospecting and life in mining camps on the Sacramento River and Rock, Middle, and Salt Creeks as well as visits to Sacramento, San José, and San Francisco. Throughout, he offers details of daily life and work and observations on native ethnic groups and European immigrants.

KIP, WILLIAM INGRAHAM (1811-1893) left New York in December 1853 to become Missionary Bishop and later the first Diocesan Bishop of the Protestant Episcopal Church for California. The early days of my episcopate (1892) contains reminiscences of his rectorship of Grace Church, San Francisco; visits to Sacraments, Stockton, San José, Monterey, Benecia, and Los Angeles; experiences in mining camps in Marysville, Grass Valley, and Nevada; and the history of church politics and rivalries.

KNOWER, DANIEL (b. ca. 1818) an Albany, New York, physician, sailed for California in 1849 with twelve prefabricated frame houses for the San Francisco market. *The adventures of a forty-niner* (1894) describes Knower's business and real estate speculations in San Francisco as well as an extended visit to a mining camp near Coloma and the life of prospectors there.

LE CONTE, JOSEPH (1823-1901) of Georgia earned a medical degree at Columbia University but devoted most of his life to the study of the physical sciences. During the Civil War, he served in the Confederate "science department" and after the war moved to California, where he became Professor of Geology and Natural History at the new University of California. *Ramblings throught the High Sierra* (1890) appeared in the Sierra Club Bulletin as Le Conte's edited version of a journal he kept in the summer of 1870, when several members of the first class of the University of California invited him to join them on a camping trip to the Yosemite Valley and the High Sierras. He describes their five week journey on horseback.

LEEPER, DAVID (1832-1900) left South Bend, Indiana, for an overland trip to the California gold fields in February 1849. The argonauts of forty-nine (1894) details Leeper's journey west and his life in California, 1849-1854: prospecting at Redding's Diggings, Hangtown, and the Trinity River; lumbering around Eureka; and early Sacramento and Humboldt Bay. Leeper shows special interest in the Digger Indians, illustrating the book with sketches of tribal garb in his personal collection.

LETTS, JOHN M. of New York sailed for California via Panama in January 1849. California illustrated (1853) describes that voyage and his landing in San Francisco. Next he travels to Sacramento and the Northern Mines of the American River, where he describes gambling and crime in the camps, Native Americans, and mining techniques. He devotes considerable attention to politics in the camps, focusing on the California Constitutional Convention and debate on slavery 1849. He describes his trip home, with stops at Sacramento and San Francisco and his return to New York via Panama, with notes on stops in Acapulco, Managua, and Chagres.

LIENHARD, HEINRICH (1822-1903), son of a Swiss farmer, sailed for America in 1843. After three years in the Midwest, Lienhard and four other young European immigrants set off by wagon for California, reaching Johann Sutter's New Helvetia in October 1846. After a few months in the U.S. Army, Lienhard returned to Sutter's settlement. In 1849 Lienhard returned to Switzerland to accompany Sutter's family to the New World. Disillusioned by the changed California he found in early 1850, Lienhard returned to Switzerland in July. A pioneer at Sutter's fort (1941) is based on a diary kept in his years in California and focuses on Johann Sutter, his family, and his settlement on the Sacramento. It also covers Lienhard's experiences as a farmer and a miner and his crossings of Panama and the Atlantic in 1849-1850.

MCILHANY, EDWARD WASHINGTON (b. 1828) left West Virginia for the California gold fields in 1849. Recollections of a 49er (1908) describes his overland journey west, gold prospecting on Feather River and Grass Valley, hunting and trapping, proprietorship of a general store and hotel in Onion Valley, the Colorado gold rush, and Missouri railroading after the Civil War.

MANLY, WILLIAM LEWIS (1820-1903) and his family left Vermont in 1828, and he grew to manhood in Michigan and Wisconsin. On hearing the news of gold in California, Manly set off on horseback, joining an emigrant party in Missouri. Death Valley in '49 (1894) contains Manly's account of that overland journey. Setting out too late in the year to risk a northern passage thorugh the Sierras, the group takes the southern route to California, unluckily choosing an untried short cut through the mountains. This fateful decision brings the party through Death Valley, and Manly describes their trek through the desert, as well as the experiences of the Illinois "Jayhawkers" and others who took the Death Valley route. Manly's memoirs continue with his trip north to prospecting near the Mariposa mines, a brief trip back east via the Isthmus, and his return to California and another try at prospecting on the North Fork of the Yuba at Downieville in 1851. He provides lively ancedotes of life in mining camps and of his visits to Stockton, Sacramento, and San Francisco.

PIERCE, HIRAM DWIGHT (b. 1810) was a successful blacksmith in Troy, New York, when news arrived of gold discoveries in California. Leaving his wife and seven children behind, Pierce set out in March 1849, crossing the Isthmus to reach San Francisco. A forty-niner speaks (1930) prints the contents of notebooks kept by Pierce from the day he left Troy until his return in January 1851. He describes his journey west and work in the gold fields near Sacramento, the Stanislas mines, and the Merced River at Washington Flat, until his return home via Panama. Pierce offers an excellent account of the details of a prospector's life and the organization of miners' camps as business companies and local government units.

PLAYER-FROWD, J.G. was an English visitor to California in the early 1870s. Six Months in California (1872) is a traveler's guide based on that visit, recounting stays in Omaha, Salt Lake City, the Sierras, Lake Tahoe, Sacramento, San Francisco, Calistoga, Stockton, and the Yosemite Valley. Player-Frowd discusses topics such as California climate, agriculture, mining, and lumbering.

ROOT, HORACE left his wife Eliza A. Root in Comanohe, Iowa in 1849 to seek gold in California.

SCHAEFFER, LUTHER MELANCHTHON, A native of Frederick, Maryland, sailed around the Horn to California in 1849. He spent most of the next two-and-a-half years in the gold fields, mining on the Feather River, Deer Creek, Grass Valley (Centerville) and other Nevada County sites. Sketches of travels in South America, Mexico and California (1860) gives an excellent picture of the international, interracial community of miners, with comments on social patterns, creation of local government, vigilance committees, and legal disputes in this society. Schaeffer also describes visits to San Francisco and Sacramento, Mexico, and Panama before his return to the East in 1852.

SCHARMANN, HERMAN left Germany as head of a company of gold-seekers bound for California in 1849. Scharmann's overland journey to California (1918) describes his family's journey from New York to their wagon train in Independence, Missouri, and the trip across the Plains via Fort Kearny and Fort Laramie. When his wife and daughter die shortly after reaching California, Scharmann and two sons push ahead to the gold fields at Feather River and Middle Fork, and the American River and Negro Bar. He offers a brutal picture of the exploitation of emigrant parties and of the drudgery of prospecting and of towns like Marysville, Sacramento, and San Francisco, 1849-1851.

SHAW, DAVID AUGUSTUS, left Marengo, Illinois, in 1850 for the overland trail to California, where he settled in Pasadena and was an active member of the local Society of Pioneers. *Eldorado* (1900) records Shaw's first stay in the West, 1850-1852, when he worked as a miner and rancher; his return to Illinois and second overland journey west, 1853, this time bringing a herd of horses; and a third round trip to the East, 1856, this time crossing at Panama. In California, Shaw worked as a miner and rancher.

SPOONER, ELIJAH ALLEN, 1811-1879 was a Massachusetts native who settled in Kansas in 1857. Spooner farmed and served as a probate judge and county clerk, also prospector who participated in the California Gold Rush of 1849. Most of his letters are addressed to Spooner's wife and were written while on the overland journey by ox team from Adrian, Michigan, to Sacramento, California, in 1849. Spooner writes of encounters with Indians, buffalo hunting, distaste for Sunday travel, a handful of deaths within his company, and traveling conditions. Spooner also mentions his religious faith in most of the letters. Many of his letters describe life in California and his distress that he has not received any letters from home

STEELE, JOHN, REV. (1832-1915) traveled overland from Wisconsin to California in 1850 and remained for three years. Returning east, he taught school, served in the Union Army, and became an Episcopal minister after the Civil War. Echoes of the past about California and... In camp and cabin (1928) reprints works by Bidwell and Steele published earlier. Bidwell's narrative was composed in 1889 and first published in 1890 in the Century Magazine. The version published here as "Echoes of the past," however, was based on a somewhat different version published in pamphlet form by the Chico, California Advertiser after Bidwell's death in 1900. This version does not include Bidwell's "Journey to California," the journal that he kept in 1841 and which was published in Missouri in 1843 or 1844 (and appears as part of his Addresses, reminiscences..., 1906). Steele's In camp and cabin, first published in 1901, recounts Steele's experiences mining in camps near Nevada City and the American River, with tales of trips to Feather River, Los Angeles, and an expedition to San Andres and camps on the Mokelumne, Calaveras, and Stanislaus Rivers. He provides numerous anecdotes of the people of the camps and their varied national and ethnic backgrounds with many tales of crime and lawlessness. He also discusses contrasting mining methods and gives special attention to Hispanic and Native American Californians whom he met.

SWAN, JOHN (1817-1896), an English sailor, settled in Monterey in 1843 and joined other Californians in the rush to the gold fields to the north in July 1848. A trip to the gold mines of California in 1848 (1960) prints a memoir written out by Swan in 1870 giving an account of his ride north to Log Cabin Ravine and daily life as a prospector on the American River. A few months in the mines satisfy Swan, and he recounts his return to Monterey, where he spent the rest of his life. His book offers lively anecdotes of mining methods and miners in 1848 as well as of the land and people.

TOLLES, JAMES overland diary from Rushville, Illinois, to California in 1849. Also included is a holograph copy of the diary made by Tolles' granddaughter, Doris Beard, in 1933. Tolles traveled to California by ox team with his father and brother, Abraham and William Tolles. Daily entries are detailed and describe the nature of the journey and distances traveled. Tolles' company of 40-odd men traded with a group of 2,000 Dakota Indians, struggled with illness, and debated over whether to travel on the Sabbath. Tolles also stopped at Salt Lake City and gives a brief description. Tolles writes extensively about life in California: the rain, disappointing mines, and his work delivering mail. The bulk of the collection is letters between Tolles, his father and brother, and other family members still living in Illinois. James eventually settled in Reno, Nevada, where he became a fruit grower. Much of the correspondence deals with family matters and James' struggle to make a living in the West.

TWAIN, MARK, See Samuel Clemens

TYSON, JAMES L., DR., sailed from Baltimore for California in January 1849, crossing the Isthmus and sailing on to San Francisco. Diary of a physician in California (1850)

recounts his 1849 tour of the Northern Mines in search
of a likely place for his medical practice and his hospital
at Cold Spring, where his patients included a number of
Oregonians. Tyson closes his hospital at the end of the
summer, sailing from San Francisco as a ship's physician,
crossing the Isthmus and landing in the United States in
December 1849. His diary pays special attention to miners'
health and working conditions.

WOODS, DANIEL B., of Philadelphia sailed to California in February 1849, crossing Mexico to San Blas,
and arriving in San Francisco in June. Sixteen months at
the gold diggings (1851) recounts those travels as well as
his experiences as a prospector in the Northern Mines on
the American River and at Hart's Bar and other camps in
the Southern Mines before starting home in November,
1850. His book offers an exceptionally realistic picture of
the drudgery of mining and the business side of miners'
companies.

WOOLLEY, LELL HAWLEY (b. 1825) left the Green
Mountains of Vermont to cross the plains in a mule train to
California in 1849. There he tried gold mining in Weaverville and Beal's Bar and hotel keeping in Grass Valley
before his marriage and the responsibilities of a home and
family took him to San Francisco. There he went into business and was active in the Vigilance Committee of 1856.
California, 1849-1913 (1913) offers anecdotes of these
adventures as well as brief notes on San Francisco person-
alities and business life in the 1850s and 1860s, with some
references to later decades.

Index

More "Golden" Books

The "Golden" Book series focuses on the life and times in Northern California and Northern Nevada in the 19th century. It is distinctive because it brings together the unique observations and viewpoints of dozens of people who were in a particular area at a particular time-frame in history.

The Golden Corridor paved the way for a more in-depth look at various Northern California and Nevada communities. We made some exciting "finds" in creating these first three books, and there is much more to discover, preserve and share. Through today's technology, information that could only be obtained looking through huge historical texts in vast research libraries is now accessible to everyone. And we'll bring it to you.

More *"Golden"* books are in the works. They will be even more informative and more fun for readers. They will include more photographic treasures and information from the archives of dozens of smaller historical societies and private collections. And, we're working with the community of historians, historical parks and friends, to discover even more new sources of information.

Over the next couple of years you'll be able to visit many places and see many scenes that few have experienced. Here are some titles and estimated release dates:

The Golden Highway, Vol II	
(Amador County & South)	Now Available
The Golden Hub - Sacramento	Spring 2008
The Golden Gate - San Francisco	Spring 2009

To pre-order copies of any of these books, or for bulk orders for schools or other organizations, please contact us at:

19thCentury Books / Electric Canvas
1001 Art Road
Pilot Hill, CA 95664
916.933.4490

If you'd like to receive an e-mail announcement when new titles are released, please contact: Jody@19thCentury.us

Thank you for your interest in our rich history. We hope you've enjoyed *The Golden Highway, Volume I* and will enjoy more of our books in the future.

Does your family have 19th century photos, journals, letters or other documents you'd like to share and preserve?

Let us help you archive your originals electronically. You will receive a copy of all your materials on CD, and you decide if you'd like to retain the originals or entrust them to your local historical society, the Library of Congress, or some other institution for safekeeping.

Please share your family's history. It'll provide one more piece to the complex puzzle that represents our rich culture and background.

Contact us today for details.